# THE
# WORLD'S
# BIGGEST

# PUZZLE
# BOOK

## CHARLES BARRY TOWNSEND

STERLING PUBLISHING CO., INC.
NEW YORK

**Library of Congress Cataloging-in-Publication Data**

10   9   8   7   6   5   4   3   2

Published by Sterling Publishing Co., Inc.
387 Park Avenue South, New York, NY 10016
This edition is a compilation from the following volumes, all pub-
lished by Sterling Publishing Co., Inc., and all copyright by
Charles Barry Townsend: *The World's Best Puzzles*, copyright ©
1986; *World's Greatest Puzzles*, copyright © 1992; *World's Hardest
Puzzles*, copyright © 1992; *World's Most Amazing Puzzles*, copy-
right © 1993; *World's Most Baffling Puzzles*, copyright © 1991; *The
World's Most Challenging Puzzles*, copyright © 1988; *World's Most
Incredible Puzzles*, copyright © 1994; *World's Most Perplexing
Puzzles*, copyright © 1995; *World's Toughest Puzzles*, copyright ©
1990; *World's Trickiest Puzzles*, copyright © 1995; *Super Brainy
Puzzles*, copyright © 1996.
Compilation © 2002 by Sterling Publishing Co., Inc.
Distributed in Canada by Sterling Publishing
C/o Canadian Manda Group, One Atlantic Avenue, Suite 105
Toronto, Ontario, Canada M6K 3E7
Distributed in Great Britain and Europe by Chris Lloyd at Orca
Book Services, Stanley House, Fleets Lane, Poole BH15 3AJ,
England
Distributed in Australia by Capricorn Link (Australia) Pty. Ltd.
P.O. Box 704, Windsor, NSW 2756, Australia

Sterling  ISBN-1-4027-0246-9

# Contents

# The
# **World's**
# Best Puzzles

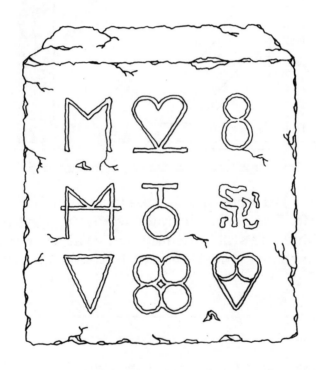

# The World's Best "Window" Puzzle

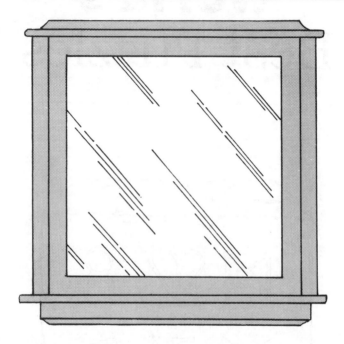

Shown here is a store window that measures 7 feet high by 7 feet wide. The store decorator wants to paint half the window blue and still have a square, clear section of window that measures 7 feet high by 7 feet wide. How would he do this?

# The World's Best "Soda Straw" Puzzle

Now here's a problem that will tax your skills. You must lift an empty soda bottle off a table using only one hand and a straw. There are two rules that must be followed: You cannot tie the straw into a knot, and the straw is not allowed to touch any part of the outside of the bottle.

# The World's Best "Fish Tank" Puzzle

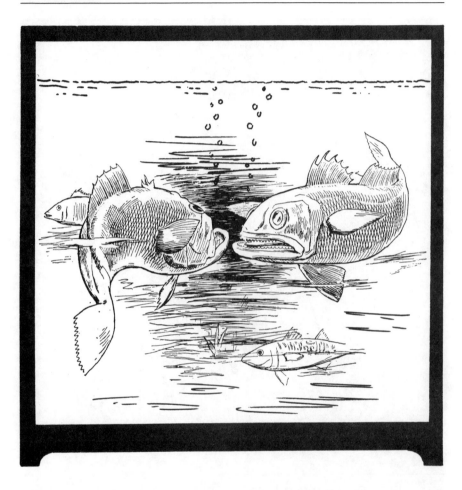

The fish tank shown here is almost filled to the top with water. Without using a measuring cup of any kind, or a measuring stick, can you remove enough water from the tank so that the water level will be exactly in the middle of the tank? The solution is easier than you think! *Note*: This can also be tried with a glass of water, which will be much less sloppy then a fish tank.

# The World's Best "Coin" Puzzle

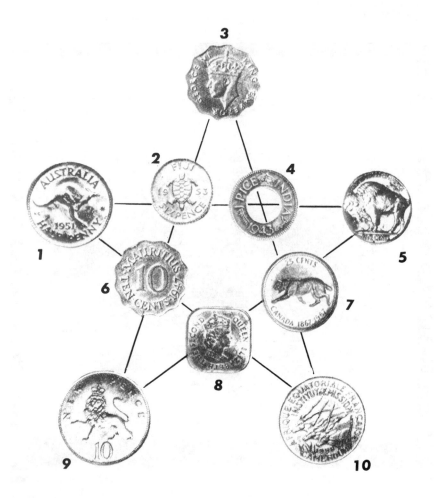

Here's a valuable puzzle for you to solve. Place nine coins on the star, one on each of the world coins except coin number eight. The object of this puzzle is to remove all but one of the coins from the star. You remove a coin by jumping another coin over it along one of the lines. The position that you jump to, beyond the coin, must be empty (the moves are the same as those you would make in a game of checkers).

If you can solve this puzzle within 15 minutes, consider yourself rich in ability.

# The World's Best "Line" Puzzle

Shown is the famous "Puzzle Kite." To solve the puzzle, you must draw the kite, and the string attached to it, using one continuous line. The line cannot cross itself at any point, nor can you go over any part of the line more than once. You must start the line at the ball of string and end it in the middle of the kite.

# The World's Best "Book" Puzzle

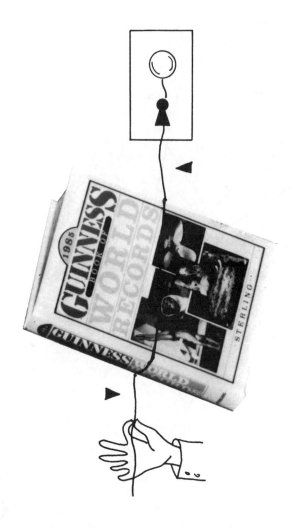

Here is a puzzle that will really perplex your friends. Tie a piece of string around the middle of a fairly heavy book, say two or three pounds. Then fasten one end of the string to a doorknob so that the book hangs about a foot down from it. Taking hold of the string below the book, tell your friends that you can pull the string and make it break either above or below the book at will. They will be astonished to discover that this can be done. Do you know how this wonderful feat of magic is accomplished?

# The World's Best "Ice-Cream-Stick" Puzzle

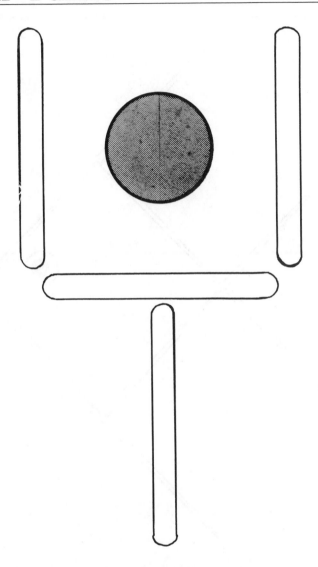

Let's pretend that the four ice-cream sticks shown represent a tall, stemmed glass, and the colored circle is a large, juicy cherry. You must remove the cherry from the glass by moving two of the sticks to new positions. You cannot move the cherry, and you must retain the exact shape of the glass.

# The World's Best "Toothpick" Puzzle

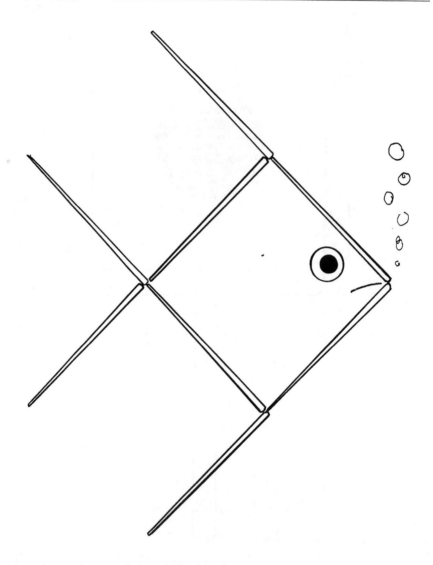

Arrange eight toothpicks as shown. Place a button in the square for an eye.

Suddenly our Toothpick Tuna sees a shark! He must turn around and swim for his life. Can you move three of the toothpicks, and the button, to new locations so that our fish will be swimming away to the left?

# The World's Best "Rope" Puzzle

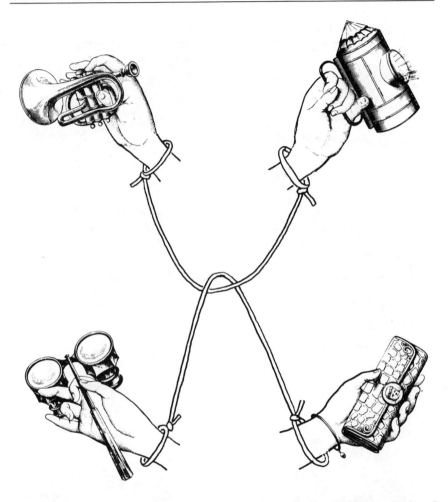

Try this puzzle with a friend. Loosely tie a short length of rope to both of your wrists. Have your friend do the same with another piece of rope that has been looped over the first rope. When this has been accomplished you will both be securely joined as shown above.

Your problem is to separate yourself from your friend without untying the knots, cutting the ropes, or slipping your hands out of the loops. It's easier then it looks!

*Note*: The objects featured in this illustration are from the turn of the century. Note in particular the flashlight on the upper right and the opera glasses on the lower left.

# The World's Best "Stamp" Puzzle

Here's a neat "Stamp Stumper." Shown are six stamps from around the world. Our problem is to arrange these stamps in the form of a cross. However, there must be four stamps in each line of the cross. *Hint*: One stamp can be in both lines of the cross.

# The World's Best "Hardware Shop" Puzzle

Shown here are four patrons of the New Old Bennington Hardware Shop. Within the past week all of them have moved into their own condominiums up the road in the Friar Briar Estates. The estates are made up of nine beautiful units overlooking Loon Lake. The customers have come to the hardware shop to buy something that the builder forgot to include with each unit. One will cost just $1.00. Eight will still only cost $1.00, but sixteen will cost $2.00. If they need one hundred and fifty, the total cost will be $3.00. Even if they order three hundred, they will still only pay $3.00. If this sounds confusing, believe me it isn't. For a total of $4.00, they each got what they came for and went away happy.

What were the items that these people purchased?

# The World's Best "Dime" Puzzle

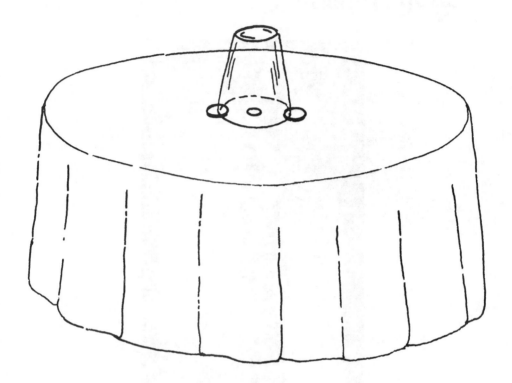

Here's another one of those "impossible" puzzles for you to solve. First, place a dime on top of a cloth-covered table. Next, place a quarter on either side of the dime. The quarters should be so placed that an inverted drinking glass will rest comfortably on the middle of each coin. After placing the glass on the coins, the setup should look like the one here. Now for the puzzle! You must remove the dime from under the glass without touching the glass or the quarters. Furthermore, you cannot slip anything under the glass in an effort to push the dime out. Impossible? Well . . .

# The World's Best "Arrowhead" Puzzle

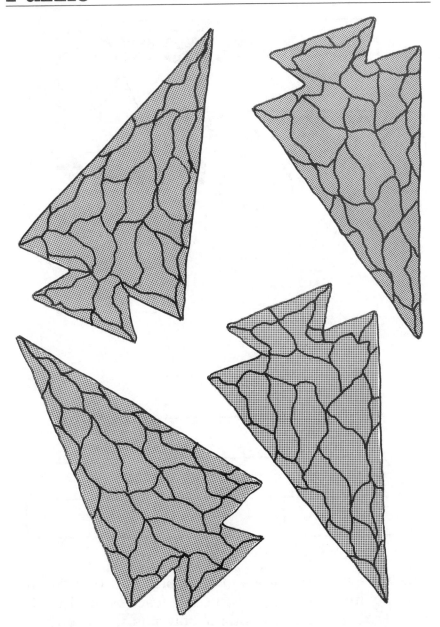

There is a way to turn these four Indian arrowheads into *five* arrowheads just by rearranging them. Let's see how good your aim is with this problem.

# The World's Best "Sugar" Puzzle

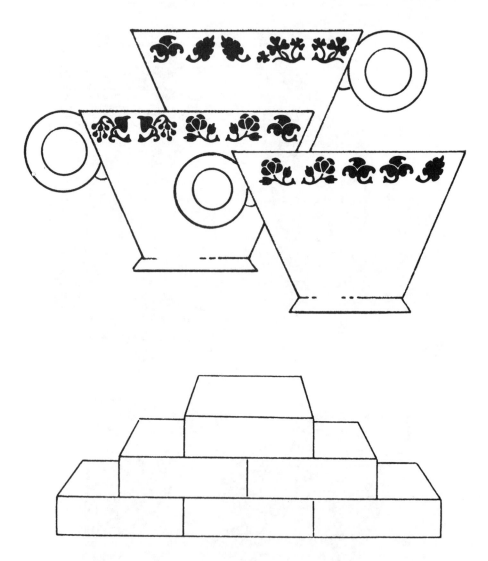

This is a sweet little problem to perplex your friends with. Place six lumps of sugar and three teacups on the table. What is required of the puzzle solver is to place the six lumps of sugar into the teacups in such a way that each cup will contain an odd number of lumps. All six lumps must be used, and none can be broken up in any way.

# The World's Best "Dollar Bill" Puzzle

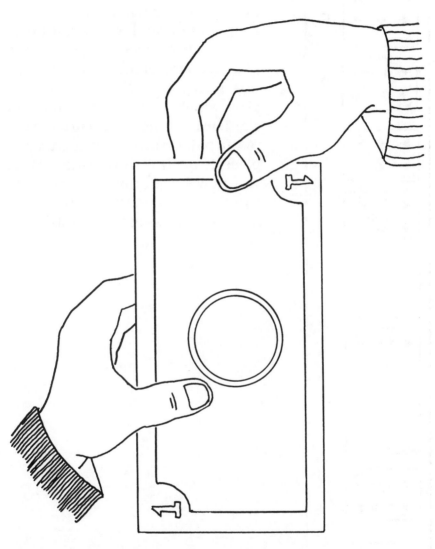

Hold a dollar bill in your right hand, at about chest level. Have someone place his left hand around the middle of the bill with the thumb and index finger about an inch apart. No part of his hand may touch the bill. Now, tell him that when you let go of the bill he won't be able to catch it before it passes through his fingers. It sounds easy, doesn't it?

# The World's Best "Card" Puzzle

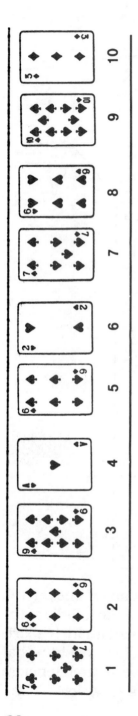

Lay out a row of ten cards on the table. Starting with any card, pick it up and move it left or right over the next two cards in the row and place it on top of the third card. You now have a pair. Next, pick up another single card and pass it left or right over the next two cards in the row (a pair counts as one card), and place it on the third single card. You now have another pair. Continue in this manner until you have five pairs upon the table.

# The World's Best "Bookworm" Puzzle

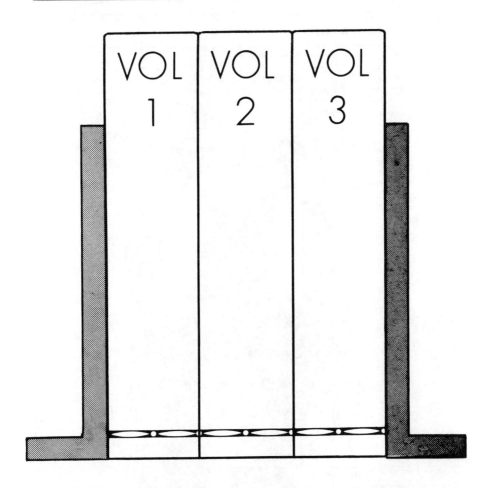

"The Case of the Ravenous Bookworm" is a great old puzzle. On top of the bookcase is a three-volume set of puzzle books. The front and back covers of the books are each 1/8 inch thick. The page section inside each book is exactly 2 inches thick. Now, if our bookworm starts eating at page one of volume 1 and eats, in a straight line, through to the last page of volume 3, how far will he travel?

# The World's Best "Code" Puzzle

During World War I, two of Europe's top spies met at Kensington House in England, to exchange information. They were, of course, talking in code. Your assignment is to break this code in 15 minutes or less. Good luck. *Hint*: This code was created by rearranging the sequence of the letters in the alphabet. It is often referred to as "The Looking Glass Code."

# The World's Best "Geometry" Puzzle

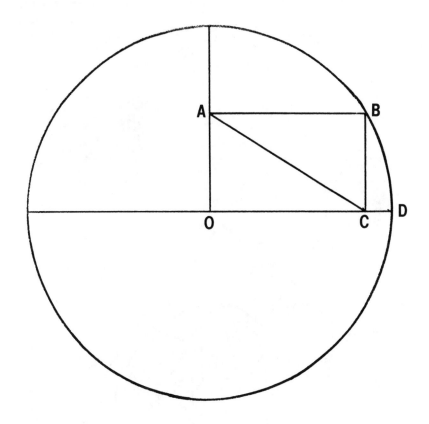

Here's a pretty geometric puzzle that's easier then it looks. The center of the circle is at O. The angle at AOC is 90 degrees. The line AB is parallel to the line OD. The segment OC is 5 inches long, and segment CD is 1 inch long. Your problem is to determine the length of line AC.

# The World's Best "Starship" Puzzle

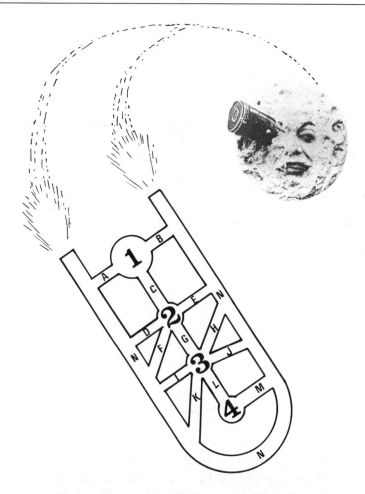

Starship 1 is heading back to Earth from the Moon. Shown here is the floor plan of the command deck of the forward module. Every hour Captain Birk makes his rounds. He has a route that will take him down every corridor that is labelled *A* through *M* once and only once. The outer corridor, *N*, can be entered any number of times. The four command centers (1, 2, 3, and 4) can also be entered any number of times. He always ends up his tour of inspection in command center 1. See if you can lay out the captain's route.

# The World's Best "Archery" Puzzle

Friar Tuck has challenged Robin Hood to solve an ancient archery problem. He has to shoot six arrows into the target so that their combined scores will add up to exactly 100. Friar Tuck looks as if he knows the answer and can already taste the prize. *Hint*: Four of the arrows ended up in the same target circle.

# The World's Best "Button" Puzzle

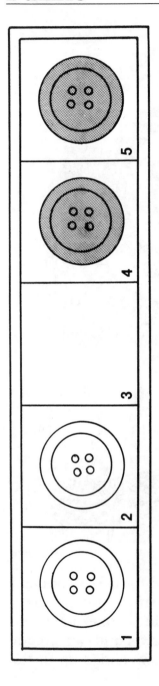

This is one of those delightful "substitution-type" puzzles. All you need are two white buttons, two red buttons, and this puzzle board. Place the buttons on the board as shown. Now, using only eight moves, you must cause these buttons to change places. The white buttons may only move to the right, and the red buttons may only move to the left. The buttons are moved by sliding them to the next empty space on the board. You can also jump one button over another button. However, the space beyond the button jumped must be empty.

# The World's Best "Chain" Puzzle

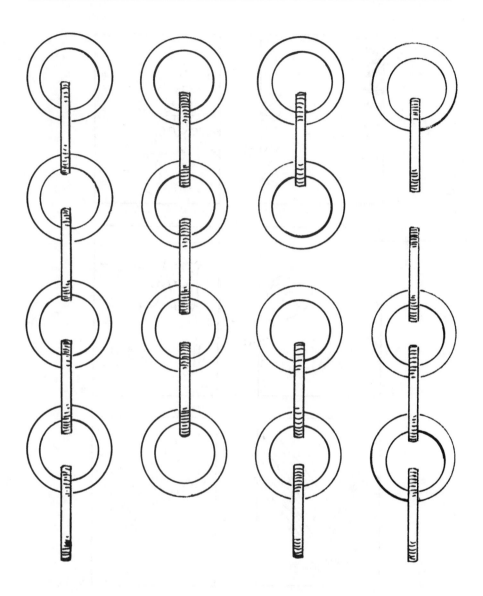

A man had six sections of chain that he wanted to join together to make one chain containing 29 links. He asked the blacksmith how much he would charge to do the job. The blacksmith told him that it would cost 50¢ to open a link and 75¢ to weld it shut. What was the cheapest price that the blacksmith could do the job for?

# The World's Best "Word" Puzzle

The six "word pictures" all stand for the names of some objects or expressions. They're tricky, but I bet that you can solve at least four of them.

# The World's Best "Block" Puzzle

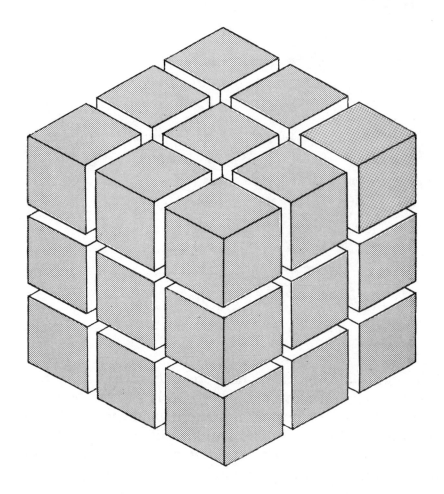

Before this block or cube was subdivided into 27 smaller cubes, it was painted a bright blue on all six of its sides. See if you can answer the following questions concerning the 27 small cubes.

(1) How many cubes have blue paint on three sídes?

(2) How many cubes have blue paint on two sides?

(3) How many cubes have blue paint on one side?

(4) How many cubes have no paint on any side?

# The World's Best "Animal" Puzzle

The administrator of a game preserve in Kenya, Africa, decided to take a count of the lions and ostriches he had in one section of the park. For some reason, he did this by counting the number of legs and heads of these animals. He came up with 35 heads and 78 legs. Do you know how many lions there were and how many ostriches?

# The World's Best "Mars" Puzzle

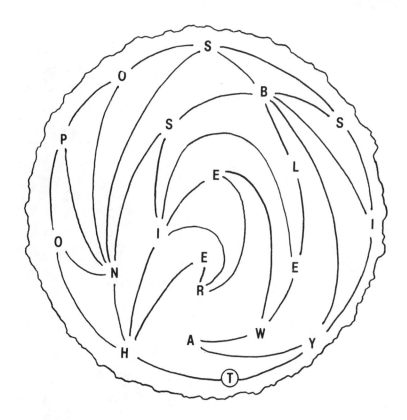

One of the oldest, and best, problems in puzzledom is the "Mars" puzzle by Sam Loyd. Shown here is a map of Mars, *circa* 1900, showing the canals that were thought to exist at that time. At the junctions of these canals are located 20 pumping stations. For the sake of this puzzle the pumping stations have been labelled with letters. If you start at station "T," and make a round-trip tour of all 20 stations, you can spell out a complete English sentence. You must travel along the canals and you cannot visit any station more than once.

When Sam Loyd first published this puzzle, over 50,000 readers wrote in, concerning the solution, that "there is no possible way." See if you can succeed where so many have failed in the past.

# The World's Best "Crossroads" Puzzle

Here we find Napoleon standing literally at the crossroads. During the night, a supply wagon knocked over a signpost at the crossing of two roads. No one in Napoleon's company knows how to replace the signpost so that the arrows will be pointing in the right directions. After contemplating the problem for a few moments, the general issues orders that cause the sign to be replaced correctly. Since Napoleon had never been to this crossroads before, how was he able to do this?

# The World's Best "Coaster" Puzzle

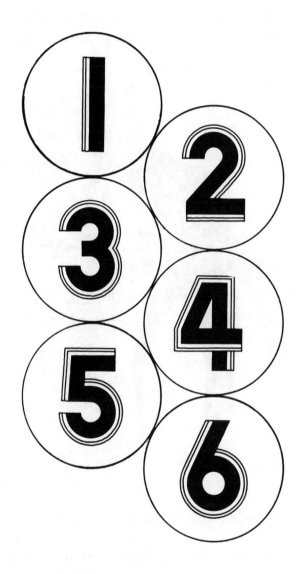

Lay out on a table six round beverage coasters as shown. The coasters should just be touching one another. You must now re-form them into a "perfect" circle by rearranging three of them. When doing this, you are allowed to move only one coaster at a time.

# The World's Best "Age" Puzzle

*"Mind your manners, you old coot! I'm over 21, and that's all the information about my age that you're going to get!"*

If "Swifty" Armbruster really wants to know Miss Prim's age, he should ask her what her shoe size is. That's right, you can determine anyone's age by the size of the gunboats that they wear. Do you know how to do it?

# The World's Best "Record" Puzzle

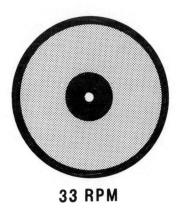

**33 RPM**

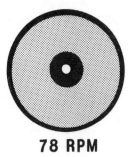

**78 RPM**

**45 RPM**

This is really a "groovy" puzzle. Shown here are three phonograph records: a 12-inch, 33 RPM record; a 10-inch, 78 RPM record; and a 7-inch, 45 RPM record. Can you guess how many grooves there are in each record? Your answers must be within 100 grooves of each record's total to be considered correct.

# The World's Best "Circle" Puzzle

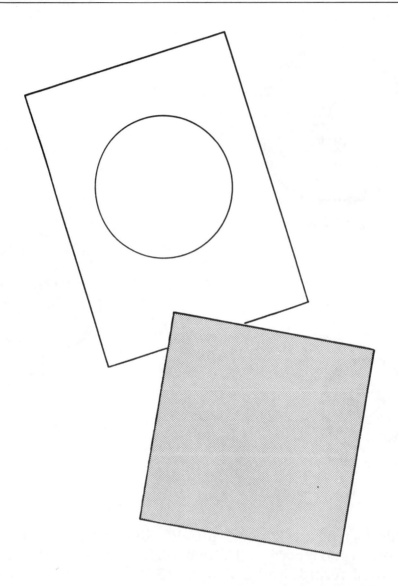

If you wanted to find the center of a circle, and all you had to work with was a pencil and a square piece of cardboard, larger than the circle, how would you go about solving the problem? It's really easier than it looks. You have five minutes to find the solution.

# The World's Best "Rune Stone" Puzzle

A recently discovered "Rune Stone," near Husavik, Iceland, had archaeologists running around in circles until a young schoolboy pointed out to them that the stone was obviously a fake since it depicted a well-known puzzle. Chiselled into the stone were nine cryptic characters. The sixth character, the third one in the middle row, was purposely left unfinished. The puzzle, then, is to figure out what this character should be. This can be done by determining what each of the other characters stands for. *Hint:* All of the characters have something in common.

# The World's Best "Truck" Puzzle

The story goes that many years ago a truck driver was flagged down by a policeman and told that his truck had to be checked for overloading. As soon as the driver had driven his truck onto the weighing machine, he jumped out of the cab and started pounding the side of the truck with a piece of wood. A bystander asked the driver why he was doing that.

"Well," he replied, "I'm carrying 5,000 pounds of live canaries in the truck. I know that my truck is overloaded, but if I can keep the birds flying around inside the truck their weight won't show up on the scales."

Is what the driver said true? If the birds are kept flying inside the enclosed box of the truck, will the truck really weigh less than if the birds were sitting on their perches?

# The World's Best "Bottle" Puzzle

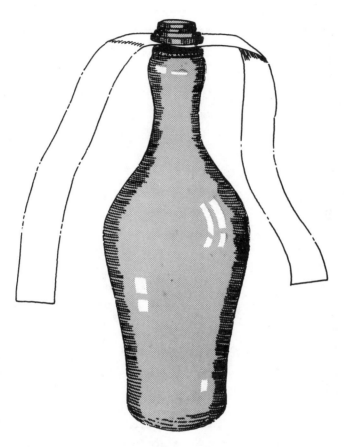

Place an empty bottle upright on the table. Next, cut a one-inch-wide strip of paper, one foot long, from a newspaper. Place the strip of paper over the mouth of the bottle as shown. Finally, place four coins on top of the paper. Start with a quarter, then add a nickel and two pennies. Now, challenge anyone to remove the strip of paper leaving the coins still balanced on top of the bottle. They cannot touch either the coins or the bottle while doing this. The only item that may be touched, in any way, by anything, is the strip of paper. Your friends will soon discover that this problem is nearly impossible to solve. Try it a few times yourself before looking up the answer.

# The World's Best "X-Ray" Puzzle

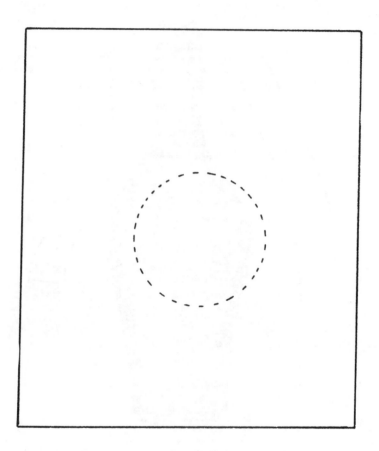

Turn your back and instruct anyone present to place a silver dollar, face up, on top of the table. Next, tell them to place a square piece of blank paper over the coin. Now, turn around and declare that you will use your superpowers to look right through the sheet of opaque paper and read the date on the coin. State that at no time will the paper be lifted from the coin, and that the coin will be fully covered at all times. Just to make things more interesting, propose the following wager. If you succeed in reading the date, you get to keep the coin. If you fail, he gets to keep it. Sounds fair to me!

# The World's Best "Frog" Puzzle

There is a story told of a frog that fell off his bicycle and ended up at the bottom of a ten-foot well. The well was too deep to hop out of, so the frog started to climb up the slippery sides. Every day he was able to climb up three feet, but during the night, while he rested, he slid back down two feet. At this rate, how many days did it take for the famous "Climbing Frog of Clavicle County" to get out of that well?

# The World's Best "Pilsner Glass" Puzzle

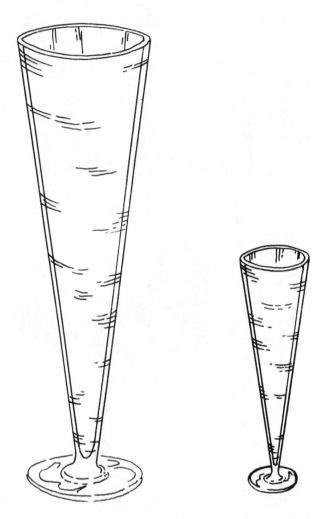

Shown here are two Pilsner glasses from Germany. The inside dimensions of the larger glass are exactly twice as great as the inside dimensions of the smaller glass. What we want to do is fill the larger glass with water using the smaller glass as a measure. We fill the smaller glass with water and then pour the water into the larger glass. The question is: How many times will we have to do this to completely fill the larger glass?

# The World's Best "Policeman" Puzzle

At the turn of the century Olaf Anderson became a policeman in a small city. He was assigned a beat in the city that covered six square blocks. Being a conscientious policeman, Officer Anderson wished to find the shortest possible route he could take that would enable him to circle each block during one complete trip around his beat. In the answer section, the route that he worked out is given. We think that it's the best possible solution. However, there just may be a shorter route, so give it a try before checking out the answer.

# The World's Best "Jealous Husband" Puzzle

Three jealous husbands travelling with their wives found it necessary to cross a stream in a boat which held only two persons. Each of the husbands had a great objection to his wife crossing with either of the other male members of the party unless he himself was also present. They also objected to leaving their wives alone with the other husbands on either side of the stream.

How was the passage arranged? Remember, though the boat held two people, one of them had to bring the boat back for the rest of the people to use.

# The World's Best "Bicycle" Puzzle

When bicycling was in its infancy, two young cyclists, Betty and Nadine Parkhurst, set out one day to visit their aunt in the country some 20 miles away. After they had covered four miles, Betty's bike broke down and she had to chain it to a tree. Being in a hurry, they decided to push on as quickly as they could. They had the choice of both walking, or of one walking and one riding the remaining bike. They both could walk at the rate of four miles an hour and ride at eight miles an hour. They decided on a plan of action that would keep their walking to a minimum and yet would get them to their aunt's house in the shortest amount of time. What combination of walking and riding did they use?

# The World's Best "Deductive" Puzzle

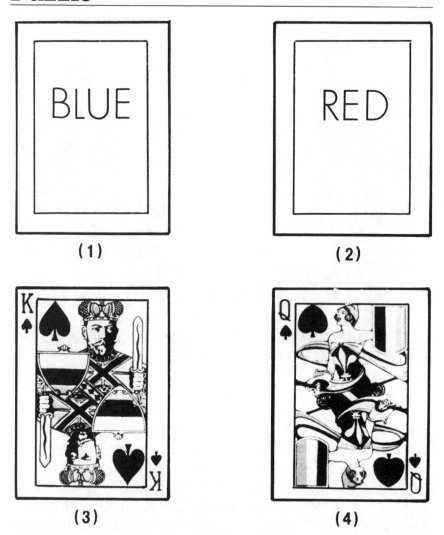

(1)

(2)

(3)

(4)

From two old packs of Australian playing cards, one with blue backs and the other with red backs, we have selected four cards and placed two of them faceup and the other two facedown on the table. Now here's the problem: "Does every blue-backed card on the table have a king on its other side?"

To solve this puzzle, you are allowed to turn two of the cards over. Which two cards would you turn over?

# The World's Best "Tennis" Puzzle

Many years ago, at the Idle Hours Country Club, they had a super turnout for the Teddy Roosevelt Mixed Doubles Tennis Tournament. One hundred and twenty-eight couples registered for the big event. Thaddeus Rackencut, the groundskeeper, was up half the night drawing up the schedule board. Do you know how many doubles matches were played before a winner was determined?

# The World's Best "Nail" Puzzle

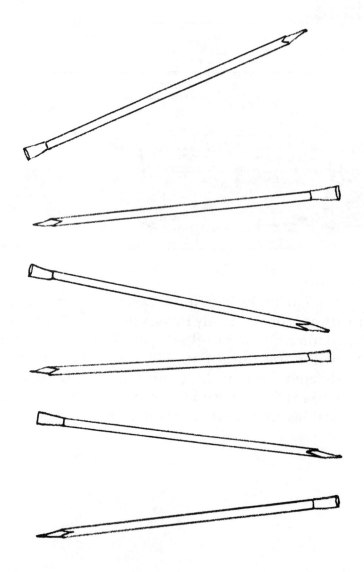

Here's an old carpenter's puzzle. You have to arrange six finishing nails so that each nail touches every other nail. It sounds easy, but watch out; you may be the one that's "finished" before you give up on this one.

# The World's Best "Travelling" Puzzle

"All right now, Alfred, pay attention! I'll repeat the puzzle one more time.
   'As I was going to St. Ives,
   I met a man with seven wives,
   Each wife had seven sacks,
   Each sack had seven cats,
   Each cat had seven kits;
   Kits, cats, sacks, and wives,
   How many were there going to St. Ives?'
It's really not very hard if you give it a little thought."

This poem is a favorite among puzzle solvers. Can you figure it out before Alfred and his friend reach their destinations?

# The World's Best "Antique" Puzzle

The other day Calvin Collectible, an antique dealer, bought a cast-iron fountain, depicting a crocodile swallowing a fish. For this marvellous work of art (?), he paid 90 percent of its "book" value. The next day, another collector saw it and offered to buy it from him for 25 percent above its book value. Calvin, no slouch at turning a quick buck, accepted the offer and made a nice profit of $105 over his purchase price. With these facts to work with, can you determine what the book value of this bubbling curiosity is?

# The World's Best "Fly" Puzzle

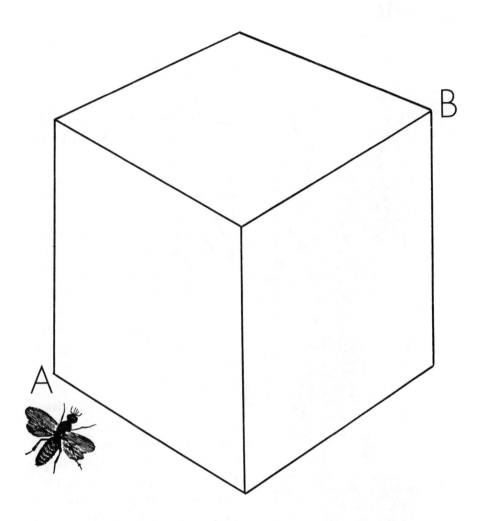

That educated fly that has appeared in so many puzzles is back for another try at stumping our readers. This time he has discovered a marble pedestal that he would like to negotiate. He wants to travel from point A, the left lower corner of the cube shown here, to point B, the upper right corner on the opposite side of the cube. The cube measures exactly two feet along each of its edges. Can you figure out the shortest possible route for our friendly fly to take?

# The World's Best "Racing" Puzzle

Two sporting gentlemen decided to stage a race where the buggy that crossed the finish line first would *lose* and the one that came in second would win. Off they went, down a one-mile course, whipping their horses to a lather. As they neared the finish line, they both slowed down until they came to a halt with only 100 yards to go. Realizing that they had made a dumb bet, the two drivers got down and went over to discuss the matter with a farmer who was watching them from his field. When the farmer heard their story, he gave them a piece of advice that sent them leaping into the buggies and speeding down the course, as each one strained to be the first to cross the finish line.

The advice that the farmer gave them in no way changed the terms of the original wager. Can you guess what it was?

be made out of four candle stubs. Since Uncle Hay bought all of his candles in Handy-Paks of 16, how many new candles was he able to make from each package?

# The World's Best "Cookie" Puzzle

Little Ariadne is very upset. Earlier in the day she received a package of fresh, homemade cookies from her mother. As she was opening her gift, four of her friends arrived and reminded Ariadne that they had shared their cookies with her and that it was now her turn to pay them back. Reluctantly, she counted out and gave half of her cookies and half a cookie to her friend Lorella. To Melva, she gave half of what was left and half a cookie. Then she counted out half of the remaining cookies and half a cookie, and gave them to Laureen. To the last girl, Margot, she handed half of what was left in the box and half a cookie. This left poor Ariadne with an empty cookie box and mayhem in her heart.

Can you figure out how many cookies were originally in the box? By the way, at no time did Ariadne cut up or break in two any of the cookies in the box.

reading that inscription, I can point out three errors in it right away."

Can you spot the errors in this "Find of the Century"?

# The World's Best "Horn" Puzzle

One year Groucho Marx bought a new horn for his brother Harpo's birthday. After having it wrapped, he took it to the post office to mail.

"I'm sorry, Mr. Marx," said the postal clerk, "but this package is too long. Regulations state that no package can be more than four feet long. This one is five feet in length."

Groucho took the horn and returned to the shop. They removed the rubber bulb, but the horn was still four feet eight inches long. Then Groucho had an idea. He had them rewrap the horn in a different way. When he returned to the post office they accepted his package because it was now regulation size. How did he do it? Remember, the horn was not cut, or bent out of shape, in any way.

# The World's Best "Wallet" Puzzle

Mr. Willard Gotrocks rushed into the police station the other day shouting that his wallet had been stolen.

"Hold on now, Mr. Gotrocks," said Sergeant Anderson. "Someone just turned in a wallet. Maybe it's yours. Can you identify its contents?"

"Well," replied Willard, "there's a picture of W.C. Fields in it, and there's my 'Everything' credit card. Oh, yes, I had exactly $63 in cash in six bills, and none of them was a $1 bill."

"That clinches it, Mr. Gotrocks. Here's your wallet."

Can you calculate what six bills he had in his wallet that added up to exactly $63?

# The World's Best "Egyptian" Puzzle

The art of puzzling started in the Valley of the Nile over 3,000 years ago. Here, we see the stonemasons polishing the head of the puzzle god, Stumpumost. The emblem on his helmet is the first recorded line puzzle. To solve it you must draw the jeweled emblem using one continuous line. At no time can you lift your pencil from the paper, nor can you allow the line to cross over itself at any point. Solve this one in five minutes and you qualify to be a scribe first-class.

# The
# World's
# Greatest Puzzles

# World's Greatest "Checkers" Puzzle

Pop Bentley, the colossus of Cracker Barrel Checkers, has just defeated Cy Corncrib for the umpteenth time. Above is the end of the game just before Pop delivered the coup de grace. Can you figure out what his moves were? The white pieces are moving up the board while the black are moving down. Pop is playing the black pieces, and it's his move.

# World's Greatest "Plate" Puzzle

Mr Maskelyne makes things spin

Pictured here is that famous 1890s plate spinologist, John N. Maskelyne. He could keep six plates and a wash-basin constantly spinning for five minutes or more. Today he has a plate puzzle for you. He challenges you to balance the center of a plate on the point of a needle that has been driven into the top of a corked bottle. You are allowed to make use of four forks and two extra corks to accomplish this seemingly impossible feat. If done correctly, you should be able to emulate Mr. Maskelyne and set the plate spinning after you've balanced it on the pin.

# World's Greatest "Match" Puzzle

> *"That was an excellent lunch, Mr. Pettibone. How about a small wager to see who gets to pay for it? I'll bet you can't arrange 15 matchsticks on the table so that they form eight complete squares all the same size. No matches may be overlapped or broken, and no square may be formed inside another. You have until post time to solve it."*

Arbuthnot Longodds, that improver of the breed, is at it again. He never picks up a check if there is a chump handy. Could you solve this matchless puzzle before poor Mr. Pettibone has to reach for his wallet?

# World's Greatest "Chess" Puzzle

Milli Sykes, a waitress over at the Humble Bishop Chess Club, is shown here checking out a puzzle that had everyone stumped last night. Put a queen on one of the corner squares, as indicated above, and see if you can move it through all nine squares in the upper left-hand corner of the board in just four moves. During any one move the queen can traverse as many squares as you want it to but may move in one direction only. See if you can beat the five-minute clock on this one.

# World's Greatest "Old Salt" Puzzle

That old seaman, Billy "the Hook" Trelawney, went into Nantucket one day with $10 and came home that night with $150.

He bought himself a new tie at the Tar and Spar Clothing Store and some birdseed for his parrot at the Binnacle Pet Lodge. Later he had his hair cut. Now Billy, who worked at the whaling museum, was paid by check every Thursday. At this time of year the banks were only open on Tuesdays, Fridays and Saturdays. The barber was always closed on Saturday, and the Binnacle Pet Lodge was not open on Thursday or Friday. Given the above facts can you determine which day of the week old Billy went to town on?

# World's Greatest "Name" Puzzle

One day, while out bike-riding, Mr. Neederwaller chanced to meet a very old friend.

"It's been years since I last saw you," he said.

"I know," replied his friend, "since we last met in Burma I've married—to someone you never knew that I worked with in Rangoon. This is our little girl."

"And a very pretty one at that," replied Mr. Neederwaller. "What might your name be?"

"Thank you, sir. My name is the same as my mother's."

"Well, you certainly look like an Eleanor. That was always one of my favorite names," answered Mr. Neederwaller.

Now, how in the world did Mr. Neederwaller know that the young girl's name was Eleanor? Could he be psychic?

# World's Greatest "Family" Puzzle

Grandpa Townsend used to tell this story. It seems that at one of his birthday parties there were 10 family members present besides numerous other guests. There were two grandfathers present, two grandmothers, three fathers, three mothers, three sons, three daughters, two mothers-in-law, two fathers-in-law, one son-in-law, one daughter-in-law, two brothers and two sisters.

Can you figure out what family members were present at grandpa's party to account for so many family ties?

# World's Greatest "Safe" Puzzle

In the annals of crime no petty crook was more petty than Knuckles Halliburton. When robbing a house he never hesitated to steal from the children's banks. Judging by the above picture he must also have been one of the smallest yeggs in history. When he cracked the Security Safe pictured here he took away exactly 100 coins. Their total worth came to $5. There were no nickels in the bank. Can you figure out what coins he came away with and how many of each there were?

# World's Greatest "Prophesy" Puzzle

"All right, Jeffords, I have a little wager for you before the next hand. I'll bet you $1,000, at five-to-one odds, that I can guess closer to the date on any coin that you remove from your pocket than you can. Of course, I get two guesses to your one, but you get to go first. What do you say, is it a bet?"

"Well, High Pockets, that bet sounds pretty good to me, but let's make the odds two-to-one. I guess that the date on the coin will be 1983!"

Even at two-to-one odds this is a cinch bet for High Pockets. How can he be sure that he will win almost every time?

# World's Greatest "Cigarette" Puzzle

Pictured here is that ne'er-do-well of cafe society, Nicotine Ned. It seems that Ned has fallen on bad times and cannot even afford to buy a decent pack of cigarettes. He is forced to roll his own with the help of that famous invention, the Rapide Cigarette Maker. For tobacco, he saves the butts of previous smokes. He can make one cigarette from three butts. Tonight he has saved 10 butts, from which he expects to make five cigarettes. It sounds impossible but Ned has a plan. Can you smoke out his modus operandi?

# World's Greatest "Poker Chip" Puzzle

The Mystic Mirror of the Great Gondolpho sees all, knows all, and tells all . . . for $25 a ticket. During his act, the Great Gondolpho illuminates the screen with famous puzzles that he has searched out from around the globe. Pictured here, the Mystic Mirror is projecting the notorious Las Vegas Poker Chip Dilemma. Many a dollar has been lost trying to solve it. The problem is to arrange five poker chips into two rows with one row containing three chips and the other row containing four chips. What makes it a tough bet is that you only have 60 seconds to come up with the answer.

# World's Greatest "Cork" Puzzle

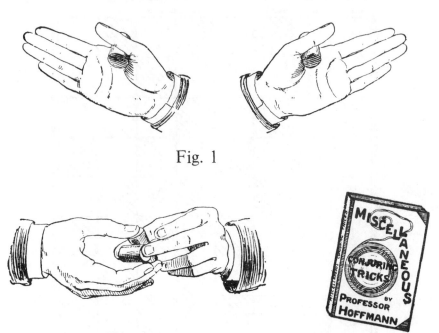

Fig. 1

Fig. 2

Here's a corking-good puzzle you can pop on your guests at your next wine-tasting party. I'm going to let that vintage puzzler from the 19th century, Professor Hoffmann, introduce it:

"Take two wine-bottle corks and hold them as shown in Fig. 1, *viz.*: each laid transversely across the fork of the thumb. Now, with the thumb and second finger of the *right* hand take hold of the cork in the *left* hand (one finger on each end of it) and at the same time, with the thumb and second finger of the *left*, take hold of the cork in the *right* hand and draw them apart.

"The above sounds simple enough, but the neophyte will find that the corks are brought crosswise, as shown in Fig. 2. The puzzle is to avoid this and enable them to part freely."

# World's Greatest "Wagering" Puzzle

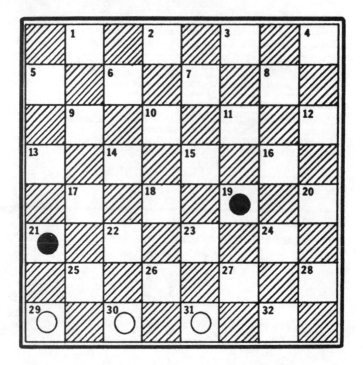

This is called the Double Whammy Wager. You win two times in a row with it. Set up a checkerboard as shown above. Tell your victim that you'll let him have the black checkers—and the first move—and that you'll bet him a dollar that he can't get the black checker on square 19 crowned a king. This looks like a sure thing, but as usual, being a prince of puzzlers, you come out on top.

After he's forked over a dollar, you set the board up again and tell him that now that he knows how it's done you'll give him a chance to win his money back. This time you'll play the black checkers and go first. To his surprise you win again, proving that lightning indeed strikes the same place twice.

The puzzle here is for you to figure out how the above Double Whammy is accomplished. It's easier than it sounds.

# World's Greatest "Planetary" Puzzle

| Q | U | O | T | H |
|---|---|---|---|---|
| L | J | T | S | R |
| R | P | U | A | M |
| I | E | N | R | E |
| T | V | Y | U | C |

Waldo Starfinder, a local amateur astronomer, is checking out our next puzzle. Hidden in the above grid are the names of the nine planets in our solar system plus the name of the star they revolve around. Your job is to spell out the names of these heavenly bodies by starting at any letter and then moving from box to adjoining box either horizontally, vertically, or diagonally. You can re-enter any box after leaving it for another. You have five light minutes to solve this one.

# World's Greatest "Horned Lizard" Puzzle

The latest acquisition at our town's nature museum is
Balshazzar, a great horned lizard from who knows where.
They placed him in a new circular-domed terrarium in our
reptile room. Balshazzar immediately set out to explore his
new domain. Starting at the door he went due north for 60
inches until he ran into the rim. He then turned due east
and scurried straight ahead for 80 inches until he again
bumped into the rim of the enclosure. Using these meager
facts can you figure out what the diameter of the terrarium is?

# World's Greatest "Number" Puzzle

SOLVE THIS PUZZLE
AND WIN A FREE LUBE
AT ABNER'S AUTO SHOP!

Back when America hit the road for the first time, competition for business was hot and heavy. It appears that Abner lured them in with puzzles and giveaways. Judging by the difficulty of this problem, I'd say that Abner wasn't losing much money.

Let's see if you'd qualify for a freebie at the lube pit. All you have to do is substitute numbers for the letters in the above math expression. The same number must be used for the same letter. The contest ends in one hour. Good luck!

# World's Greatest "Poker" Puzzle

MELVIN      HARVEY

BRUCE      ROLLO

Many years ago, in the old baseball bush leagues, the players would be paid after every game. Many hot poker games ensued into the wee hours of the morning. One such game concerns four players from the Bayside Buzzards. When the game began the four players—Melvin, Harvey, Bruce and Rollo—had $233 between them. When the cock crowed and the game was over, Melvin had $20 more than Harvey, $53 more than Bruce, and $71 more than Rollo. How much money did each of the Buzzards take home that morning?

# World's Greatest "Toy Train" Puzzle

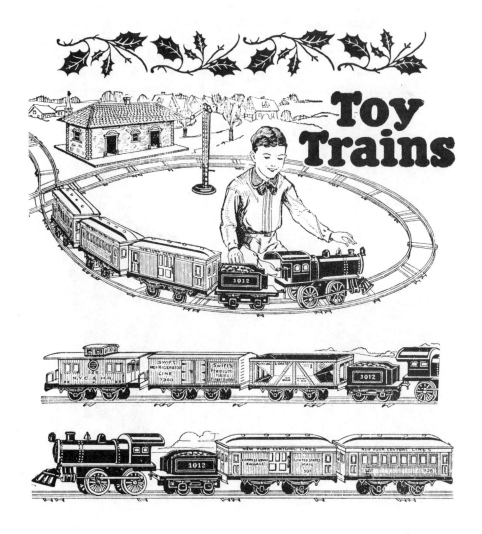

When I was a young lad my dad gave me a set of trains for Christmas. Besides the regular cars that it came with, he bought 20 extra cars for an additional $20. Passenger cars cost $4 each, freight cars were $0.50 each, and coal cars were $0.25 each (this was a long time ago). Can you figure out how many of each type he bought for his $20?

# World's Greatest "Punishment" Puzzle

*"We are not amused, Master Throckmorton! You will stay after school until you discover a number, written with only odd figures, that is equal in value to an even number. Now, sweep yourself back to the classroom!"*

Will Throckmorton ever learn? Mr. Pennypacker has given him tough meat to chew on. He can only use the figures 1, 3, 5, 7, and 9 to make this number. Obviously, numbers like 333, or 753, or 917 are not even numbers. Can you help Throckey get out of detention and out to the baseball diamond?

# World's Greatest "Play Store" Puzzle

"Doris, I'm returning this peach jam. I want a strawberry jam instead."

"Okay, Hally, here's your jam. However, you now owe me an additional 10 cents!"

Hally and Doris are playing store. Hally originally bought three jars of strawberry jam and four jars of peach jam from Doris for $3.10. Now she owes her 10 cents more. From all of this can you figure out the price of a jar of strawberry jam and a jar of peach jam?

# World's Greatest "Word" Puzzle

"My, what an extraordinary find! According to the local puzzle club there is a five-letter word containing five other words within itself. The letters that make up the word do not have to be rearranged in any manner. Also, each word is complete with no intervening letters. It says that the answer is on page 15, but someone has pinched that section of the paper. I'll be here all day trying to figure this one out!"

Malcolm Dolittle, prominent young socialite, dropped into his club to relax and found consternation instead. The funny thing is that if you read over his thoughts you'll see the answer as plain as the shine in his hair.

# World's Greatest "Bullet Hole" Puzzle

In the lore of the Old West, Cattle Kate was one of a kind. Her prowess with a six gun was legendary. Here we see her winning a bet by shooting 12 bullets into the wall while looking in the other direction. Her bet was that she could line up the holes into seven rows with four holes in each row. Of course, some of the holes would be in more than one row. Sam, the piano man, doesn't seem a bit worried. Where do you think the slugs were drilled into the wall?

# World's Greatest "Car Sale" Puzzle

Well, Daphne, I finally sold that old crock today. I originally priced it at $1,100. When no one was interested I dropped the price to $880. Still no nibbles. I then cut the price to $704. Finally, in desperation, I slashed the price once more and Orvile Winesap came in this morning and bought it. Can you guess the amount he paid for it?

# World's Greatest "Playing Card" Puzzle

Pictured here is an 18th century manufacturer of playing cards. He was certainly a walking advertisement for his product. Back in those days some folks considered a deck of cards an evil waste of time. A deck of cards has many similarities to a calendar. In fact there are at least seven ways in which a deck of cards bears a striking resemblance to a calendar. I'll bet that you can't think of more than five of them.

# World's Greatest "Hoop Gun" Puzzle

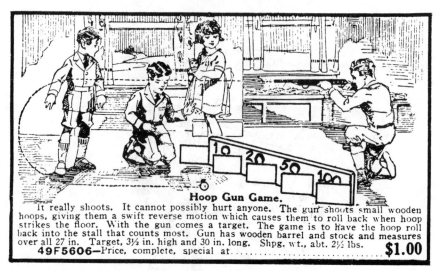

**Hoop Gun Game.**

It really shoots. It cannot possibly hurt anyone. The gun shoots small wooden hoops, giving them a swift reverse motion which causes them to roll back when hoop strikes the floor. With the gun comes a target. The game is to have the hoop roll back into the stall that counts most. Gun has wooden barrel and stock and measures over all 27 in. Target, 3½ in. high and 30 in. long. Shpg. wt., abt. 2½ lbs.

**49F5606**—Price, complete, special at.................................... **$1.00**

A great old pastime was the Hoop Gun Game, and it wasn't very expensive either. Here we see Ned Sureshot winning another game from his sister and the Whimpwhiler boys. Ned put 25 straight hoops into the target slots for a total score of 500 points. There are four target slots with point values of 10, 20, 50, and 100. Can you figure out how many hoops Ned placed in each of the slots?

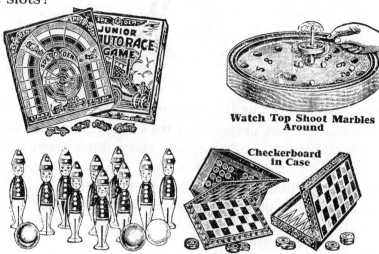

Watch Top Shoot Marbles Around

Checkerboard in Case

# World's Greatest "Royal" Puzzle

> "I say, Clive, when this rubber is over I have a smashing card puzzle for you. I'd be willing to bet my Bentley against your Rolls that you can't solve it in 30 minutes!"

Here's how Reggie expects to gain a new car. To solve the puzzle, you have to take the four kings and the four queens and arrange them into a packet that can be dealt out as follows: king, queen, king, queen, king, queen, king, queen. They must be dealt in the following manner:

(1) Take the top card and turn it face up on the table.

(2) Take the next card and place it on the bottom of the deck.

(3) Repeat steps 1 and 2 seven more times.

This is quite a tricky little problem and Reggie just might get to drive a Rolls home. See if you can solve it under 30 minutes!

# World's Greatest "Rebus" Puzzles

Complete each sentence with the help of the associated rebus clue.

# World's Greatest "Computer" Puzzle

Our puzzle computer has been grinding away for hours with no end in sight. The problem that it is working on is to take the numbers 1 through 9 and arrange them into three rows where the value of the three-figure number in the middle row is twice that of the number in the first row and the value of the three-figure number in the third row will be three times that of the number in the first row. Let's see if you can beat the number-cruncher to the answer!

# World's Greatest "Kissing" Puzzle

"All right, Elvira, let's stop kidding around! Will you give me a kiss if I can prove to you that I can take one away from 29 and have a total of 30 left?"

"Caleb, that's not fair! You know how much I love a good puzzle. Okay, I accept your wager."

Caleb's puzzle is an old, but good one. Do you know how this oily Casanova will win Elvira's lips?

# World's Greatest "Rope Ladder" Puzzle

When the U.S.S. *Extravagantic* pulled into New York Harbor last week it needed some maintenance on its hull. A rope ladder was let down that reached from the deck to the water. The rungs were spaced one foot apart, and there were 50 of them above the water at low tide. The water in New York Harbor rises at about 6 inches an hour. Can you calculate how many rungs will still be above water six hours later when the ocean will be at high tide?

# World's Greatest "Bottle" Puzzle

The following note in a bottle was brought to Professor Flunkum by one of his students. He challenged the learned man to figure out what famous sea captain would have written the poem contained in the note:

"A mighty ship I now command,
With cargo rare from every land.
No goods have I to trade or sell;
Each wind will serve my turn as well;
To neither port nor harbor bound,
My greatest wish to run aground."

Do you know who this poetic pilot was?

# World's Greatest "Ballot" Puzzle

"Get lost, Wolfram, your time has come!"

"Not so fast, your ladyship. I'm a tenured servant protected by the Royal Ballot!"

When King Bowen of Gallstonia died, Queen Olga decided that the time was ripe to fire his manservant, Wolfram, whom she had always hated. However, since he was entitled to the Royal Ballot she had to let him draw ballots to try and hold his job. She placed two folded pieces of paper in her crown. One had "Get Lost" written on it, and the other was supposed to have "Stay" on it. However, the queen wrote "Get Lost" on both slips to make sure Wolfram would be dismissed. In spite of her conniving, Wolfram outwitted the queen and retained his position in the royal household. How did he do it?

# World's Greatest "Addition" Puzzle

Daddy Bruin sounds a little upset over the puzzle he's reading in the *Peltville Gazette*. Let's see what the problem is before he really explodes:

"The row of figures shown here neatly adds up to 45. Can you, by changing one of the plus signs to a multiplication sign and adding one set of parentheses, make this row of figures add up to 100?"

# World's Greatest "Vacation" Puzzle

*Palmas, Calif., July 10, 1902.* Pictured here is that well-known socialite, Ursala Uppercrust of Chevy Glenn, New York, regaling the other vacationers at the fashionable Palm Cliff Hotel with her witty puzzles and stories concerning her many friends around the world. Can you solve the maharanee's problem?

# World's Greatest "Magic Store" Puzzle

Well, here we are at Bland's Magical Palace, that famous Victorian emporium of mystery on New Oxford Street. This is the haunt of the famous puzzle writer, Professor Hoffmann. We're to meet him at 1:00 P.M. Let's go in.

"Hello, professor, we're right on time. Do you have any new puzzles for us today?"

"I certainly do! Please sit down and try your hand at the Three Legacies problem. A gentleman, making his will, left legacies to his three servants. The parlour maid had been with him three times as long as the housemaid, and the cook twice as long as the parlour maid. The gifts were distributed in proportion to the length of service. The total amount to be given out was $700.

"What was the amount received by each of his servants?"

# World's Greatest "Substitution" Puzzle

While the master magician was rummaging through a crate of books, he came across a perplexing math problem that he thought our readers would be interested in. The board he is holding illustrates the puzzle. To solve it you must substitute the digits 1 through 9 for the dots in such a manner that a true mathematical problem is created. There are no zeros, and each digit is only used once. Let's see if you can conjure up the answer in 30 minutes.

# World's Greatest "Bubble" Puzzle

Granddad used to say that one of the great joys of his youth was going to bubble parties. Everyone was given a clay pipe, and prizes were awarded to those who blew the biggest bubbles or who had the most bubbles in the air at one time. When asked what the most bubbles he ever had in the air at one time were, his reply was:

"I'll make a puzzle out of that question, young man!" Granddad loved a good problem. "If I had as many more, and half again as many more, and yet seven more, I should have had 32 bubbles in the air."

From his confusing hints can you figure out exactly how many bubbles he had in the air at one time?

# World's Greatest "Camera" Puzzle

Four avid collectors went to an old camera auction and came home with a bonanza. One of the items on the block was a case containing 233 antique cameras. The collectors pooled their money and made the winning bid. When they got home they divided the cameras up in proportion to the amount of money each of them chipped in.

Flash Farrington received 20 more cameras than Shutters Smollet, 53 more than Wet Plate Pennington, and 71 more than Bellows Barlow. Can you develop an answer to the question, "How many cameras did each of the collectors receive?"

# World's Greatest "Transpositional" Puzzle

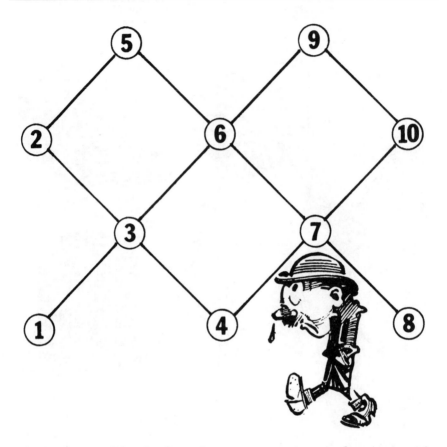

Lonesome George has been going in circles trying to solve this one. Let's help him out. Place two pennies on numbers 1 and 2 and two dimes on numbers 8 and 10. We have to make these four coins change places in just 18 moves. The rules for moving the coins are: You can move one coin at a time to any numbered circle on any straight line. You can move any coin during a turn, but you can't move the same coin twice in a row. The big no-no is that at no time can a penny and a dime come to rest on the same line at the same time.

Those are the rules. You have 15 minutes to solve this puzzle.

# World's Greatest "Carnival Wheel" Puzzle

Jingles, the carnival clown, is right. The boss is a very superstitious man. He always wants the numbers on the wheel, 1 through 11, placed so that any three numbers in a straight line will add up to 18. Can you place them correctly before someone yells, "Hey, Rube?"

# World's Greatest "Tips" Puzzle

"Mike, I think that you cheated me when we divided up the luncheon tips!" Pat complained.

"Why, I just thought you were being generous, Pat!" Mike replied innocently.

Here's the problem: After lunch, when they were trying to divide up their tips, Pat gave Mike as many dollars as Mike already had. Mike then said, "This is too much" and gave Pat back as much money as Pat now had left. Pat then said, "No, Mike, this is too much," and gave Mike back as many dollars as Mike now had left. Pat now had no money left and Mike had a total of $80. Pat obviously needs a keeper . . . book, that is. How much money did both waiters have before they started their transactions?

# World's Greatest "Beehive" Puzzle

The bees pictured here are busy trying to rearrange the numbers 1 through 14 in their hive into a more random order. What they are trying to do is to place the numbers in the cells so that no two consecutive numbers are in adjacent cells. And to top it off, no number can be next to a number that divides it evenly. (The number 1 is excluded from consideration.) Try to wax, not wane, on this one.

# World's Greatest "Castle" Puzzle

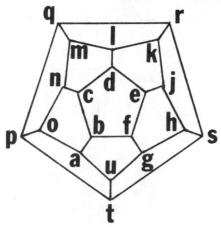

Pictured above is the layout of a mountain castle. The points on the battlements where the sentries are posted are marked with letters. All the posts are connected with walkways, as indicated. What route would the sergeant-at-arms take if he wanted to inspect each post only once during his tour and end up back at his starting point?

# World's Greatest "Marbles" Puzzle

Pictured above is the famous North Jersey shoot-out between "Dutch" Doberman and "Spike" Callahan, back in the summer of 1908. Both players came with bulging marble bags to settle once and for all who had the best thumb in the Oranges. They started the game with the same number of marbles. After the first round Dutch was up 20 marbles. However, on the second and final round, he lost two-thirds of what he had. Spike then had four times as many marbles as Dutch. Can you figure out how many marbles each started with and how many they each had when the game was over?

# World's Greatest "Balloon" Puzzle

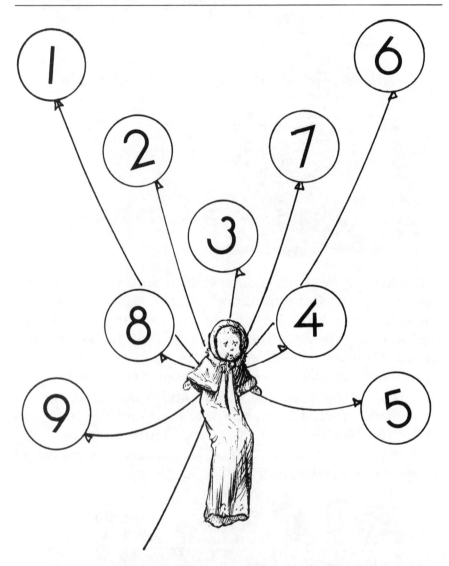

Little Gwendolyn does not look happy about her brother's idea of creative babysitting. However, the numbered balloons remind us of an old puzzle. Can you rearrange the balloons so that the numbers in each of the two rows of five balloons add up to 27? Then tell her brother Pugsley to haul her down.

# World's Greatest "Wine" Puzzle

Here's a puzzle from old Bacchus himself. To get into his party you have to figure out how much wine is in each of two 10-gallon barrels. The barrels are labeled *A* and *B*. Barrel *A* contains more wine than barrel *B*.

First, you pour from barrel *A* into barrel *B* as much wine as barrel *B* already contains. Next, you pour from barrel *B* back into barrel *A* as much wine as barrel *A* now contains. Finally, you pour back from barrel *A* into barrel *B* as much wine as barrel *B* now contains.

At this point both barrels contain 48 pints of wine. How much wine did each barrel contain at the start?

# World's Greatest "Domino" Puzzle

This is one of the few domino puzzles that you are ever liable to run across. Pictured above are four blank dominoes. What you have to do is to figure out where to put 18 spots on them according to the following rules:

The total number of spots on the top halves of the dominoes must be equal to the total number of spots on the bottom halves. Also, the first domino will have twice as many spots as the last domino. One of the pieces has only one spot on it and another one is a double (the top has as many spots as the bottom).

Finally, three dominoes have the same number of spots on their top halves, and two have the same number of spots on their bottom halves.

It sounds confusing, but I bet you can solve it in less than 15 minutes.

# World's Greatest "Primate" Puzzle

It's lunch time at the local zoo, and down at the primate pavilion the cry is for bananas. Every day 100 bananas are divided up among 100 limb swingers. Each gorilla gets three bananas; each ape gets two. The lemurs, being the smallest, get a half a banana each.

Using these facts to work with, can you figure out how many gorillas, apes and lemurs there are?

# World's Greatest "After Dinner" Puzzle

Back in the pre-television days when people actually sat around the dinner table and talked, puzzles were a popular form of after-dessert amusement. Here we find "Scissors" Symington showing off his famous Triangle Problem. The puzzle is to take the paper equilateral triangle that he is holding and cut it into five pieces that can subsequently be used to form four smaller equilateral triangles. Not all the pieces will be needed to form each of these triangles. All five pieces are cut in the shape of triangles. I'll have another piece of pie while you're working on this one.

# World's Greatest "Tinsmith" Puzzle

Back in 1776 Timothy of York was the best tinsmith in Boston. As soon as he finishes making the drinking cup he is working on, he's going to tackle a giant puzzle for the owner of the Bloody Marlin Grog Shop down the road. Sitting on the back bench is a large piece of tin that Timothy has to cut into five pieces that can then be arranged to form a perfect square. Can you figure out how he's going to do this?

# World's Greatest "Hot Dog" Puzzle

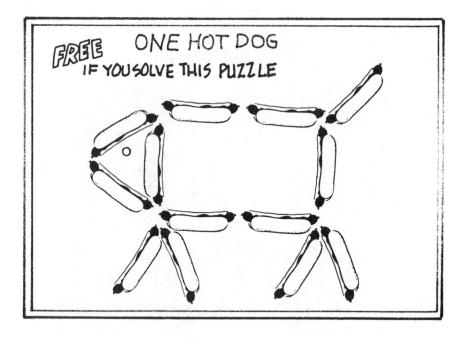

"Hi, kiddies, I'm back with another Murbles stumper. I've arranged 13 hot dogs into a picture of a dog facing west. Can you change the picture so that the dog is now facing east by moving only two of the hot dogs to new positions? The dog must keep his upturned tail. His eye is a quarter, and you can also move that. The first one to solve it gets a Murbles Masterpiece in mustard!"

# World's Greatest "Chemistry" Puzzle

Jimmy: "Hey, Ma! I've done it! I've done it! I just isolated the chemical compound *HIJKLMNO!*"

Mother: "That's nice, Jimmy, don't burn the carpet!"

Well, it looks like Jimmy A. Chiver, the boy wonder of Ashtabula, Ohio, has made a chemical breakthrough. Can you figure out what uses he'll discover for his new compound, *HIJKLMNO*?

# World's Greatest "Vitascope" Puzzle

During the early days of the movies, theatres would often have "Puzzle Parties" to help bring in the crowds. Before the movie began, they would flash puzzles on the screen and the patrons would jot down the answers on their programs and hand them in hoping to win something. The puzzle being projected above shows a Roman numeral nine. The problem is to add one line to this figure so that it is turned into an *even* number. Your answer must be a conventional number.

# World's Greatest "What" Puzzles

"What's best when it's cracked?"
"What's the hardest thing to deal with?"
"What key is hardest to turn?"
"What has 18 legs and catches flies?"
"What flowers are kissable?"
"What men have made their mark in the world?"
"What's worse than raining cats and dogs?"

The winners of the Lake Running Bear Middle School "What" contest of 1906.

# World's Greatest "Triangle" Puzzle

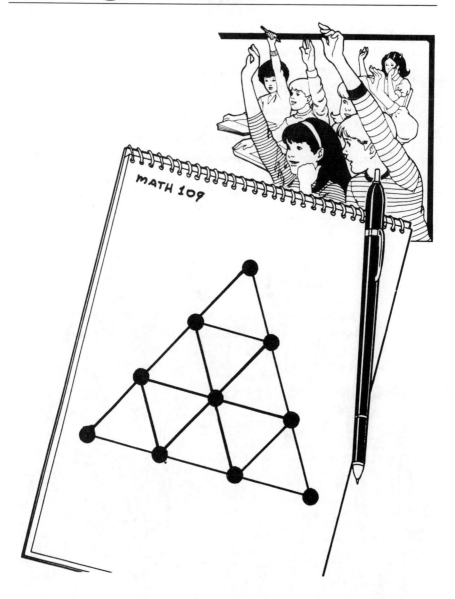

Last night's homework included a geometry stumper. The assignment was to remove four bars from the above drawing so that five triangles remained. Will the teacher see your hand raised?

# World's Greatest "Thinking Cap" Puzzle

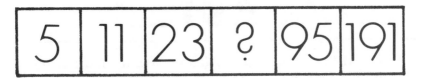

| 5 | 11 | 23 | ? | 95 | 191 |

Professor Warwick Barnstable, inventor of the Barnstable Electronic Thinking Cap, has come out of retirement to answer a challenge from the Maplewood Middle School Computer Club. He has donned his famous thinking cap and is attempting to solve the above progression problem before the mighty mites in the background. Can you figure out what the fourth number in the above sequence should be?

# World's Greatest "Spelling" Puzzle

## "__KST__"

"Win a free weekend in Altoona, Pennsylvania, by being the first to solve this puzzle: What eight-letter word has the letters KST in its middle, in the beginning, and at the end? Strangely enough, the letters K, S, and T only appear once in the word."

"That's easy! Mommy, pack our bags, We're going to Altoona!"

It looks as though that precocious child, Mehitabel Well-read, the Wunderkind of Wheeling, West Virginia, is headed for the Keystone State. Could you have beat her to the answer?

# World's Greatest "Movie Star" Puzzle

The Dish sisters, Ima and Sucha, were all the rage when they came to Hollywood back in the 1920s. The studio refused to reveal their ages, but a playful press agent teased the reporters with this puzzle.

"Added together, their ages come to 44 years. Right now, Ima is twice as old as Sucha was when Ima was half as old as Sucha will be when Sucha is three times as old as Ima was when Ima was three times as old as Sucha. From that you should be able to tell me how old the women are."

# World's Greatest "Statuette" Puzzle

When Calvin Collectible opened his New Antique Shoppe some 20 years ago, these two statuettes were proudly displayed in the front window. Up until last week, they were still there. Then in two days, he sold the first one for $198 and made a 10 percent profit on it, and then he sold the second one for $198 and took a 10 percent loss on it. Taken together, did Calvin make a profit on the two sales or did he sustain a loss?

# World's Greatest "Travel" Puzzle

Time out for a short vacation. Where would you like to go? In this hidden-places quiz, we've buried the names of 10 places. There's one hidden in each sentence. We supply the answer to the first one to show you how it's done.

1. He thinks I *am her st*upid sister. (Amherst)
2. Let no woman or man dye his or her hair.
3. His overwrought exasperation filled the enemy with dismay.
4. The wounded were brought in nine vehicles.
5. The calmest man is sometimes made irate.
6. The sale must commence at one o'clock.
7. I should be proud to entertain such a guest.
8. The escaping prisoners crossed the river on a raft.
9. He has my R.N. as a monogram on all his notepaper.
10. He must cross the Atlantic or keep quiet.

# World's Greatest "Radio" Puzzle

"All right, Mr. Puzzle Answer Man, let's see you answer this one:

*A word I know*
*Six letters it contains;*
*Subtract just one*
*And twelve you'll find remains.*

What is that word?"

In 1930s radio, the Puzzle Answer Man was very popular. Can you help him prove that six minus one equals twelve? If you succeed, pay yourself one shiny, silver dollar, the standard radio prize in those days.

# The
# **World's**
# Hardest Puzzles

# World's Hardest "Checkbook" Puzzle

*"Could you please get me a pot of coffee, Ms. Upshot. I fear that I'm going to be up all night trying to reconcile this confounded checkbook."*

```
Beginning balance for the month... $54.00
Check #0221    $20.00    Balance    $34.00
Check #0222    $20.00    Balance    $14.00
Check #0223    $10.00    Balance    $ 4.00
Check #0224    $ 4.00    Balance    $  .00
=========================================
        Total  $54.00        Total   $52.00
```

Thaddeus Tightwad has been trying for hours to figure out why the two sides of his checkbook ledger are not the same. Can you determine where the missing two dollars have gone?

# World's Hardest "Checkerboard" Puzzle

Cy Corncrib will be pulling out his goatee if he loses one more game of checkers to Pop Bentley. He hasn't won since Hoover was President. Shown above is the ending of their last match. Pop was playing the white pieces and it was his turn. The white pieces move up the board while the black move down. What devious moves did Pop make to seal Corncrib's fate?

# World's Hardest "Plywood" Puzzle

Our local handyman, Hiram Ballpeene, just returned from his reunion at Carpentry College where he stumped everyone with his new plywood puzzle. He showed them a piece of wood composed of five equal squares. First you must make two straight cuts across the panel, dividing it into three pieces. Then fit these pieces together so that they form a perfect square. How did Hiram do it?

# World's Hardest "Line" Puzzle

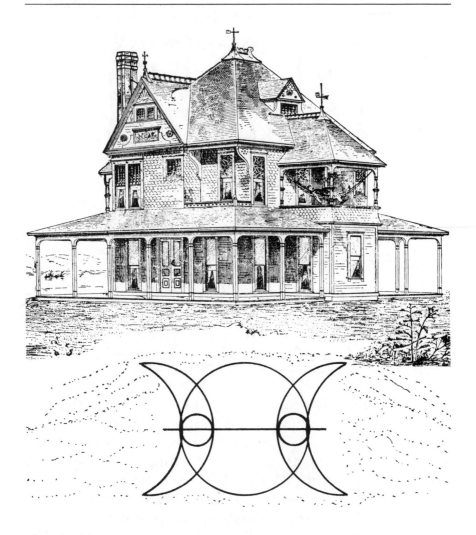

Amos Edelhagen is napping in his hammock when he should be out on the beach, enjoying his vacation. It seems that he spent all morning on the beach drawing in the sand, attempting to solve a line problem. He wanted to draw the above figure, using just one continuous line without letting any part of the line cross any other part of the line. Truly a puzzle to ruin anyone's vacation!

# World's Hardest "Flour" Puzzle

While checking his supplies, Cy Corncrib noticed something interesting about his flour sacks. The sacks were stacked three to a shelf and numbered one through nine. On shelves one and three, he had a single sack next to a pair of sacks, while the middle shelf held three sacks grouped together. Now, if he multiplied the number on the single sack (7), by the number on the pair next to it (28), he got 196, the number on the middle sacks. However, if he tried multiplying the numbers on the third shelf, (34) and (5), he got 170.

Cy then came up with this problem: How do you rearrange the sacks, with as few moves as possible, so that when you multiply each pair by its single neighbor, you will come up with a product equal to the number on the middle shelf?

# World's Hardest "Animal" Puzzle

The eighty-one squares in the puzzle picture contain the names of forty-four animals. They may be spelled out by what is known in chess as the "King's Move," namely, one square at a time in any direction. Thus, from the first *O* on the second line, you could move to *X, N, Y, L, F, U, I* or *S*. Thus, *DOG* might be found in the squares 75, 65, 56; and *PORCUPINE* in 33, 43, 35, 45, 54, 63, 62, 70, and 71. Perseverance is necessary if you hope to find all forty-four animals.

# World's Hardest "Glass" Puzzle

J. Wellington Moneybags, the Prince of Gamblers, is back with a "glass" stumper. Place two inverted glasses close enough together so that you can prop a stick match between them about halfway up, as shown. Now, Wellington will bet that he can remove *one* glass and the match will remain suspended in air. You may not touch the match with anything other than the second match on the table, and you must do that prior to removing the glass. Anyone care to wager?

# World's Hardest "Paper" Puzzle

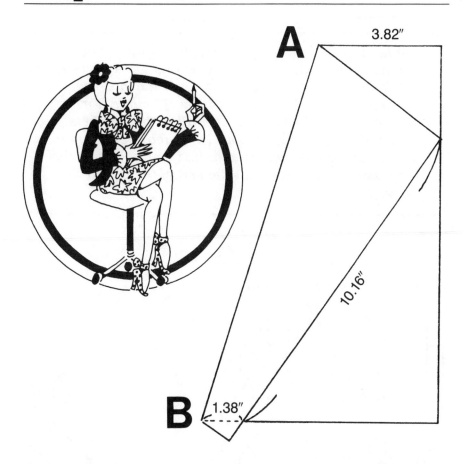

Harriet is not only the prettiest woman in the secretarial pool, she's also the best puzzler in the office. One day, when the boss's son challenged her to prove how good she was at puzzles, she took out a sheet of 8½-by-11-inch typing paper, folded it once, and marked some measurements on it.

"All right, Herbert, I'll bet you lunch that you can't calculate the length of the fold (A–B) without measuring it. I've marked down three lengths on the paper. This is all the information you'll need to solve this simple problem."

Can you succeed where Herbert failed?

# World's Hardest "Division" Puzzle

*"Well, students, I see by the teaching guide that you are working on division problems this week. Let's see just how far you've progressed. On the board I've written a problem in long division. To make it more difficult, I've substituted X's for all of the numbers except the lucky 7's. It's your job to reason out what these numbers were and to write them back into the expression. You have until the end of the period to solve this one."*

Ms. Priscilla Sunshine is once again our substitute teacher for the day. Make sure that your erasers are handy.

# World's Hardest "Hardware" Puzzle

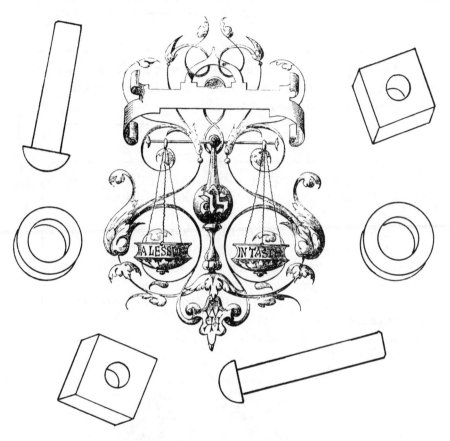

Last Sunday, down at Tutwyler's Hardware Store, Ben was playing with the balance scale that Grandfather Tutwyler had brought over from the old country in 1903. After a while, Ben observed:

(1) Three nuts plus one bolt were equal in weight to twelve washers.

(2) One bolt was equal in weight to one nut plus eight washers.

Using this information, he came up with a puzzle—How many washers are equal in weight to one bolt?

# World's Hardest "Age" Puzzle

"Really, Madge, we've been seeing each other for over a year now. Don't you think that it's about time you told me your age?"

"Roger, only a cad would ask a young lady how old she is. However, to satisfy your morbid curiosity, I'll give you a hint:
I come from a very large family. Five years ago, I was five times as old as my youngest sister, Veronica. Today I'm only three times as old as she is. That's all the information you're going to get from me. And, knowing your prowess in mathematics, I'm sure my secret will remain closely guarded."

Can you help Roger discern Madge's true age?

# World's Hardest "Chess" Puzzle

Over a hundred years ago, Kempelen's famous Automation Chess Player could not only beat most players that challenged it, but it could also formulate chess puzzles that stumped the best minds of the day. Here's one of the hardest. You are required to place four black queens and a black bishop on a chessboard so that they control the entire board. In other words, after the five pieces have been positioned, it will be impossible to place the white king on any vacant square without being in check.

# World's Hardest "Antique" Puzzle

Mercator Wins $10,000 For Antique Puzzle

Alex Mercator, proprietor of the Nothing New Antique Mart, is seen here happily reading the news of his unexpected win at last month's puzzle convention. He challenged the contest judges to take the seventeen antique items he brought with him and arrange them in four straight lines on the floor, with each line containing five items. Can you succeed where the eminent panel of experts failed?

# World's Hardest "Archaeology" Puzzle

"Well, Petrie, there it is—Plato's Cube. They said it didn't exist, but our perseverance has paid off. According to Plato, the huge central cube was made up of many smaller marble cubes. Also, the square central plaza that it sits on is made of these same smaller cubes. On top of that, the plaza has the same number of smaller cubes in it as the huge central cube is made of."

"Quite right, Hawkings. For once, we're in agreement. Another point that you should note is that the length of one side of the plaza is exactly twice the length of one side of the cube, which brings us to the nature of Plato's puzzle. Without going over to the plaza, can you calculate how many smaller cubes were used in building both the cube and the plaza? Although there are several answers to this problem, we are looking for the one that uses the smallest number of cubes to satisfy all the rules of construction that we have related."

# World's Hardest "Number" Puzzle

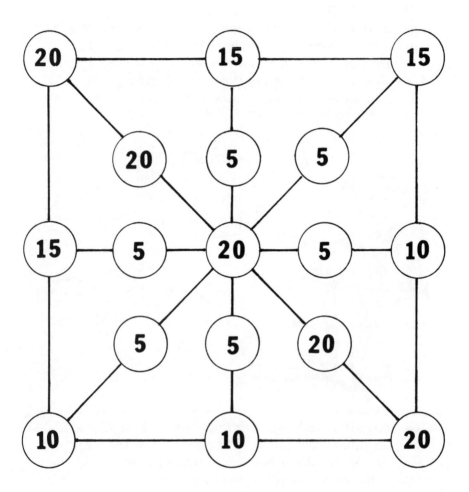

This is a rather neat number puzzle. You are challenged to rearrange the 17 numbers in this diagram so that they add up to 55 along any of the eight straight lines that make up the grid.

# World's Hardest "Dots" Puzzle

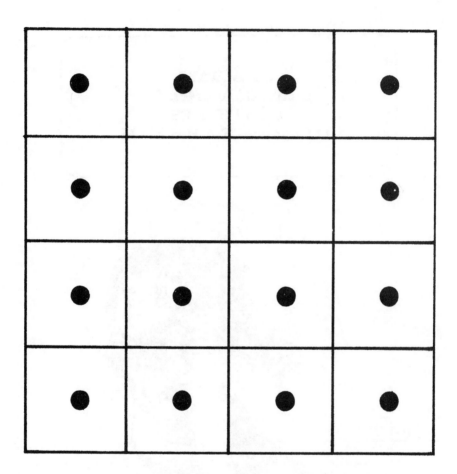

Draw the above sixteen-square grid on a separate sheet of paper, and place a dot in the middle of each square. Now for the puzzle: Try to draw six straight lines that will pass through every dot in the grid—without lifting the pencil from the paper. Here's a slight hint: you will have to pass through two of the dots twice. Also, your first line must start outside the grid.

# World's Hardest "Rebus" Puzzle

2 B ALWAYS
E co X nf Aid Men S t
I d S i H m ES
111 chances T 4 H 6 E s M

Our Victorian puzzler is working on one of the hardest rebus problems anywhere. The advice to students, once deciphered, will prove as apt today as it was a hundred years ago.

# World's Hardest "Floating Paper" Puzzle

Last night at the Paper Mill Ball, betting achieved a fever pitch. Waldo Pennypacker, shown above, simultaneously dropped two sheets of writing paper from shoulder height. Which piece of paper will touch the floor first? Hundreds rode on each foot the paper fell. How could you ensure that paper *a* would land first? Of course, nothing could be attached to or added to either sheet of paper.

# World's Hardest "Magic Square" Puzzle

This gentleman is reading about the prize-winning magic square puzzle. To solve it, replace the X's in the grid with the correct numbers to create a square that adds up to 34 in each column, row, and the two major diagonals. Use numbers 1 through 16; no number may be used more than once.

# World's Hardest "Newspaper" Puzzle

"Hello, Eddie, this is Horatio Stumpwell. Here's the copy for today's puzzle column:

'The Ancient sat and pondered well,
The following puzzle I'm about to tell.
From six you remove nine,
Now isn't that fine!
From nine you remove ten,
Don't try that again!
From forty you remove fifty,
That's what I call nifty!
A six is all that's left over,
Solve the puzzle and you'll be in clover.'

Rush that down to the printer!"

"Yes, sir, Mr. Stumpwell, I'm on my way!"

You're going to have to go back nearly 2,000 years to solve this one.

# World's Hardest "Steamship" Puzzle

Back in the golden age of steam, great steamships entered and left New York Harbor on a daily basis. On one day, three ships cleared the Narrows and headed for Portsmouth, England. The first ship made the round trip to Portsmouth and back in 12 days. It took the second ship 16 days to complete the round trip. The third ship came limping back to New York in 20 days. Since the turn-around time in port was 12 hours, the ships were always back at sea the same day that they arrived. How many days will pass before all three ships again leave New York on the same date, and how many round trips will each ship make in the meantime?

# World's Hardest "Typewriter" Puzzle

1.
H
A
N
G

2. HEAD
D

3. ONCE
8AM

4. LO HEAD HEELS VE

5. DAYDAYOUT

6. sopBACTRIAN

7. Sympho

8. BED
BED

The *doodle words* shown here represent a proper name, common saying, or familiar object. The first doodle word stands for "hang-up." If you got that one, it should be a cinch to solve the remaining seven.

# World's Hardest "Gold Bar" Puzzle

Patrick O'Donald, the famous Nome gnome, spent days digging for gold and nights drinking at the Northern Lights Saloon. At the beginning of each month, Patrick cast his gold into a 31-inch-long bar. Every night he ate and drank the equivalent, in gold, of one inch of the bar. Instead of cutting the bar into 31 pieces, Patrick figured out the smallest number of pieces necessary to pay the bartender each night. The first night, for example, he gave the barkeep a one-inch piece; the second night, he paid with a two-inch piece and took back the one-inch piece. What are the fewest number of pieces he would need to cut the bar into so that he could get through any month of the year?

# World's Hardest "Chicken" Puzzle

Farming neighbors Amy and Bessie went to market every day to sell their chickens. Bessie sold 30 chickens a day, at two chickens for $1.00, and brought home $15.00. Amy sold 30 chickens a day, at three chickens for $1.00, and brought home $10.00. One day Amy was sick, so she asked Bessie to sell her chickens for her. Bessie took the 60 chickens to market and sold them all at the rate of five chickens for $2.00. She brought home a total of $24 for the day's work. This was a dollar less than the two women usually made each day when they sold their chickens separately. What happened to the extra dollar? Did Bessie pocket it?

# World's Hardest "Progression" Puzzle

| HOLE | 1 | 2 | 3 | 4 | 5 | 6 | 7 | 8 | 9 | TOTAL |
|------|---|---|---|---|---|---|---|---|---|-------|
| Divots Davenport | 4 | 5 | 5 | 6 | 3 | 4 | 5 | | | |
| Sandy Bunker | 12 | 9 | 3 | 6 | 3 | 1 | | | | |

Sandy Bunker, one of Idle Hours Country Club's golf pros, is having a spotty day on the links. His score for the first six holes reads like a roller coaster. The funny thing is that Sandy's score, hole by hole, has been moving according to a set progression. Can you figure out what Sandy's score was on the seventh hole?

# World's Hardest "Coin" Puzzle

"She'll being coming round the Alps when she comes, when she comes!"

TIP BUCKET

The Bellowing Bavarian Belters had another poor night at the local rathskeller. When they finished their last set, only a few American tourist coins lay in the tip bucket. Rudi commented that with these coins he could pay the exact amount for anything costing from one cent to one dollar. He also said that the group had the smallest number of coins that you could do this with. What coins were in the bucket?

# World's Hardest "Logo" Puzzle

Posing here is Woo Ling Yu, advertising agent for the famous Spicy Tea Export Company. He has his arm around the company logo, a cross inside a square—a symbol recognized around the world. Many years ago, Woo created a puzzle with this logo. Using an oriental fountain brush, Woo claimed that he could draw the logo without lifting the brush from the paper and without going over any line more than once. Can you figure out how he did it?

# World's Hardest "Rug" Puzzle

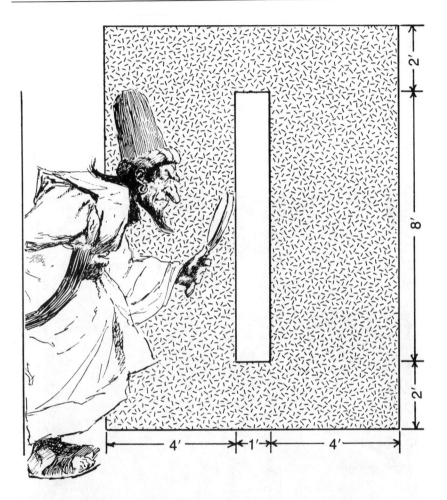

Abdul, the rug merchant, is in deep trouble. He has to deliver a ten-foot-by-ten-foot rug to a wealthy client by sundown. He planned to make it out of a piece of nine-foot-by-twelve-foot carpet in his warehouse, but when he unrolled the carpet, he found that someone had cut a one-foot-by-eight-foot piece out of its center. Quick as a genie, Abdul figured out a way to cut the rug into two pieces that could then be sewn back together to form a solid ten-foot-by-ten-foot rug.

147

# World's Hardest "Gulliver" Puzzle

> "We are little airy creatures,
>   All of different voice and features;
> One of us in 'glass' is set,
>   One of us you'll find in 'jet',
> T'other you may see in 'tin',
>   And the fourth a 'box' within.
> If the fifth you should pursue,
>   It can never fly from 'you'."

Gulliver here is entertaining the Queen of Lilliput with Jonathan Swift's puzzle poem. The problem involves figuring out the five "little airy creatures" the poem describes.

# World's Hardest "Political" Puzzle

Election years in the United States seem to always have encouraged wild rhetoric and slogans. We've taken one of the most famous political slogans and made it into a puzzle. See if you can read the slogan in the frame of letters above. Beginning with any letter, go around the frame twice, reading every other letter as you go. You'll be up a creek if you miss this one!

# World's Hardest "Clock" Puzzle

Waldo Snoozingham fell asleep while reading *War and Peace*. Sometime later he was awakened by hearing one chime from his downstairs clock. His clock strikes once every quarter-hour and gives a full number of chimes on the hour. Since Waldo was too tired to get up, how long would he have to sit in his cozy chair until he could be sure of the right time? There are two possible answers to this puzzle.

# World's Hardest "Toy Box" Puzzle

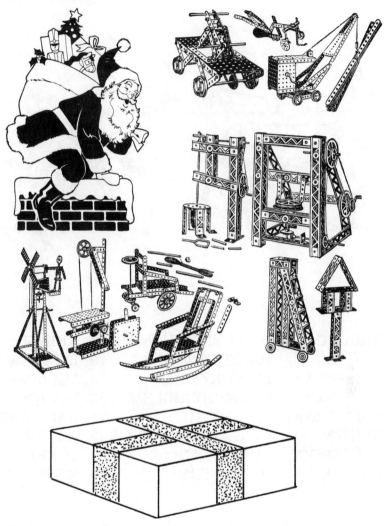

Before the invention of the silicon chip, building blocks and construction toys were among children's favorite Christmas gifts. The items shown here were built with materials that came in a box with these measurements: the top—120 square inches, the side—96 square inches, and the end—80 square inches. Can you figure out the length, width, and height of the box?

# World's Hardest "Sports" Puzzle

1. TRUCEOQ
2. ORCSEC
3. ICOBEC
4. TALFOLOB
5. LOLBVALYEL
6. NSIETN
7. SALSEROC
8. CARGIN

9. LEEHTSEEPCAS
10. OTSNOHGI
11. RCRYAEH
12. DOGBEBDLSNI
13. KYOCHE
14. GLASNII
15. SGTKANI
16. HGSFIIN

17. NKIBGI
18. LIBLGOAONN
19. LEBLBAAS
20. TUOIQS
21. BADLNAHL
22. BGUYR
23. TCEKICR
24. MSGIWMIN

In this puzzle we salute the wonderful world of sports. Below the names of 24 outdoor games are listed, but the letters have been scrambled. To win the match, you have ten minutes to unscramble them.

# World's Hardest "Word" Puzzle

"I say, Livermore, is this really the man you claim to be the world's most intelligent waiter?"

"Quite right, Doubtington, and I'll prove it to you. Barlowe, how would you say to Mr. Doubtington here, in one word, that he had a late dinner between nine and eleven o'clock?"

"That's an easy one, sir. The word that I'd use is . . . !"

Can you serve the answer before it's time to pay the check?

# World's Hardest "King" Puzzle

"So, you think that I've had trouble with women! Well, I'm not the only ruler who has run afoul with the so-called weaker sex. Let's see if you can fathom the name of this famous king from this little ditty.

'Five hundred begins it, five hundred ends it,
Five in the middle is seen;
The first of all figures, the first of all letters,
Take up their stations between.
Join all together, and then you will bring
Before you the name of an eminent king.'"

# World's Hardest "Racing" Puzzle

Here is Professor Betsalot, that avid horse player. He's studying the racing form for the next race and has narrowed the field to three horses: Sway Belly at 4 to 1, Aunt Sara at 3 to 1, and Thunder Hooves at 2 to 1. The professor is trying to figure out how much he must bet on each horse so that he will win $13, no matter which of the three horses comes in first.

For example, if he bets $5 on each horse and Sway Belly wins, he'll win $20 on Sway Belly and lose $10 on the two other horses. See if you can solve the professor's problem before the race begins.

# World's Hardest "Nationality" Puzzle

"So tell me, Myra, who had the most difficult pair of hands you ever worked on?"

"So ask me a hard one, why don't you! Last week a little old Oriental woman came into the shop. I thought the gloves she wore were ten sizes too big before she took them off. Her nails were a foot long if they were an inch. I must have used a whole bottle of nail polish on them when I was through. She told me that all the old women where she came from never cut their nails. It seems that she was . . . E, E, E."

Myra has some great cuticle stories, all right. She also likes to show off her puzzling ability as exemplified by her way of specifying the long-nailed lady's origin. Can you figure out what Myra meant when she said the lady was "E, E, E"?

# World's Hardest "Route" Puzzle

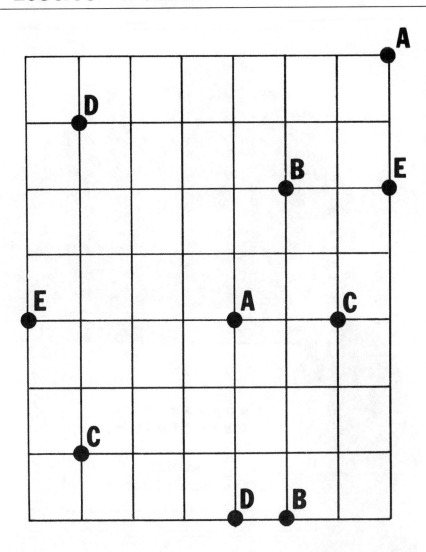

This is an old and rather interesting puzzle. On the grid above are five pairs of dots, labeled A through E. Connect these pairs: A to A, B to B, C to C, D to D, and E to E. The routes you lay out must follow the lines on the grid. No two routes may cross or touch each other. Now, take charge of traffic control.

# World's Hardest "Inspirational" Puzzle

On his way to vespers, the Reverend I. N. Spire pauses to study a rather cryptic inspirational message carved on a monument. The stonemason from long ago was something of a puzzler since he rendered advice in the form of a rebus. Can you solve the puzzle as quickly as the good reverend?

# World's Hardest "Hopscotch" Puzzle

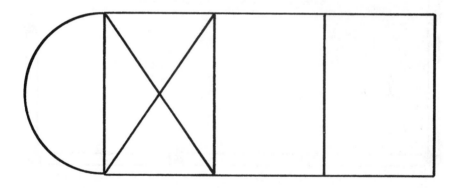

Here we see a group of 19th century lads passing time with a lively game of hopscotch. Under the illustration is a "puzzlescotch" pattern. To solve this puzzle, trace these puzzlescotch chalk marks using one continuous line without lifting your pencil from the paper and without crossing over any part of the line. Also, you may not go over any part of the line more than once. Don't skip to the answer section before trying this game.

# World's Hardest "Wooden Match" Puzzle

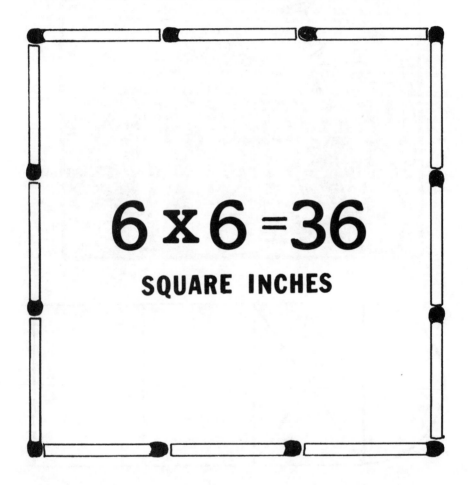

6 x 6 = 36
SQUARE INCHES

Here are twelve wooden matches arranged in a square. Each match is two inches long, which gives us a square measuring 6 inches by 6 inches. So, the matches enclose a 36-square-inch area. Rearrange these twelve matches into a new shape that will enclose an area of 12 square inches.

# World's Hardest "Circle" Puzzle

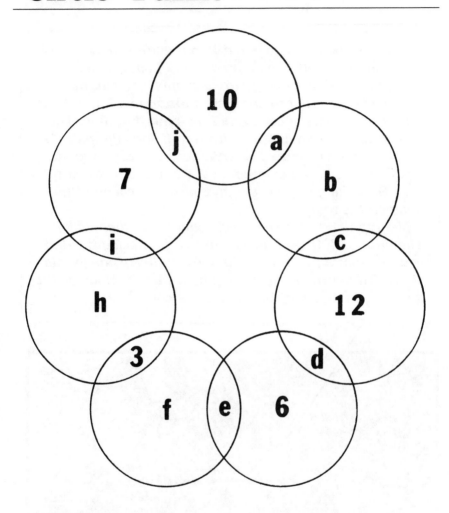

You may find yourself "seeing circles" before you finish this puzzle. The figure above is composed of seven interlocking circles. There are fourteen enclosed areas within the drawing. Replace the letters in the drawing with numbers so that all numbers from 1 to 14 will appear in the drawing. The puzzle involves doing this in such a way that the numbers within any one circle will add up to 21. There's no time limit on this one.

# World's Hardest "Bread" Puzzle

"This story is true! Clive told it to me himself. It seems that young Forsythe wandered away from Kitchener's army and became lost. Near starvation, he met two native chaps about to eat their midday meal. One chap had three loaves of bread and the other had five. They agreed to share their food with him if Forsythe paid for what he ate. Of course, he said yes, and all three ate equal shares of the eight loaves. When the meal was over, Forsythe gave them eight coins and eventually rejoined his regiment.

Meanwhile, the two natives fought over the money. The man with three loaves wanted the money divided equally, while the other chap wanted five coins for his share. This turned out to be quite a puzzle. How would you, ladies, have fairly divided the coins?"

# World's Hardest "Safe" Puzzle

At the turn of the century, a Hall's safe offered the ultimate protection for valuables. The safe shown here was owned by Timoney O'Shay, a man of great wealth who had a short memory. For the life of him, he couldn't remember the three numbers of the safe's combination. However, he had these clues pasted on top of the safe to help jog his memory:

"Multiply the 1st number by 3 and the answer is all ones. Multiply the 2nd number by 6 and the answer is all twos. Multiply the 3rd number by 9 and the answer is all threes."

If the safecrackers above had stayed in school, they may have been able to turn those clues into cash. Can you make those old tumblers fall into place?

# World's Hardest "Transposition" Puzzle

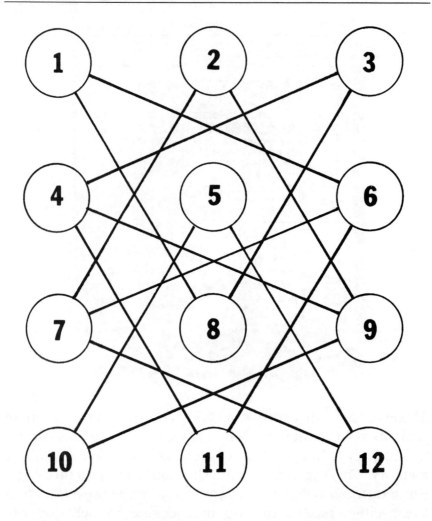

Here's a neat changing-places puzzle. Place three red checkers on positions 1, 2, and 3, and three black checkers on positions 10, 11, and 12. In just 22 moves, you must cause them to change places. Alternately move one checker at a time along the lines from one circle to another. At no time may a checker of one color be on a circle that a checker of the opposite color could reach on the next move. Only one checker may be on a circle at any one time.

# World's Hardest "Poker Chip" Puzzle

The next time the cards are running against you and you're in a cold sweat, try this little puzzle to calm your nerves. Draw up a sixteen-square playing board similar to the one above and attempt to place ten poker chips in ten of the squares so that you form the greatest number of rows, with each row containing an even number of chips. The rows may be horizontal, vertical, or diagonal. Let's see how you stack up with this puzzle.

# World's Hardest "Square" Puzzle

Here we see Fenton Catchall, Society Juggler, winding up his act with his famous Triangles-of-Death feat. Fenton holds no fear for the razor-sharp shards of steel. And, like the rest of the props in his act, they are derived from a famous puzzle. If you were to cut one of these five triangles in half, you could then take the resulting six pieces and fit them together to form a perfect square. Care to try your hand at this one?

# World's Hardest "What?" Puzzle

*"What occurs once in a second, once in a month, once in a century, but not at all in a week or a year?"*

*"What has a foot on each end and one in the middle?"*

*"What is black and white and has fuzz inside?"*

*"What is it that nobody wishes to have and nobody likes to lose?"*

*"What word will, if you take away the first letter, make you sick?"*

# World's Hardest "Moving" Puzzle

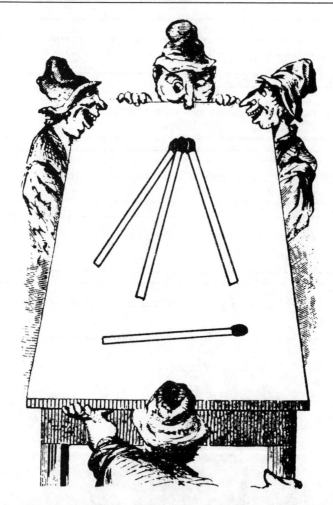

This puzzle should prove a moving experience. You'll need four wooden matches. Take three of the matches and balance them in the form of a pyramid, as shown above. Next, hand the fourth match to your victim. Challenge him to *lift* the three upright matches, using only the fourth match, transport them across the room, and place them on another table, still standing in pyramid form.

The old cronies down at the local hardware store have been working on it all afternoon.

# World's Hardest "Cork" Puzzle

The cork from the "Bottle" Puzzle landed in Ms. Smedwick's water glass. It's strange but true that a cork will not stay in the center of a glass of water. Instead it will slowly drift over to the side of the glass, where it will remain. There is, however, a simple way to make the cork remain floating in the center of the glass. (Swirling the water is not the answer.)

# World's Hardest "Rectangle" Puzzle

Mr. Gotrocks is mulling over the famous rectangle puzzle. The twelve black dots above are all evenly spaced from one another. How many rectangles, of varying sizes, can you find that would use any four of these dots for their vertices (corners)? Remember, a square is also considered a rectangle.

# World's Hardest "Ballooning" Puzzle

Ballooning is one of the hottest new sports in the country. During a recent puzzle fair, ballooning became a new presentation category. Above is the winning entry of the Montgolfier brothers. Each brother piloted a balloon with four large words suspended beneath. Jacques's balloon is on the left and Joseph's is on the right. Determine which word suspended below the right balloon logically belongs with the four words under the left balloon? Anyone care to float a guess?

# World's Hardest "Suitcase" Puzzle

The Fabulous Frontenacs was one of the strangest musical acts of the century. Bertha and Reinhold played two instruments called the Berthaphone. Just before they began to play, Reinhold placed an old suitcase on a table. The suitcase hung slightly more than one-third over the table edge. They then launched into a medley of classical favorites. Sometime later, to everyone's surprise, the suitcase suddenly up-ended and tumbled to the floor. This closed their concert. No clockwork mechanization was inside the suitcase. Can you figure out how the Frontenacs timed their soirees?

# World's Hardest "A to Z" Puzzle

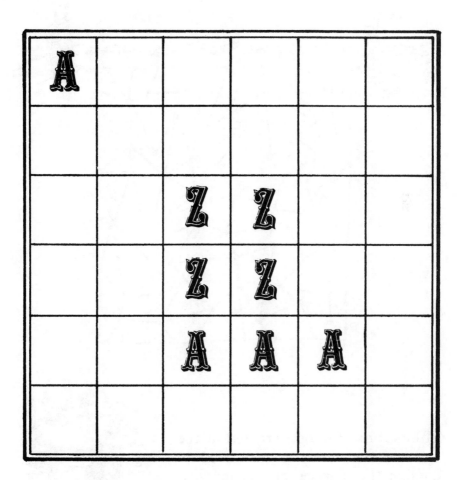

All right, puzzlers, it's time to tackle a really hard one. This six-by-six square grid contains four letter A's and four letter Z's. Cut this board into four pieces. All the pieces must be the same size and shape, and there must be one letter A and one letter Z in each of the pieces. You must cut the board along the grid lines. Good luck! You have one hour to solve this one.

# World's Hardest "Submarine Net" Puzzle

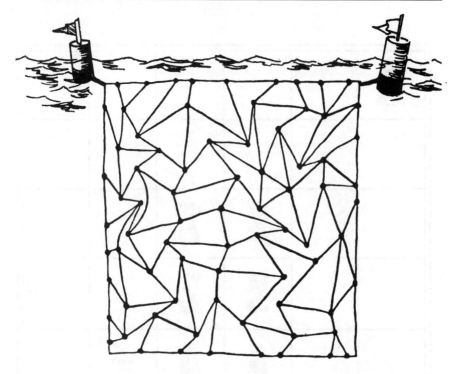

This submarine net, created at the turn of the century, was used to combat the menace of the new underseas submersibles. To counter this threat. Monsieur Gamonet from France invented his famous underwater diving suit. Using this device, see if you can divide the net in two, from top to bottom, with the fewest number of cuts. None of the cuts may be through the knots. Suit up and start snipping.

# World's Hardest "Will" Puzzle

"And to my beloved family, who have waited so long for this moment, I bequeath the following:

'What does man love e'en more than life,
Hate more than death or mortal strife?
That which contented men desire,
The poorest have and the rich require,
The miser spends and the spendthrift saves,
And all men carry to their graves.'"

The will of the Earl of Eastwich, some centuries ago, was certainly colorful. Can you figure out from the poem what his lordship gave his heirs?

# World's Hardest "Film" Puzzle

The · ·
Improved
Folding
KODAKS

$60.00
to
$100.00.

Fitted with Double Swing Back, Rising front, and
Iris Diaphragm Shutter. Can be used with plates
and films, and are adapted to stereoscopic work.

EASTMAN KODAK CO.,
ROCHESTER, N. Y.

Send for
Catalogue.

When Grandpa Townsend was a young man, he bought a new Kodak Iris Diaphragm Shutter camera for Christmas. The camera had a super film capacity. When Grandpa counted up all relatives present, he found that if he took four pictures of each relative, he needed a second roll of film because he ran four photos over the number that fit on a film roll. However, if he took only three photos of each relative, twelve unexposed frames would be left on the original roll. How many relatives did Grandpa have to photograph, and how many photos could he shoot from one roll? You should solve this one in a flash.

# World's Hardest "Toothpick" Puzzle

Doctor Stall and Professor Quackenbush are having dinner at the Toronto Inn and amusing themselves with after-dinner toothpick puzzles. Doctor Stall has laid out an equation using Roman numerals. The equation is incorrect, but he claims that by shifting just one toothpick to a new position, he can correct it. Professor Quackenbush is not so sure about that. Can you pick out the correct move?

# World's Hardest "Billiard Ball" Puzzle

Pockets Prendergast, Idle Hours Billiard Academy impresario, has a hundred ways of parting clientele from their cash. One of his favorites is shown above. He lines up eight billiard balls, alternating a colored object ball with a white cue ball. He'll bet that in four moves you can't end up with the four white balls on the left and the four colored balls on the right in a row. During each move, you must move any two *adjacent* balls to a new position in the row. Let's see if you can solve this one before Pockets runs the table.

# World's Hardest "Keyboard" Puzzle

Neither of these two relics from an office at the turn of the century would be much help in solving this puzzle. We include them here only for atmosphere. What we're interested in is the keyboard of a modern typewriter. The second row from the top contains these letters:

## QWERTYUIOP

Our question is simple. What is the longest English word that you can type using only the letters from this row? You may use the letters more than once. If you miss the answer, you'll find yourself asking, "Why didn't I think of that?"

# World's Hardest "Doggie" Puzzle

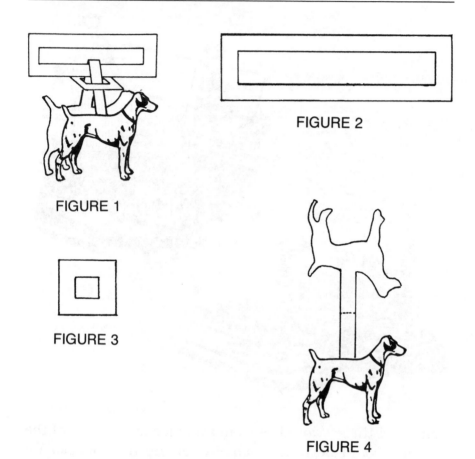

FIGURE 1

FIGURE 2

FIGURE 3

FIGURE 4

This ingenious paper puzzle is dedicated to my dog, Jackie. Figure 1 shows the assembled puzzle. It's constructed of three fairly stiff pieces of paper. Discover how they were put together without tearing or mutilating any of the fragile pieces. Note that the dog is firmly locked onto the large paper link by the smaller paper link. The hole in the small link, however, is far too small for either dog to fit through it. The three pieces that make up the puzzle are shown in figures 2, 3, and 4. See if you can fetch the answer before chow time.

# The
# **World's**
# Most Amazing
# Puzzles

# World's Most Amazing "Astronomical" Puzzle

Willard Starfinder is checking out his latest find. He has discovered a super solar system containing six suns revolving in three overlapping orbits. Willard had better name it quickly, before they converge and produce a supernova. Willard has numbered the suns one through six and has created a stellar puzzle. Can you renumber the suns, so the total of any four suns within one orbit will be 14? This puzzle implodes in exactly 10 minutes.

# World's Most Amazing "Abracadabra" Puzzle

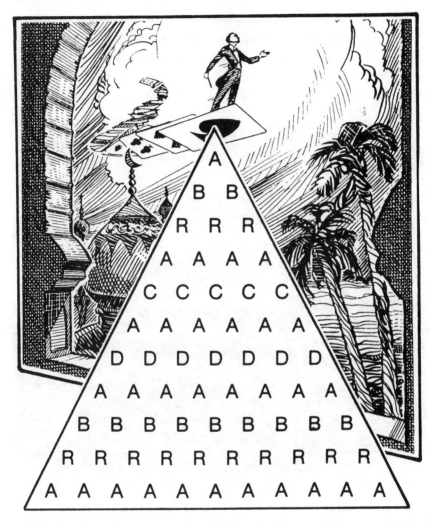

From the mystic East, our magician friend has brought us the famous Abracadabra pyramid puzzle. Starting at the top of the pyramid, try to figure out how many times it is possible to spell *abracadabra*, going from the "A" at the top down to the bottom row of letters. As you go down the 11 steps of the pyramid, you can branch either to the left or to the right to the two letters immediately below.

# World's Most Amazing "Billiards" Puzzle

*"The seven ball in the side pocket for the win, Rexford!"*

Here we see "Cushions" Halliburton about to sink the winning ball and walk away with the 1903 Manhattan Pocket Billiards Championship. During his five turns with the cue, he sank 100 balls. During each turn, he sank six more balls than he did during his previous turn. Can you chalk up a win by calculating how many balls he sank during each of his five turns?

# World's Most Amazing "Egyptian" Puzzle

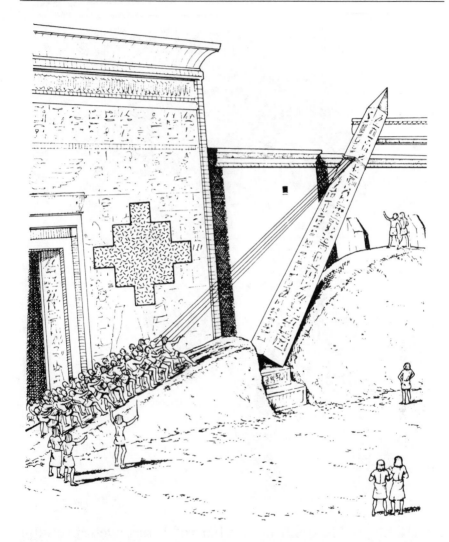

The year is 1480 B.C.; the place, the newly built temple of the Egyptian god Stumpumost. Chiselled on the front of the building, next to the entrance, is the first recorded change-the-shape puzzle. The problem is to cut the 20-sided figure into four pieces, each the same size and shape. These four pieces must then fit back together so that they form a perfect square.

185

# World's Most Amazing "Age" Puzzle

Ned Noble, the fictional sports hero of dime novels, probably played college sports longer than any other student in history. For the first quarter of his life Ned played touch football. For the next fifth of his life he was a college freshman. The next third he spent as a sophomore and junior. The final 13 years were spent as a senior, after which he finally hung up his helmet and graduated at the bottom of his class. How old was Ned when he got his sheepskin?

# World's Most Amazing "Rearranging Bee" Puzzle

The three winners in the Scramble Club rearranging bee are toasting their victory at this year's convention. They successfully unscrambled the names of nine state capitals to walk away with the laurels. Let's see if you, too, can decipher the jumbled clues being presented above!

# World's Most Amazing "Gong" Puzzle

Woe to this unfortunate Roman soldier who fell into the hands of his enemies. If he failed to solve the mystery of the gong, he quickly became a sacrifice to the sun god. Can you divide the gong into more than four pieces by making two straight cuts across it? You are not allowed to place one piece on top of another when making the second of these two cuts.

# World's Most Amazing "Substitution" Puzzle

> "Watch out, Smedley! There's a crossroads puzzle ahead! We don't want to miss it!"

CROSS
+ROADS
―――――
DANGER

"You're wrong, Pop! That sign is the puzzle! All you have to do to solve it, is to replace each of the letters in the sign with a number, using the same number for the same letter wherever it appears. If you do it correctly, you will have a valid mathematical expression. See if you can solve it before we get to the beach!"

# World's Most Amazing "Math" Puzzle

Today, Ms. Priscilla Sunshine is our substitute teacher. Please pay attention.

"All right, students, it's been several weeks since I was here last, so I have a puzzle treat for you. I want you to arrange the eight numbers I've written on the board into two groups of four numbers each. When you add up each group, the sums must be the same. All those who fail to solve this problem will be eligible to help clean my new car."

# World's Most Amazing "Coin Counter" Puzzle

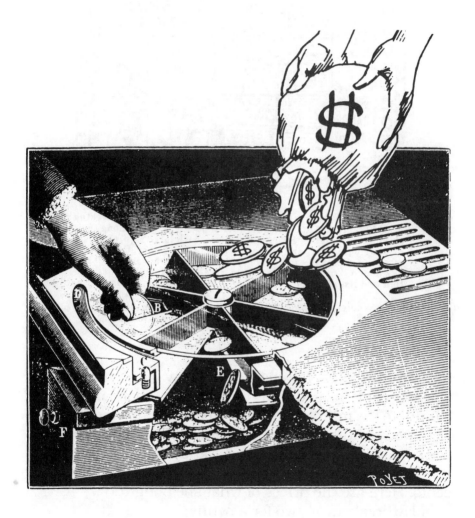

Pictured here is the Crichton coin counting machine just installed in our local bank. Mr. Tremayne is testing it with a bag of 50 coins. Their total value is $1.00. How many coins of each denomination are in the bag?

# World's Most Amazing "Candy Store" Puzzle

Active, intelligent Boys, who can count money, are making from 50 cents to $1.00 per day, after school, at home, among their playmates. Each one a complete Store, with large sign, circulars to distribute, etc., and over 450 articles of Fancy Candies, to retail at one cent each. Money doubled in a few days. "It's lots of fun." Sent by express on receipt of $2.00; full description and list of articles sent on receipt of three-cent stamp.

**MITCHELL & WHITELAW,**
Wholesale Confectioners, 70 Walnut St., Cincinnati, O.,
Manufacturers of all kinds of Confectioners.

Back in the 1890s, Mitchell & Whitelaw didn't miss a trick when it came to peddling their candy. Their aim was to eliminate the middleman and sell directly to the consumer. Here we see little Hermione Reinholder about to spend her week's allowance at Billy Boss's Candy Store. Before she is finished she will have bought 25 pieces of candy for 25 cents. Here are the prices of what she bought:

Jawbreakers @ two for a penny;
Stick candy @ a penny a stick;
Peerless butterscotch @ two for a nickel;
Cream chocolate drops @ 5 cents each.

Can you figure out how many of each candy Hermione bought and how many times a year she visited the dentist?

# World's Most Amazing "Kite" Puzzle

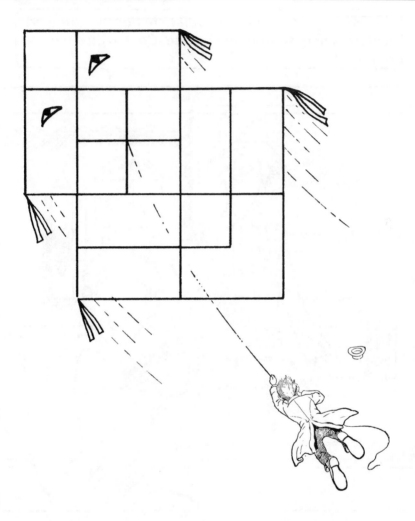

Calvin Barnstable is in real trouble this time. His overly ambitious kite is about to take him on a trip to Oz, if the wind doesn't calm down. Besides being highly aerodynamic, the kite also has a puzzle built into it. The struts form a series of interlocking squares of various sizes. Let's see if you can correctly count the number of squares, large and small, on the face of the kite. You have just 60 seconds to come up with the correct total.

# World's Most Amazing "Soda Straw" Puzzle

"Hi! You're just in time. Treetall here has me stumped with this new soda-straw puzzle. Care to give me a hand?"

Treetall Bentley has come up with a humdinger this time. Lay out 24 soda straws, as pictured here, so that nine small squares are formed. First, remove four straws, so that five squares are left. Next, set up the straws as before, and this time remove six, leaving five squares again. Finally, set up the straws as before, and remove eight straws, leaving—you guessed it—five squares. Every square should have one straw to a side.

# World's Most Amazing "Hidden Word" Puzzle

"Rubens just look at that superb Angora cat!"

Wonderful! He plays in A flat and she sings in G sharp!

Hidden in the description at the bottom of each picture is the locality of the incident depicted. You have one minute to find each town.

# World's Most Amazing "Bank Robber" Puzzle

Here we see America's most famous bank robber, Willie Sutton, contemplating either the money he lost, or when to make his next jail break. When asked why he robbed banks, Willie said, ". . . !" This famous quotation is hidden in the above frame of letters. To find it, start at any letter and go around the frame twice, reading every other letter as you go. Lights out in 10 minutes!

# World's Most Amazing "Santa" Puzzle

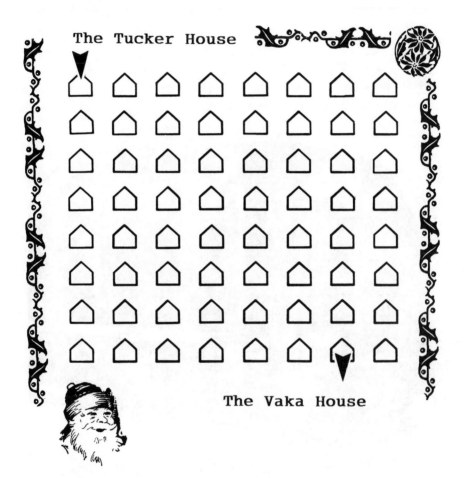

The Tucker House

The Vaka House

Before leaving the North Pole, Santa stopped to study his flight plan for the town of Pleasant Dale. There are 64 homes in Pleasant Dale, laid out in the pattern depicted above. Every house is on his list. Santa wishes to start with the Tucker house and end with the Vaka house. In between, his route should always be a series of straight lines, moving horizontally or vertically from house to house, never backtracking or crossing any previous line of flight. Can you help Santa draw up a flight plan that will use only 21 straight lines?

# World's Most Amazing "Packing Case" Puzzle

Here we see Herman Ganzer piloting his Ganzer Pipe Gazing Motor Tram through New York's 100-year-old water system. I hope he gets out of there before the water is turned back on. When they shipped his tram down from his factory in Oriskany, they had to build a special box to contain it. The box had 14 corners and 21 edges. Can you figure out how many faces the box had? The losers get to ride Herman's Folly from Wall Street to the Bronx.

# World's Most Amazing "Puzzle Machine" Puzzle

Which of the following words doesn't belong? Why doesn't it belong?

**GANG**
**REGATTA**
**CHARCOAL**
**EDUCATOR**
**TAXICAB**
**AKIMBO**

You must solve the card machine's puzzle before entering the Sphinx Puzzle Museum.

# World's Most Amazing "Magic Square" Puzzle

Billy Thorpe, puzzle genius, is shown here facing his greatest challenge. During his stage performances, he accepts puzzles from the audience. Recently, the president of a local puzzle club was so sure that Billy couldn't solve the above magic-square problem in three minutes, he offered to donate $100 to Billy's favorite charity if Billy succeeded. In this puzzle, Billy had to rearrange the numbers in the above grid so that no two identical numbers would appear twice in any row or column. Also, no number could appear twice across the two diagonals. When solved correctly, every row and column totals 10. Billy solved it in three minutes flat. Can you?

# World's Most Amazing "Knight's Tour" Puzzle

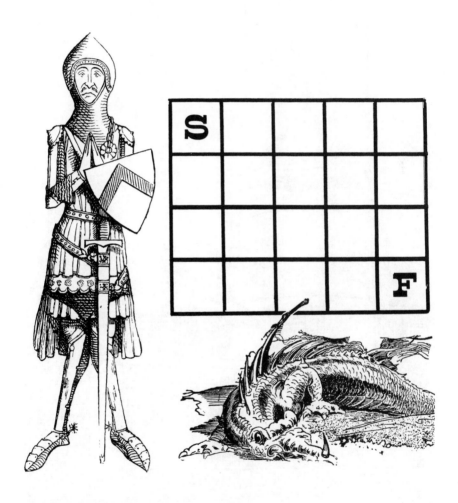

Peter the Pious is in a puzzling predicament. He must solve this chess puzzle by nightfall or be cast in the pit with the dragon. The object of the puzzle is to move a chess knight from square $S$ to square $F$. He can only use knight's moves. The knight must land once on every square. The last move must find the knight on square $F$.

# World's Most Amazing "Line" Puzzle

When Barlow Wingate retired to the mountains, he made sure that his TV antenna was big enough to pull in his favorite programs. Can you draw this antenna using one continuous line that doesn't cross itself at any point or go back over any part already drawn?

# World's Most Amazing "Cross" Puzzle

That ancient wizard Merlin has an interesting problem for you. Lay out five rows of five dots each. Now, try to connect these dots with one continuous line until you have formed a Greek cross. When the cross is complete, there should be eight dots outside the cross and five dots inside. (All arms of a Greek cross are the same length.)

# World's Most Amazing "Racing" Puzzle

Barry      Bert      Harry      Larry

The famous Fontana Brothers, kings of the unicycle, used to take their daily workout on four circular tracks that were each exactly one-third of a mile in length. At noontime, starting at the center of the circles, each brother started riding around one path. They rode at the rate of 6 miles, 9 miles, 12 miles, and 15 miles per hour, respectively. They kept on riding until they met for the fourth time at the center of the circles. How long did they have to ride?

# World's Most Amazing "Toy" Puzzle

It's Puzzle Fair time once again in Culpepper, and all the merchants have decorated their windows with contest problems. Tilli Turner, owner of Tilli Turner's Tivoli of Toys, has come up with a great one this year. Using a child's building toy, she constructed a pyramid consisting of nine equal-size triangles. To win a place in the puzzle finals, you have to remove four of the girders, so you are left with five equal-size triangles. Care to enter the contest?

# World's Most Amazing "Egg" Puzzle

Try stumping your friends at the next Easter party with this *eggstraordinary* problem. Since it can get messy, it's best to present it in the kitchen. Challenge everyone present to an egg-balancing contest. Place an egg, two forks, a cork, and a cane on the table. State that you can balance the egg on the end of the cane with the aid of the two forks and the cork. Let the others try first. After cleaning up their mess, show them how it's done—but, first, make an appropriate wager or two.

# World's Most Amazing "Snake" Puzzle

"Well, what do you think of it, Cynthia? It's a genuine Dudeney line-puzzle painting."

"It's nice, Basil. What's the problem?"

"You're required to draw as much of the serpent as you can, using one continuous line. You can start anywhere and end anywhere, but you cannot lift the pencil from the paper, and you cannot cross over or retrace any part of the line already drawn. It's an excellent puzzle-painting, and well worth every cent of the asking price."

# World's Most Amazing "Measuring" Puzzle

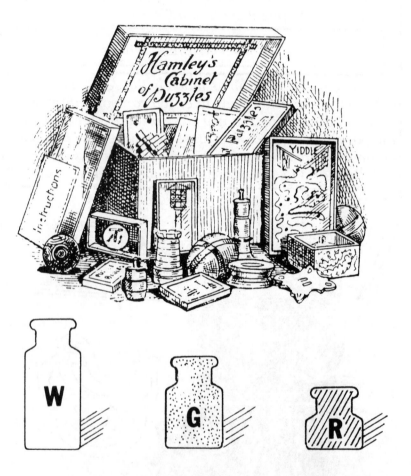

At the turn of the century, Hamley's department store in London sold a most wonderful box of puzzles. In the box, pictured above, are three jars of different colors: white, green, and red. The green jar holds three pints more than the red one, and the white jar holds four pints more than the green. The problem is to use these three jars to measure out exactly one quart of water. How would you do it in just nine pourings?

# World's Most Amazing "Adam and Eve" Puzzle

$$\frac{\text{EVE}}{\text{DID}} = .\text{TALKTALKTALKTALKTALKTALK} \dots$$

*"You ain't heard nothing yet, pal!"*

Adam is about to hear from someone else. However, his observation concerning Eve presents us with a pretty problem. Can you replace each letter with a number, using the same number for the same letter wherever it appears, so that you will have a correct mathematical expression?

# World's Most Amazing "Taffy" Puzzle

Business must be good for Mrs. Murbles, that purveyor of all things good and sweet. This is certainly a sweet problem she has placed before you. If you can keep from eating the taffy, arrange 21 pieces into nine straight lines, with each line containing five pieces. Of course, each piece will be in more than one line.

# World's Most Amazing "Transpositional" Puzzle

Using the above puzzle board, place three pennies on squares 1, 2, and 3, and three nickels on squares 5, 6, and 7. Then, make the pennies and nickels change places. To do this, you may move a coin to an adjacent empty square, or you may jump a coin over an adjacent coin to a vacant square beyond. Move either horizontally or vertically. Try to transpose the coins in 15 moves or less.

# World's Most Amazing "Domino" Puzzle

Here's a neat wager you can make next time you sit down for a game of dominoes. Take seven dominoes, and build a small tower, as pictured above. Next, place a single domino in front of it, and state that you wager that no one can use this domino to remove from the tower the one labelled A without knocking down the rest of the tower. Nothing can touch the tower other than domino B. The answer is a snap to figure out.

# World's Most Amazing "Executive" Puzzle

When Percival Pembroke lost his high-paying job, he thought finding another would be a piece of cake. He had a rude awakening when he applied at Bullion Investments. They made him take an aptitude test . . . and he flunked it! He was given four squares and eight triangles and told to assemble them into a square in five minutes flat. Could you have passed Bullion's test?

# World's Most Amazing "Rebus" Puzzle

# World's Most Amazing "Hero" Puzzle

"Ferris, you're my hero for winning this year's puzzle contest!"

"Nonsense, Eldrida. It was absurdly simple. All I had to do was arrange the numbers 1, 2, 3, 4, 5, 6, 7, 8, and 9 in such a manner that when they were added up they would total 99,999. It was the merest bagatelle."

You, too, can be a hero if you can solve this one.

# World's Most Amazing "Bug" Puzzle

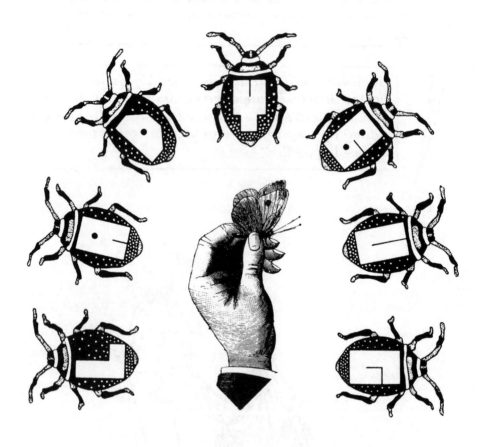

The butterflies have finished their act, and now it's time for Santini's Magnificent Performing Ladybugs—the greatest show of precision bug-marching ever presented. Within the space of three minutes, the seven ladybugs will line up and then will form every possible arrangement of the seven letters painted on their shells. Can you figure out how many arrangements there are?

# World's Most Amazing "Toe Skiing" Puzzle

Here's the perfect way to win a hot chocolate at the warming hut the next time you're out toe skiing. Wager your friends that they can't arrange six toe skis so that they form eight perfect triangles. If you're not out on the slopes you can try it using soda straws.

# World's Most Amazing "Fencing" Puzzle

"I'm sorry, sir! I've sent Timothy to town for more supplies."

"This won't do, Syms! Time is money, and you're wasting both. One more mistake like this, and you're through!"

Squire Chapman wanted to run a new fence along his property next to the road. The section was 99 yards long. The fence posts were to be nine feet apart with three rails between each pair. Syms came back with 33 fence posts, 99 rails, and 99 yards of wire fencing. Where did he make his mistake?

# World's Most Amazing "Party" Puzzle

Back in the good old days, home birthday parties were the rage. Naturally, they played lots of games. Pictured above is a famous old party puzzle. Lay out 12 plates on the table, and place a penny in each plate. Next, pick up a penny from one of the plates. Moving counterclockwise, pass it over two pennies, and place it on the next plate that has a penny on it. Repeat this action, always in a counterclockwise direction, starting at any plate that has a single penny on it. It doesn't matter if the two pennies you pass over are on one plate or two. After six such moves, you should have six empty plates and six plates each containing two pennies. After the sixth move, walk around the table until you arrive back at the plate you started from. The object of this puzzle is to make the fewest number of complete circuits around the table.

# World's Most Amazing "Battery" Puzzle

*"Pack the kids, Mildred; we're on the way to Ocean Grove!"*

Elmer Lazlo, owner of Battery City in Racine, Wisconsin, ran a contest they're still talking about. He arranged 36 batteries in the form of a square on his showroom floor, and offered anyone a two-week, all-expenses-paid vacation in Ocean Grove, New Jersey. The catch: Contestants had to remove six batteries from the display, leaving an even number of batteries in each row, horizontally and vertically. It looks as if Willard here is going to beat you to the solution.

# World's Most Amazing "Teddy Bear" Puzzle

The three women pictured above all pitched in and worked the teddy-bear booth during the recent local church fete. At the start of the day, they all sold the same number of bears for $10. In the afternoon they changed the number of bears they sold for $10. The funny thing was, that at the end of the day, although they each had sold different numbers of teddy bears, each ended up with the same amount of money. Can you figure out how this was possible?

# World's Most Amazing "Medical" Puzzle

The young and restless interns at St. Billum's Hospital thought they could catch old Doc Stall with the ancient parts-of-the-body puzzle. He might be past his prime, but he's as quick as ever. The problem: In one minute, name 10 parts of the body that are spelled with only three letters.

# World's Most Amazing "Clock" Puzzle

The great two-ton Detroit clock was the hit of the 1876 Centennial Exhibition in Philadelphia. Not only did it give the time in 13 cities, but it kept track of the seasons and plotted the orbits of the planets around the sun. It also inspired the following problem: At noon the big and little hands of the clock meet. How many times do they meet between noon and midnight?

# World's Most Amazing "Robot" Puzzle

From the world of surrealistic dreams comes this robot puzzle. Various segments of Robbie are numbered from 1 to 12. For some strange reason, he can't leave this weird planet until the numbers are rearranged so they total 26 in seven different ways. This would include the two horizontal rows, the two vertical rows, the four inner numbers, the four arm numbers, and, lastly, the four numbers in the neck and legs. Don't expect logic in a dream puzzle.

# World's Most Amazing "Stove" Puzzle

> **If the B empty put:**
>
> **If the B full . putting:**

Cy Corncrib was always stressing to his wife, Columbine, that a penny saved was a penny earned. In the kitchen, over the stove, he had a catchy admonition concerning the maintenance of the cooking stove. He had it printed in the form of a rebus. You have five minutes to cook up the answer.

# World's Most Amazing "Plywood" Puzzle

Hiram Ballpeene, local handyman supreme and amateur puzzler, has his work cut out for him. Mel, his faithful assistant, brought him a sheet of plywood containing three square holes. Mel challenged Hiram to cut it into two pieces, which could then be fitted back together into a solid rectangular sheet with no holes in it. Where do you think Hiram should make his cuts?

# World's Most Amazing "Anagram" Puzzle

> *"And now, ladies and gentlemen, the Anagram Quiz. Our contestants are ready, so let's get to it. I'll give you the answer to the first one. After that you're on your own."*
>
> 1) *Thelma = Hamlet.*
> 2) *to love ruin = ?*
> 3) *great help = ?*
> 4) *best in prayer = ?*
> 5) *a stew, sir? = ?*
> 6) *Erin lad = ?*
> 7) *mad policy = ?*
> 8) *moon-starers = ?*

A short-lived program on early radio was Anagram Quiz. In an anagram, you take the letters in a word or name, and rearrange them to form other names or words that, ideally, have something in common with the original word. Let's see what kind of contestant you would have been.

# World's Most Amazing "Spanish" Puzzle

"What Spanish instrument's familiar name
And fisher's occupation are the same?"

The Madrigals and Guy are packing them in at the local opera house with their new orchestration of "Puzzles and Preludes." The above selection is sung to the accompaniment of "Habañera" from Bizet's *Carmen*.

# World's Most Amazing "Sailor" Puzzle

> *"The six men sail around the _____*
> *Eagerly waiting for the _____*
> *To put an end to the dreadful _____*
> *In which the mate, a man of fearsome _____*
> *Had tried to prove that _____ was _____*
> *Their rum he'd doped and made their _____*
> *A useless thing; they were too _____*
> *To _____."*

The jolly tars above are rowing back to their ship after a less-than-happy shore leave. To find out what happened, fill in the spaces in the above verse with nine words. Every word contains the same last four letters, all arranged in the same order.

# World's Most Amazing "Dog Biscuit" Puzzle

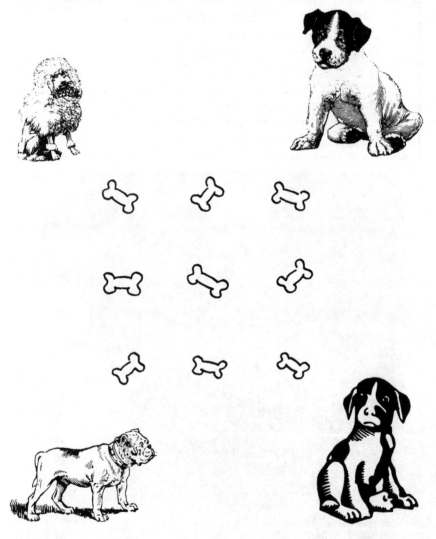

Our dog, Jackie, had a few friends over for a dog-biscuit puzzle party. As usual, her pals ate the puzzle before anyone could solve it. The problem that came out of the party is shown here. You're required to join the nine biscuits together, using four straight lines, without lifting the pencil from the paper. Chew on this one for a while.

# World's Most Amazing "Carousel" Puzzle

Here's a puzzle inspired by the carousel at old Olympic Park in Irvington, New Jersey. Place eight pennies, heads up, on the circled animals above. Then, try to turn seven of these coins tails up in seven moves. During each move, start counting from a coin that is heads up. Count out four coins, and turn the fourth one tails up. Count every coin, regardless of whether it's heads or tails up. Solve this in 10 minutes, and win a brass ring.

# World's Most Amazing "Charade" Puzzle

*"My first is often at the front door."*

*"My second is found in the cereal family."*

*"My third is what most people want."*

*"My whole is one of the United States."*

The Heidelberg Four are shown here gearing up for the charade-word division of the 1910 International Puzzle Symposium in London. In a charade puzzle, various parts of a chosen word are cryptically hinted at. See if you can figure out what English word they had in mind.

# World's Most Amazing "Counting" Puzzle

*"All right, students, here's a 20-point question for you. Fill in the blank, so the sentence is correct. There are three possible answers. If you get all three, I'll give you 60 points."*

**"This sentence has _____ letters."**

This is certainly an interesting final question on today's exam. Can you earn 60 points and a smile from Miss Wilson?

# World's Most Amazing "Scholar" Puzzle

"You'll never believe this! I wrote on the board, 'One of the words in this sentence is mispelled. What word is it?' Not one of my students got it!"

"I believe it. I gave my students an age-old puzzle that goes: 'A girl is twice as old as her brother and half as old as her father. In 22 years, her brother will be half as old as his father. How old is the daughter now?' They're still working on it!"

# World's Most Amazing "Rumor" Puzzle

"What do you think, dear; is Netty playing around behind Bevan's back?"

**I am Madam, man making mischief wife.**

Can you decipher the above cryptic reply to his companion's gossipy question?

# World's Most Amazing "Trolley" Puzzle

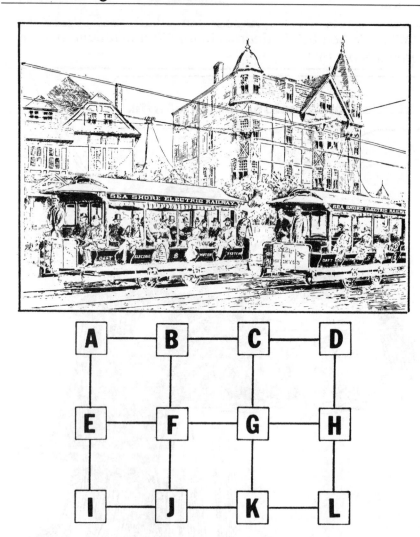

The old Asbury Park trolley line had 12 stops connected by 17 lines of track, each one mile in length. Barton Crull, the line's inspector, had to check all 17 miles every day. To do this, he had to travel over some of the lines more than once. Can you figure out the best route for Barton to take, so he travelled the shortest distance during his daily inspections?

# World's Most Amazing "Cologne Bottle" Puzzle

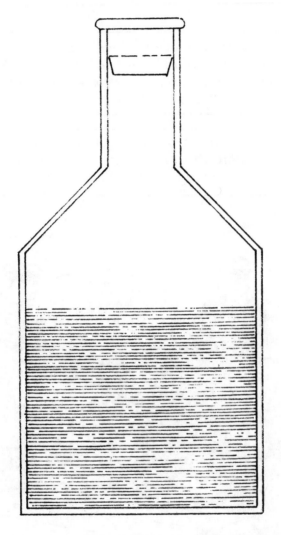

Pictured here is a partially filled round bottle of cologne with a stopper in it. Your problem is to calculate what percentage of the total volume of the bottle is filled with liquid, not counting the area filled by the stopper. You can only use a ruler to figure this out, and you cannot remove the stopper from the bottle. You have five minutes to uncork the answer to this one.

# World's Most Amazing "Progression" Puzzle

"I know how much you love puzzles, Sibyl, so I rushed right over as soon as I heard this great new stumper. It's a progression puzzle. What number comes next in this series: 1, 2, 6, 24, 120, 720, _____?"

"Well, Sidney, it's nice that you thought of me as soon as you heard this puzzle, but I wish you'd brought me a box of candy to munch on while I solve it!"

Sidney has a lot to learn when it comes to romance. See if you can solve the problem before he gets back from the local confectionery shop.

# World's Most Amazing "Contest" Puzzle

The Coltrane Bank is having its yearly puzzle contest, and the first prize is nearly out of this world. Here's a hint that will help you get in the running. Find the smallest number of coins that, when divided by 2, 3, 4, 5, 6, 7, 8, 9, and 10, will always give you a remainder of one.

# World's Most Amazing "Robbery" Puzzle

When Black Bart hit the Denver stagecoach for the 13th time, his luck finally ran out. The only cash he found was in a salesman's travelling bag, and that only amounted to $5.00 in coins. The $5.00 was made up of exactly 100 coins from the Denver mint. Can you tell the value of the coins and how many of each were in the bag?

# World's Most Amazing "Playing Card" Puzzle

Professor Pepper is shown here in 1896 giving his famous Puzzle Slide Show at the Egyptian Hall in London. In this problem, three playing cards are placed in a row, facedown. The following clues to their identities are given: There is a two to the right of a king (though not necessarily right next to it); next, a diamond will be found to the left of a spade; an ace is to the left of a heart; finally, a heart is to the left of a spade. Now you should be able to identify each of these cards easily.

# World's Most Amazing "Barber" Puzzle

A small town in France had two barbers, Henri and Pierre. Henri was well groomed, his shop was neat and always clean. Pierre's shop was dirty, the chairs were broken, and Pierre always had a bad haircut and needed a shave. Henri often said that he would rather cut the hair of two Germans than one American. Do you know why? One other question: If you were to visit that town, whose barber shop would you go to for a haircut?

# The
# World's
# Most Baffling
# Puzzles

# The World's Most Baffling "Number" Puzzle

To solve the puzzle just arrange the four *fives* in the above winning picture so that their collective value equals 56.

# The World's Most Baffling "Ornament" Puzzle

Old Saint Nick has a smashing Xmas puzzle for you. After fastening an ornament to one end of a three-foot piece of string, he tied the other end to an overhead bunch of mistletoe.

"I'll double your Xmas present," he said, "if you can cut that string right in the middle and not have the ornament fall and smash on the floor. Remember: Once you've cut through the string you can't touch the string or the ornament in any way."

What's it going to be, reader, two Mercedeses for Xmas or the old bituminous coal?

# The World's Most Baffling "Card" Puzzle

You don't have to be a magician to solve this problem, but your friends will think you are. Tell them you're going to show them a puzzle based on lightning calculation. After discarding all the face cards and tens from the pack, take the remaining cards, and start laying them down on the table in groups of three. Explain to your audience that each group of three cards forms a three-digit number that can be divided by 11 without leaving a remainder. You form these three-digit numbers as fast as you can lay down the cards.

In our example we have the number 231. Eleven goes into this number exactly 21 times. How is this marvelous feat accomplished?

# The World's Most Baffling "Cross" Puzzle

The Reverend I. N. Spire is once again in a spiritual quandary. Last night, during a tremendous rainstorm, a gust of wind toppled the cross from the church steeple, sending it spinning to the ground where it split into five pieces. Sexton Winslow has vowed to mend the cross and return it to its perch of distinction, if he can only figure out how to reassemble the pieces. A revelation is definitely in order. Can you help the Reverend and Winslow see the light and solve this mystery?

# The World's Most Baffling "Business Survey" Puzzle

From the looks of things, I'd say Sylvester's Surveys is a booming concern. Just don't ask them about the mustard account that got away. They were hired by the Volcano Mustard Company to find out how many people like hot mustard and how many like mild. The report they presented reads:

Number of people surveyed..................300
Number of hot mustard users ................234
Number of mild mustard users ...............213
Number who used both hot and mild.........144
Number who never used mustard ............. 0

After the Volcano Mustard Company digested this report, they erupted and promptly fired Sylvester's Surveys for gross inaccuracies. Can you spot the errors in their report?

# The World's Most Baffling "Water and Wine" Puzzle

Mr. Percy Poindexter, the famous after-dinner puzzle expert, is shown here at his wit's end trying to solve the old Water and Wine puzzle. It goes like this: You have two glasses each filled with exactly the same amount of liquid. One contains water, the other, wine. First take a teaspoon of water from the water glass and pour it into the wine glass. Next stir the wine and water until well mixed. Then take a teaspoon of the water and wine mixture and pour it into the glass of water.

The question now is: is there more wine in the water glass than water in the wine glass, or is there less?

# The World's Most Baffling "Planchette" Puzzle

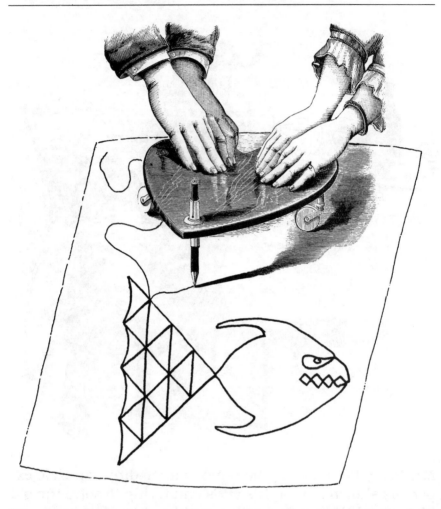

You don't have to be clairvoyant to solve this puzzle, but it sure would help! Paul and Vivian are shown here communicating with what looks like the spirit of a Siamese Fighting Fish. I don't know how they did it, but I'm told that the planchette drew this picture with a single line and that the pencil never left the paper nor did the line ever cross itself at any point. Do you think that you can duplicate this drawing while adhering to these other-worldly rules?

# The World's Most Baffling "India Squares" Puzzle

This Indian prince of puzzlers is on his way to a puzzle convention in Agra. Printed on the cloth that covers the royal elephant is his contribution to the lively arts. To solve it, you must determine how many squares, both big and small, are contained within the drawing. You have five minutes before the caravan moves on.

# The World's Most Baffling "Geography" Puzzle

Our next problem is a lesson in geography. Hidden in the above chart are the names of four cities, all beginning with the same letter. To find them, you must first find the letter in question and then proceed to spell out the names going in four different directions. With the exception of the first letter, no letter in the chart is used twice.

# The World's Most Baffling "Cocoa Tin" Puzzle

In this sweet problem you are given a sealed tin of Baker's Breakfast Cocoa, full of cocoa, and a twelve-inch ruler. Can you measure the inside of the tin, without opening it, to determine the length of the box's major diagonal line?

An example would be a line from the right bottom front corner (B) of the can to the left top back corner (A). There are four of these lines inside the tin. Disregard the thickness of the tin's sides, top, and bottom. Your final measure may be within a quarter inch of the actual length. You could solve the problem by resorting to mathematical calculations, but there's an easier method that relies on straight measuring with the ruler only. We want this method.

We've excluded dimensions from the problem, since the solution is not dependent upon them. Do you think that you can brew up a quick solution to this rich puzzle?

# The World's Most Baffling "Counter" Puzzle

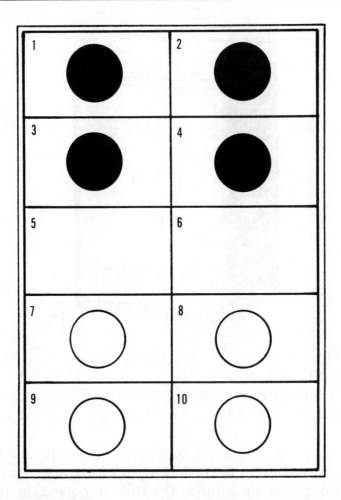

For this problem you'll need four black and four white counters placed on your puzzle board as shown above. What you're challenged to do is to make these eight pieces change place in exactly ten moves.

The rules of play are simple. Black moves down the board and white moves up. All pieces must either move forward to an empty square or jump over one or two counters to get to an empty square. You have ten minutes to solve this one.

# The World's Most Baffling "Bathtub" Puzzle

Professor Willard Wordsworth, a resident of Ma Bascomb's boardinghouse, has made these observations about the gas-fired Victorian tub in the second-floor bathroom: You can fill the tub from the cold water tap in 6 minutes and 40 seconds, while it takes exactly 8 minutes to fill it from the hot water tap. Furthermore, after the tub is full, if you pull out the stopper, it takes the water exactly 13 minutes and 20 seconds to run out.

Now comes Willard's puzzle. If you leave the stopper out and open both the hot and cold water taps all the way, how long will it take to fill the tub? Don't get all wet trying to solve this one.

# The World's Most Baffling "Touching" Puzzle

You may think that you'll have to resort to some magical solution to solve this problem after you've worked at it for awhile. Place the five magician's palming coins here so that each coin will be touching every other coin. If you're out of palming coins, you may use quarters or half-dollars. Our Baffling Bunny thinks that ten minutes is tops for finding the answer to this problem.

# The World's Most Baffling "Milling" Puzzle

*"What do you say, Ian, will you mill my corn for one-twentieth of the amount of corn I bring you?"*

*"Are you daft, Angus? You know full well that my price is one-tenth of the corn brought to my mill!"*

Oh well, you can't blame Angus for trying. However, he's faced with a problem. How much corn must he bring to the mill so that after giving Ian his ten percent he will come away with exactly 100 pounds of cornmeal?

Assume there will be no waste during the milling.

# The World's Most Baffling "Soda Straws" Puzzle

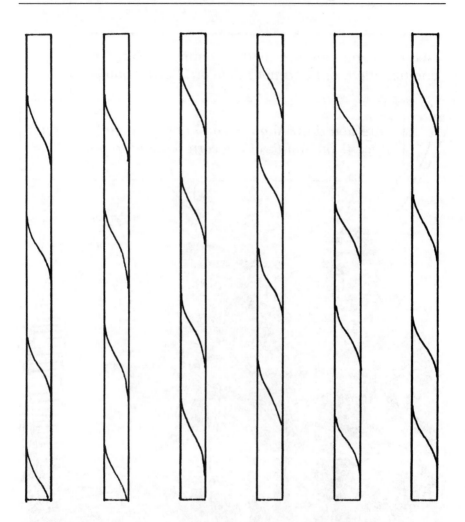

The next time you go down to the local malt shop, try stumping friends with this one. As shown here, lay out six soda straws on the table and say: "Using these straws, I can prove to you that six plus five equals nine. By adding five more straws to the ones on the table, I'll end up with nine instead of eleven."

Can you figure out how to do this ex-straw-dinary puzzle?

# The World's Most Baffling "Math" Puzzle

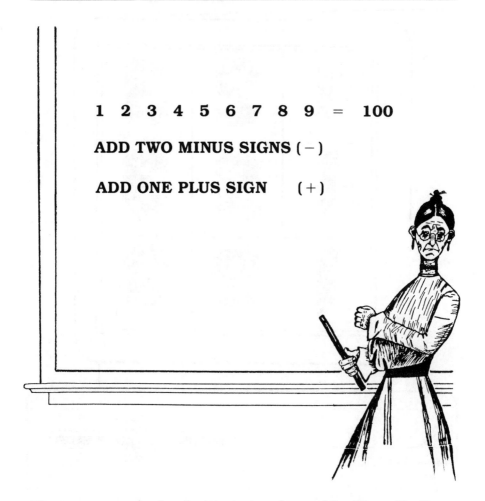

1  2  3  4  5  6  7  8  9  =  100

**ADD TWO MINUS SIGNS ( − )**

**ADD ONE PLUS SIGN     ( + )**

That nonpareil of substitute teachers, Ms. Priscilla Sunshine, is back to test your mathematical prowess.

"All right students, pay attention! The problem on the board is patently incorrect. However, if you were to place two minus signs ( − ) and one plus sign ( + ) between certain of the numbers on the left side of the equation, you would end up with a correct mathematical expression that equals 100. You have until the end of the period to discover where to place these signs."

# The World's Most Baffling "Magic Square" Puzzle

Puzzle Computer

Our famous Puzzle Computer seems to have contracted some sort of hacker virus. The program was supposed to have generated a magic square that would add up to six in every horizontal, vertical, and diagonal direction. Instead, it came up with the above dismal display. Can you rearrange the numbers on the screen so that the correct magic square is formed?

# The World's Most Baffling "Sculpture" Puzzle

"I say, Millicent, that's a smashing new puzzle sculpture you've put in your garden. What's the problem behind it?"

"It's an original Oliver Weldright creation, Percy. To solve the puzzle you must figure out where Oliver could weld three straight bars across it so that the bars would cut once through each of the squares that make up the sculpture. I'll give you until teatime to come up with the answer!"

# The World's Most Baffling "Ports of Call" Puzzle

(1) GLSOLESANE

(2) NONODL

(3) IEDERIJOONAR

(4) SNILOB

(5) LHANCTORSE

(6) LMRSLAEEIS

(7) BGNOYMEATO

(8) DVNOMIOETE

(9) SREBT

(10) NDNGELRIA

The old salt pictured here has had many a landfall in his fifty years at sea. In his snug harbor at Shelter Cove he challenges you to unscramble the names of ten world seaports that he has visited. You have until four bells to come up with the answers.

# The World's Most Baffling "Shooting" Puzzle

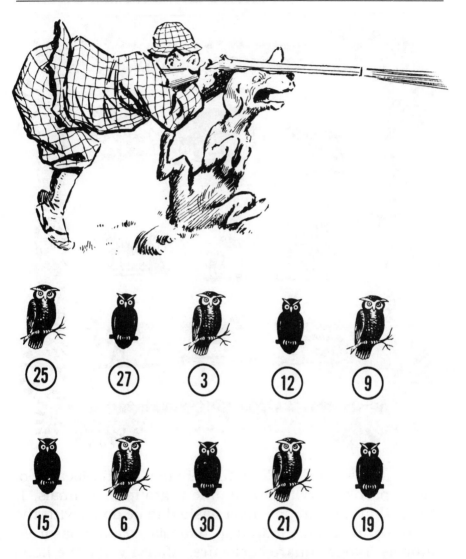

At a recent charity fete Barney Blunderbuss, the local skeet champion, was trying to win a prize at the shooting gallery concession. You get three shots for ten dollars, and if you knock down three birds whose numbers add up to exactly 50, you win a stuffed alligator. Care to take a turn after Barney runs out of money?

# The World's Most Baffling "Zoo" Puzzle

Walter Snaretrap, park commissioner at the local zoo, had a problem trying to confine a group of animals. It seems that the lion no longer wished to lie down with the lamb, so to speak. Snaretrap had placed nine assorted animals in one square enclosure. After a while the lions started nipping at the camels, and the elephants stomped on the lions. So, no one was very happy. Snaretrap decided it was time for each of the animals to have a pen of its own. To do this, he built two more square enclosures inside the first enclosure. This created nine separate pens. Do you know where he placed these enclosures?

# The World's Most Baffling "Clock" Puzzle

It never rains but it pours for the good Reverend I. N. Spire. Not only did he lose the steeple cross during that monumental rainstorm (see page 12), but the clockface was also broken into four pieces by a flying branch. When he examined the damage, he noted an extraordinary thing. The Roman numerals on each piece independently added up to twenty. Can you figure out how the clockface split to make this occur?

# The World's Most Baffling "Poem" Puzzle

YYURYYUBICURYY4me

Here we see Mr. and Ms. Gotrocks leading their dinner party to the table. Mr. Gotrocks has been entertaining his guests with a series of puzzles and stumpers. I think that his wife has had quite enough of his posturing, as evidenced by the puzzle she's giving him as they enter the dining room. Can you decipher the cryptic four-line rhyme contained in the above poser?

# The World's Most Baffling "Baseball" Puzzle

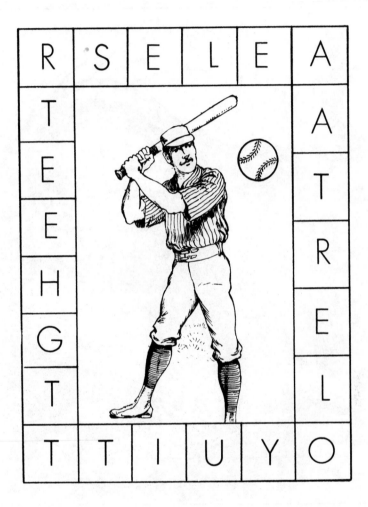

Here's a grand slam puzzle for all of you baseball fans. Over the past 100 years, much has been said about our national pastime. We've picked out one of the most famous quotations concerning the philosophy of the game and arranged the letters round the ballplayer above. Let's see if you can find the quotation. Starting at any letter, go around the frame twice reading every other letter as you go.

# The World's Most Baffling "Big Fish" Puzzle

The fisherman pictured here certainly had a whale of a story to tell his friends when he got back to shore. It seems his prayers were answered; the leviathan passed him by. How big was this fish? Well, the fisherman's best guess is that the fish's head was 60 feet long, the fish's tail was as long as its head and half of its body, and the fish's body was half of its entire length. How long do you calculate this denizen of the deep was?

# The World's Most Baffling "State" Puzzle

"We've been aloft for two days now. What state do you think we're flying over?"

"That's an easy question, Wilbur. It's the only state whose name begins with, ends with, and has every other letter the same. I'll give you until we land in ten minutes to solve that one!"

# The World's Most Baffling "Dice" Puzzle

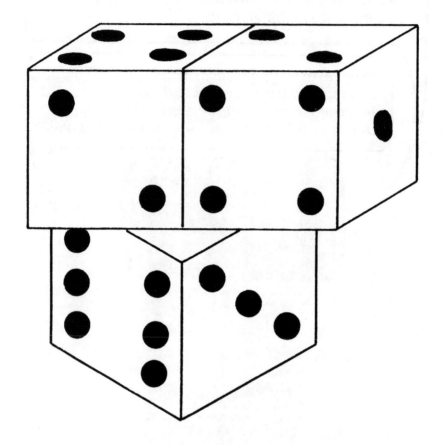

You'll need three dice for this problem. Place one die on the table, and hold the other two between thumb and forefinger. Wager those present that they cannot place these two dice side-by-side on top of the die on the table at an angle as depicted in the above picture. Needless to say, they will fail every time. When they finally concede defeat, pick up the dice and balance them without hesitation. The only question is . . . how are you going to do it?

# The World's Most Baffling "Shopping" Puzzle

Tilly the Tireless was certainly born to shop. When the notice about a mallwide sale appeared, she beat it down to the Bon Ton department store for some serious outfitting. At the checkout counter of one store, her total bill, including tax, came to $103. Tilly rummaged through her purse and came up with eight bills that totaled exactly $103. The funny thing was that none of them were one-dollar bills. Can you figure out what combination of greenbacks Tilly used to pay her bill with?

# The World's Most Baffling "Proofreading" Puzzle

"Frankly, Professor, I can't solve this problem. I was up all last night trying to find the blasted third incorrect item!"

"Same here, Professor. I've studied the paragraph for two days without finding it!"

**Their are three errers in this paragraph. Study it carefully and see if you can find all of them.**

# The World's Most Baffling "Handshake" Puzzle

Once again it's graduation at the Apex Santa Claus School. This year eight new Kriss Kringles are ready to assume their duties at department stores across the city. As they get ready to leave, each santa shakes hands with each of the other santas. This brings us to our puzzle. How many handshakes will there be?

# The World's Most Baffling "Logic" Puzzle

You'll need all of the pyramid power you can generate to solve this neat little logic problem. The numbers in the above triangle follow a certain pattern. If you can discern what this pattern is, you will then be able to calculate what numbers should replace the five question marks within the triangle. You have until the desert sands in this hourglass run out to find the answer.

# The World's Most Baffling "Crown" Puzzle

Here we find a tower guard hard at work protecting the crown jewels of England. This stout lad spends many an hour gazing upon the greatest collection of riches in the world. While staring at a case containing 12 mounted crowns, Harold was suddenly struck with a puzzle inspiration. Would it be possible to connect these 12 crowns using 5 straight lines? Each line, of course, would have to start at the end of the previous line. After ten minutes of thought, Harold came up with the answer. Solve this one and we'll crown you Prince of Puzzlers!

# The World's Most Baffling "Waiter" Puzzle

Clumsy Callahan was the fastest and the sloppiest waiter down at the Bavarian Gardens Restaurant. He drenched more diners than Hurricane Hugo. Finally, one day a disgusted customer left Callahan a one-cent tip and the following note: "You ruined my suit, so I'm leaving you a penny tip. However, if you can remove the penny from the plate without touching the table, the plate, or the penny, I'll give you a twenty-five dollar gratuity." Clumsy never solved this problem. Can you?

# The World's Most Baffling "Mental" Puzzle

"Yes, I'm getting it now! The complete number is 198. Is that correct?"

Once again the Mental Wizard has read your mind. Here's how the feat is done. Ask someone to write down any three-digit number in which each digit is a different number. Next, tell him to reverse the number and then to subtract the smaller number from the larger number. Finally, ask him to tell you what the last digit of the difference is. In the above example that would be eight. With this information you can tell him what the complete number is. See if you can figure out the Wizard's modus operandi before looking in the answer section.

# The World's Most Baffling "H₂O" Puzzle

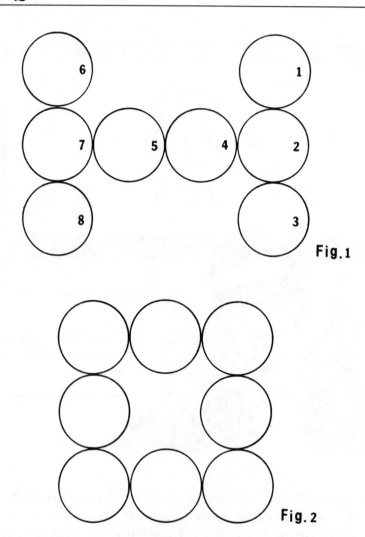

Fig. 1

Fig. 2

This is one of those delightful shifting coin problems. You have to change the *H* in Fig. 1 into the *O* in Fig. 2 in just five moves. A move consists of sliding one coin at a time to a new position without disturbing any of the other coins. When the coin reaches its new position, it must be touching two other coins. Don't end up all wet at the end of this slippery puzzle.

# The World's Most Baffling "Rearranging" Puzzle

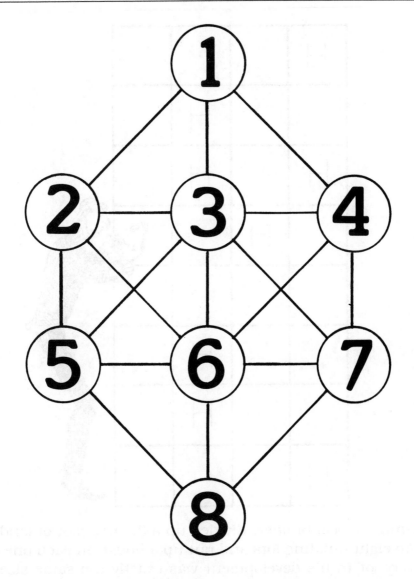

Here's a nice little problem to tax your puzzling abilities. The above connected circles contain the numbers 1 through 8. Your problem is to rearrange these numbers in the circles so that no two consecutive numbers will be joined by any one of the lines.

# The World's Most Baffling "Real Estate" Puzzle

Sidney, a local builder, divided up a 32-acre plot of land into eight building lots and put up a house on each one. Every lot in his development was exactly the same size and shape. Sidney's problem is that someone stole all the boundary markers from the lots and his estate plans are missing. He suspects foul play. Can you help Sidney determine where the original boundaries of each lot were? (The H's indicate where each house was built.)

# The World's Most Baffling "Weighing" Puzzle

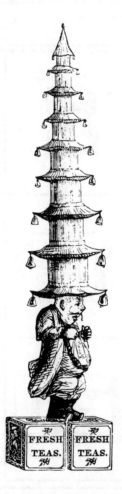

Pictured here is High Hat Louie, a famous old tea merchant in New York's Chinatown. He's standing here trying to figure out how to divide 20 pounds of tea into 10 2-pound packets using a simple balance scale. He could only find two weights around his shop; one was 5 pounds and the other was 9 pounds. He knows that it can be done in just nine weighings, but he's forgotten how to do it. Can you help High Hat solve this mystery before his customers start coming in?

# The World's Most Baffling "Mystical Square" Puzzle

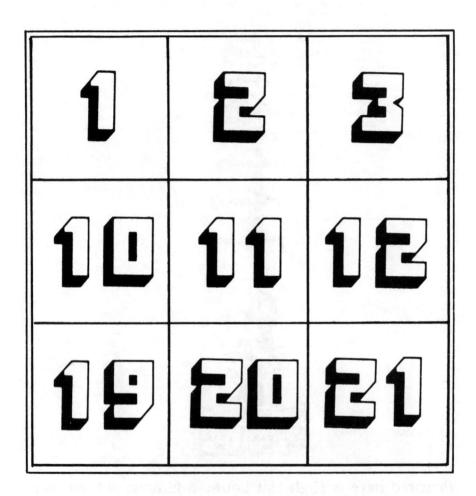

Let's take time out for another of those delightful (?) mystical square puzzles. All you have to do is rearrange the nine numbers in the above square so that every horizontal, vertical, and diagonal line adds up to 33. I hope that you can conjure up the answer in five minutes or less.

# The World's Most Baffling "Substitution" Puzzle

It looks like everyone has the answer to the extra credit problem in Ms. Sunshine's math class. In case you're not familiar with this type of puzzle, you must substitute the numbers 0 through 9 for the ten different letters in the above math expression. The finished product must be a correct addition problem. The same number is given to each occurrence of the same letter.

# The World's Most Baffling "Progression" Puzzle

## 8 5 4 9 1 7 6 3 2 0

"Gee, Mom, this homework puzzle is too tough!"

"No, it isn't, Timmy. All you have to do is to discover the order they're written in!"

Here we have an old-time kid trying to solve an old-time puzzle. Some things just never change!

# The World's Most Baffling "Train" Puzzle

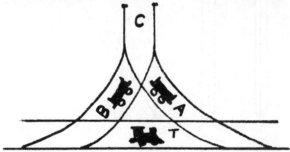

When Peter Cooper built his famous locomotive, the Tom Thumb, there were only about 13 miles of railroad track in the United States. Near Baltimore there was a funny little siding that caused all kinds of mix-ups. In the diagram below, T is the engine and A and B are two cars on the siding. Position C is only long enough to hold one car or the engine. Your problem is to make cars A and B change places and to end up with the engine back where it started in the fewest possible moves.

# The World's Most Baffling "Stirring" Puzzle

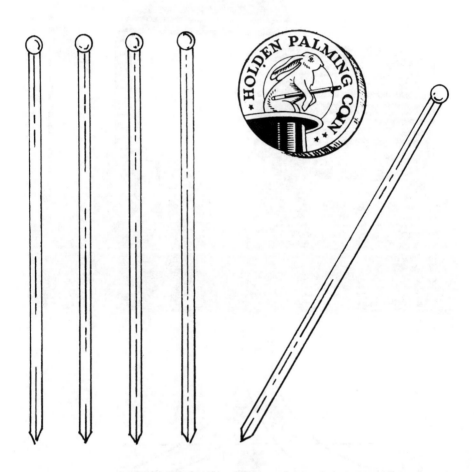

Here's a neat bet you can use the next time you're at the local soda fountain. Place four plastic stirrers and a coin on the table. Wager those present that they cannot pick up the four stirrers and the coin all at once using only a fifth stirrer. The catch is that after lifting them clear of the table the person must be able to turn the lifting stirrer over and still not have the other stirrers, or the coin, fall off. Levitate on that one for a while.

# The World's Most Baffling "Time" Puzzle

The gentleman pictured here is having nightmares over a puzzle he heard at work and has been unable to solve all day. The problem states that a woman had two clocks in her house. One of the clocks didn't run at all, and the other clock always loses an hour a day. Now, which of the clocks will have the correct time most often during any given week? Please solve this one in a hurry so this distraught man can get some sleep before dawn's early light.

# The World's Most Baffling "Pie" Puzzle

There's nothing like a good pie puzzle when Turkey Day rolls around. This problem is so old that Governor Bradford probably used it at dessert during that first Thanksgiving Day so many years ago. What you have to determine is: What are the most different-size pieces you can cut this mincemeat pie into, by making four straight cuts across it?

# The World's Most Baffling "Domino" Puzzle

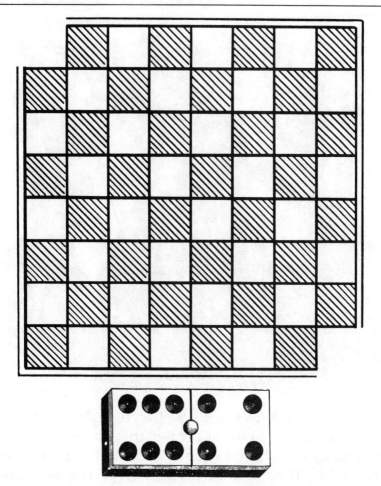

Here's your chance to play both checkers and dominoes at the same time. Let's say we have 32 dominoes and that each domino is big enough to cover two squares on a checkerboard. We could then place all of them on the board, and they would cover all 64 squares. Fair enough?

Now, let us cut off two opposite corner squares from the board and discard one of the dominoes. Could you then cover the remaining 62 squares on the board with the 31 dominoes you have left on the table? If you can, prove it. If you cannot, explain why.

# The World's Most Baffling "Chocolate Candy" Puzzle

Many years ago three travelers shared a table at the Black Eye Tavern. At the end of dinner they ordered a plate of chocolates to be shared equally. Before the candy arrived at the table, they had all fallen asleep. The first one to wake up saw the candy, ate his equal share, and fell back to sleep. The second man soon awoke and, seeing the chocolates, ate what he thought was his equal share and promptly went back to sleep. Finally, the third traveller awoke, looked at the candy, and ate what he thought was his equal share. He then drifted back to the Land of Nod.

While they snored away the rest of the evening, their waiter removed the dish with the candy on it. There were eight pieces left. Can you figure out how many pieces were originally brought to the table?

# The World's Most Baffling "Tire" Puzzle

Not long ago our puzzle club set out for a day's outing at the local beach. Halfway there we had a flat tire. Our driver jacked the bus up, removed the bad tire, and went to get his spare. As he was about to put the spare on the wheel, he kicked the hubcap on the ground so hard that it flew off the side of the road and over a cliff, taking along the five lug nuts used to hold the tire on the wheel.

"Well, that does it," he said, "I'll have to walk back to the last town we passed and try to find some replacement lug nuts."

"Not so fast, sonny," Aunt Bertha piped up, "all you have to do is . . . !"

What was Aunt Bertha's solution to this motoring mishap?

# The World's Most Baffling "Shape" Puzzle

Back in 1877 Professor Reynaund put on quite a show. One of his most popular features was a puzzle slide show presented with the aid of his famous invention, the Praxinoscope. Here we see him presenting the problem known as "The Puzzling Shape." Shown on the screen, top to bottom, are the front and side views of a solid block of wood. After studying these two pictures, you should be able to figure out what the three-dimensional shape of the object is. Focus in on this one.

# The World's Most Baffling "Family" Puzzle

"All the Anderson children, get down here on the double. Hup, hup, hup!"

Well, it looks like the Andersons really mean business this time. They've hired Cedric Longnose, the toughest baby-sitter in town, to watch their brood tonight. The Andersons have a great bunch of kids, but are they hard to handle. I forget just how many kids they have, but I do know that each daughter has the same number of brothers as she has sisters. Also, each of the boys has twice as many sisters as he has brothers. Using this information, can you figure out how many Anderson children there are?

# The World's Most Baffling "Unicycle" Puzzle

Young Austin Tightcollar was a dutiful son who visited his mother for dinner every Sunday. Austin lived in Rivergrove and his mom lived in Center City. Austin left promptly at noon after coffee hour at his church. Long ago he figured out that if he rode his unicycle at 15 miles an hour, he would get to her house an hour before dinner. But if he rode at the rate of 10 miles an hour, he would arrive an hour late for dinner.

Can you figure out at what speed Austin rode to arrive precisely at dinner time? Also, what was the distance between his home and his mother's?

# The World's Most Baffling "Groucho" Puzzle

*"Any puzzle club that would accept me as a member is a club I wouldn't want to join!"*

| PUZZLE CLUB ENTRANCE PROBLEM | | | | | |
|---|---|---|---|---|---|
| 4 | 5 | 6 | 7 | 8 | 9 |
| 61 | 52 | 63 | 94 | 46 | ? |

It looks like Groucho is in no mood to join our club. I wonder if he could have solved the above entrance problem? All you have to do is to figure out what the last number should be!

# The World's Most Baffling "Diet" Puzzle

Our overweight diner is so flabbergasted over the size of the bill that he has lapsed into number talk at the end of his reply to the waiter. Can you translate his numbers into words?

# The World's Most Baffling "Betting" Puzzle

J. Wellington Moneybags is back in town with a new bag of bets to separate the local wagering gentry from their money. We were sitting around the Bits-and-Grits Coffee Shop one night when Wellington presented us with this one. Putting a sheet of paper and a pencil on the table, he said, "I'll wager anyone a hundred dollars that I can prove that you can take four away from four and be left with eight."

We all knew that there had to be a trick to it, but finally Elmer Wormwood put a dollar on the table and said: "Take it or leave it, Moneybags. My money says, 'You can't prove it.'"

Well, of course, J. Wellington took it and showed everyone that you can indeed take four away from four and end up with eight. How did he do it?

# The World's Most Baffling "Floating" Puzzle

*"See how easy it is! Now I'll show you how to make a solid piece of steel float on water."*

*"I say, Lorenzo, do you have to?"*

Uncle Lorenzo is quite an after-dinner entertainer. Although not in the same class as J. Wellington, he pulls off a good one now and then. He's not kidding about being able to make a solid piece of steel float on water. See if you can figure out how it's done before turning to the answer section.

# The World's Most Baffling "Arrow" Puzzle

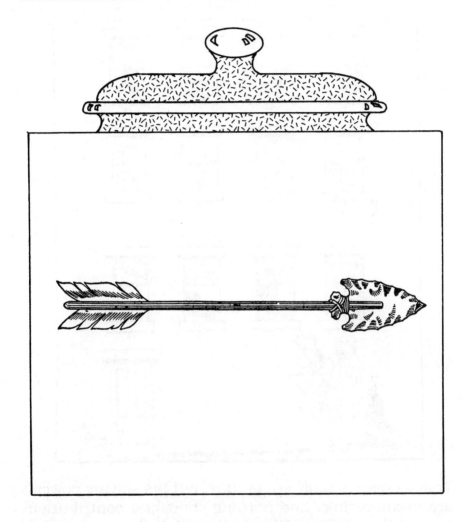

Here's a clever bit of trickery that will fool them every time. On a small piece of cardboard, draw an arrow, the fancier the better. Next, prop the drawing up against some object on the table so that the arrow points to the right. Now, bet anyone that you can make the arrow turn around and point to the left without touching the card or moving the table in anyway. It sounds impossible, but . . .

# The World's Most Baffling "Monkey" Puzzle

Tony's organ is sadly out of tune, but his staying powers are inexhaustible, and nothing short of a contribution from each person in the picture will bribe him to stop grinding and move on to other quarters.

Now that his audience is ready to capitulate, can you show Jocko the shortest possible route by which he can move from window to window with his little tin cup to collect his dues? The monkey must start from his present position and end his tour by resting on his master's shoulders.

# The World's Most Baffling "Dirt" Puzzle

"Another urgent message from Panama. Jackson is always having trouble with his excavation calculations. See if you can figure this one out, Henderson. How many cubic yards of dirt are there in a ditch that is 12 yards wide, 20 feet deep, and 600 feet long?"

"I'll need pencil and paper to work that one out!"

President Theodore Roosevelt is dealing with a problem concerning his famous canal. Can you help Mr. Henderson answer the president's question?

# The World's Most Baffling "Triangle" Puzzle

Down along the Nile people often contemplated pyramids and triangles. The young woman shown here is trying to calculate the number of triangles depicted in the above drawing. There are many different-size triangles within the drawing. Let's see how many you can find in 60 seconds.

# The World's Most Baffling "Entrance" Puzzle

TOOP ENGA TE PU SH!

This young lady is on her way to a costume party for charity being presented at the local zoo. However, there is no one in attendance to let her in. On the fence post there's a badly lettered sign with instructions on how to proceed. Can you interpret this sign so that Cleo will be on time for the ball?

# The World's Most Baffling
## "Geometry" Puzzle

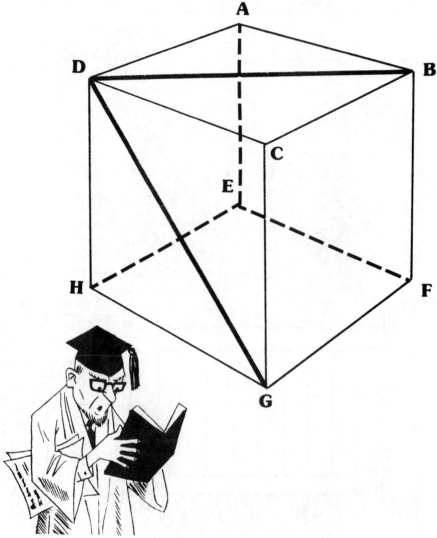

The professor is in a quandary. He's forgotten the answer to the puzzle pictured above and class begins in five minutes! Two lines, *BD* and *GD*, are drawn on the faces of an imaginary cube. Both lines converge at point *D*. Can you calculate the angle between these two diagonal lines and help the professor out?

# The
# **World's**
# Most
# Challenging
# Puzzles

# The Most Challenging "Tombstone" Puzzle

Sacred to the memory of
**MR. EDWARD FOUNTAIN**
of this parish, who died
on the 28th Oct. 1823:
*AGED 66 YEARS*
also of
**MRS. SARAH FOUNTAIN**
his widow, who died
on the 23rd Sept. 1812
*AGED 82 YEARS*

The Reverend I. N. Spire chanced upon the above tombstone while on his way to vespers. Something about the inscription bothered him. After a moment's reflection he discovered an error in it. Can you find the Reverend's revelation?

# The Most Challenging "Magic Square" Puzzle

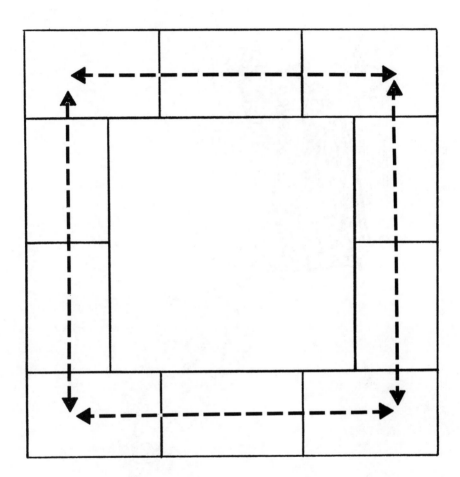

Now, here's a novel way to construct a magic square. From a deck of playing cards remove ten cards, ace through ten, and, counting the ace as one, arrange them in a square in such a way that the sum of the cards on any side is eighteen. If you set them down as shown above, the three cards in the top and bottom rows must add up to eighteen and the four cards in each of the side columns must also add up to eighteen.

# The Most Challenging "Tennis Ball" Puzzle

Harriet has discovered a gopher hole on the courts of the Idle Hours Country Club. The hole where her tennis ball now resides is too deep to reach into and the bend in its middle makes retrieving the ball with a stick out of the question. Undaunted, Harriet quickly figures out the best way to free the ball and has it back in service within two minutes. How can she do this without digging up the court?

# The Most Challenging "Thimble" Puzzle

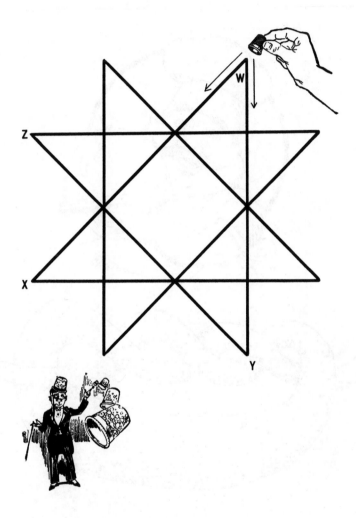

Thomas Thackery, the King of Thaumaturgical Thimble Trickery, presents this problem: Put seven thimbles on seven points of the above star by placing a thimble on an empty point of the star and then sliding it over to another empty point. On the move pictured here, the thimble could end up either at point X or point Y. Don't get stuck by this puzzle.

# The Most Challenging "Bakery" Puzzle

This is a puzzle with a twist. Olaf has just removed a piping-hot loaf of his famous "Poppy Seed Pretzel Puzzle Bread" from the oven. As his customers draw near, he asks them, "If I take my knife and make one straight cut across any part of the loaf, what is the maximum number of pieces I can divide it into?" Can you taste the answer to this delectable problem?

# The Most Challenging "Bicycle" Puzzle

At the turn of the century, Atlantic City was famed for its miles and miles of boardwalk. Every summer, Waylan Armstrong was out on the boards perambulating Mother Armstrong down to the Steel Pier and back. Waylan was very consistent in his rate of speed: Against a stiff wind he could pedal a mile in four minutes, but with the same wind at his back he could pedal a mile in three minutes. Given these facts, can you figure out how long it took him to ride a mile on a calm day? If you solve this in less than five minutes you deserve a box of Salt Water Taffy.

# The Most Challenging "Coin" Puzzle

"All right, Dear, listen carefully. On the table are three coins: two quarters and a nickel. The nickel is between the quarters. The problem is to place one of the quarters in the middle instead of the nickel. When moving the coins you must adhere to the following rules: The first quarter can be moved but not touched; the nickel can be touched but not moved, and the last quarter can either be touched or moved. This is the quarter that we want to place between the other two coins. Think that you can solve the puzzle?"

"Farlow, hit the road. It's three in the morning."

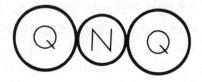

# The Most Challenging "Magnet" Puzzle

The monthly Puzzle Club meeting is about to start. To be admitted, you have to answer a question propounded by the Sergeant at Arms: "You are given two identical iron bars. One is a magnet, the other an ordinary piece of iron. You are to identify which of the bars is the magnet by placing them together in a certain way. You can only do this once and nothing else may be used in your determination." How will you go about solving this problem?

# The Most Challenging "Card" Puzzle

"I give up! This blasted puzzle can't be solved!"

Our hero seems to be at the end of his rope. Let's help him out. The puzzle states that you must take the four fives from a deck of cards and lay them out on the table face up in such a way that only sixteen of the twenty *large* pips on the cards show. You have ten minutes to solve this one.

# The Most Challenging "Rope" Puzzle

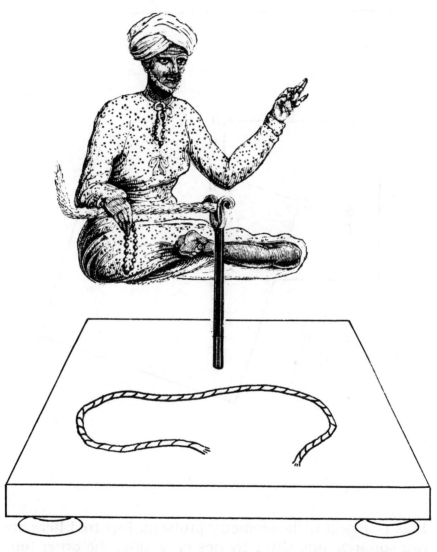

Our levitating swami has his own version of the "Indian Rope Trick" for you to solve. On his platform is a plain piece of rope. Pick up the ends of the rope, one in each hand, and tie a knot in the middle. The catch is that you are not allowed to let go of either end of the rope while doing this. Don't get up in the air trying to work this one out.

# The Most Challenging "Area" Puzzle

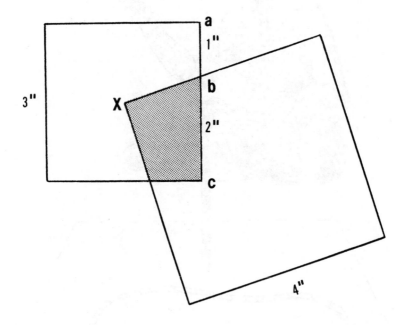

This is a neat little geometry problem. Pictured here are two squares, one three inches on a side, the other four inches on a side. The upper left corner of the four-inch square is anchored to the middle of the smaller square at point X. The larger square has been rotated until its upper side crosses line ac at point b. Using the information given in the illustration, can you quickly calculate the area, in square inches, of the shaded portion of the drawing?

# The Most Challenging "Lunch" Puzzle

"I'll take that bet—and if I lose I'll buy dinner, too!"

When the boss's lunch arrived, a $6.00 triple-decker sandwich from the Stage Door Deli, Treadmill walked over and placed an empty wastebasket over it and said, "Chief, I'll bet you 50¢ that I can eat your sandwich without touching the wastebasket, the table or the plate it's on. In fact, I won't touch anything in the room nor will anyone else help me out in any way. Do we have a wager?"

How did Treadmill win his bet?

# The Most Challenging "Rectangle" Puzzle

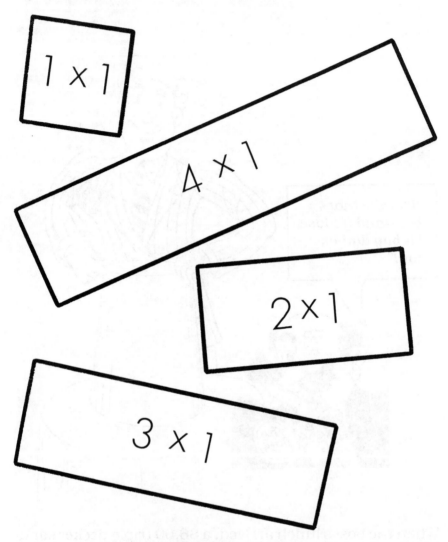

Here's a great "gotcha" problem. Place these four rectangular pieces of cardboard on a table and invite a friend to arrange them so that they form a perfect square. The numbers indicate the size of the pieces in inches. Suffice it to say that after all fail you will show them the way. Of course, you have to try it yourself before turning to the solution.

# The Most Challenging "Cord" Puzzle

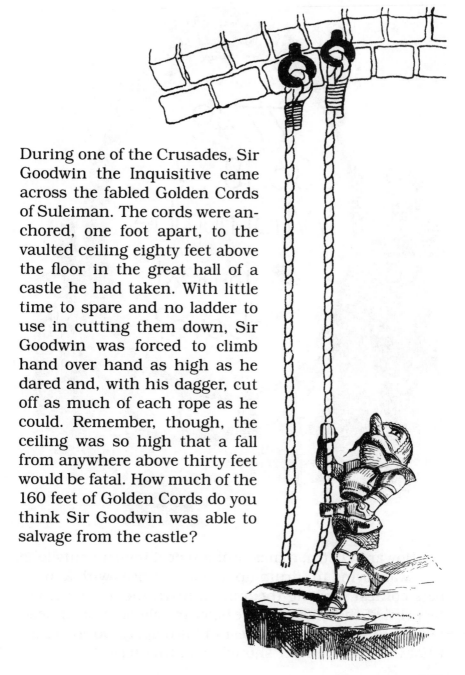

During one of the Crusades, Sir Goodwin the Inquisitive came across the fabled Golden Cords of Suleiman. The cords were anchored, one foot apart, to the vaulted ceiling eighty feet above the floor in the great hall of a castle he had taken. With little time to spare and no ladder to use in cutting them down, Sir Goodwin was forced to climb hand over hand as high as he dared and, with his dagger, cut off as much of each rope as he could. Remember, though, the ceiling was so high that a fall from anywhere above thirty feet would be fatal. How much of the 160 feet of Golden Cords do you think Sir Goodwin was able to salvage from the castle?

# The Most Challenging "Number" Puzzle

77, 49, 36, 18...? What number is next above?

Mr. Howard Distin, a maker of musical instruments long ago, was trying to "drum up" some business with a numbers contest. During the annual instrument convention he printed the above progression puzzle on a drumhead hoping to snare some interest in his display. Do you know what the next number should be in this series?

# The Most Challenging "Salt and Pepper" Puzzle

It seems that Gwendolyn has seen her boss perform this trick once too often. Herbert loves to amaze his friends with this puzzle. After pouring a small mound of salt on the table he then sprinkles it with a liberal amount of pepper. The puzzle, he tells his guests, is to remove the pepper from the salt without touching either the salt or the pepper. Although this sounds impossible, clever Herbert can do it in one minute flat. Can you discover the secret and make Gwendolyn yawn, too?

# The Most Challenging "Pencil" Puzzle

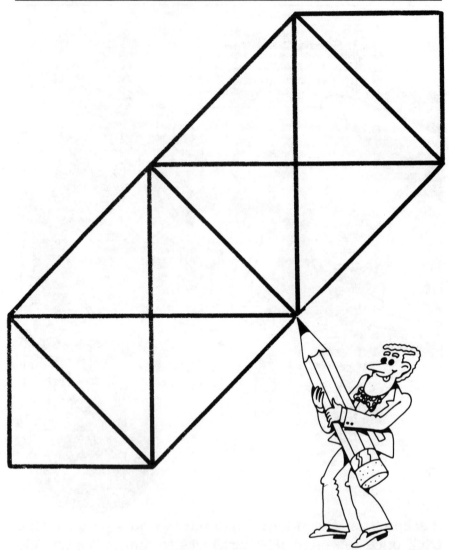

This is one of those "continuous line" puzzles that we all love so much. Take pencil in hand and duplicate the figure shown above. To accomplish this you have to use one continuous line; the line cannot cross itself at any point, cannot go over any part of the line more than once, and must end at the point indicated by the tip of the pencil in the hands of the young artist pictured here.

# The Most Challenging "Theatre" Puzzle

Back in 1905 that famous theatre of magic, the Sphinx, opened to an enthusiastic audience. The theatre had one hundred seats and on that first day they sold every one of them and took in exactly $100. The admissions were as follows: men, $5.00 each; women, $2.00 each; and children, 10¢ each. Using this information, can you calculate how many men, women and children took in this premiere performance?

# The Most Challenging "Sting" Puzzle

Be prepared to get stung on this one. On the table are nine coins totalling 80¢. As you can see, there is 20¢ in heads showing and 60¢ in tails showing. The puzzle is to turn over 25¢ worth of coins and leave 40¢ in heads showing. I think that I'll be "buzzing" along before you read the answer to this one!

# The Most Challenging "Fish" Puzzle

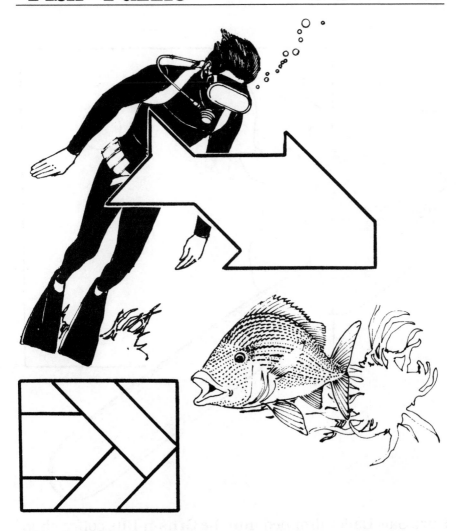

Certainly one of the most enduring forms of mechanical puzzles in the world is the tangram. It has been around for hundreds of years.

Pictured is an oblong set of tangram tiles. Above it is the outline of an oriental fighting fish. The puzzle, of course, is to rearrange the seven tangram tiles into the shape of this fish. Can you picture how this is done? Don't get hooked now; it's not as easy as it looks.

# The Most Challenging "Buzz Saw" Puzzle

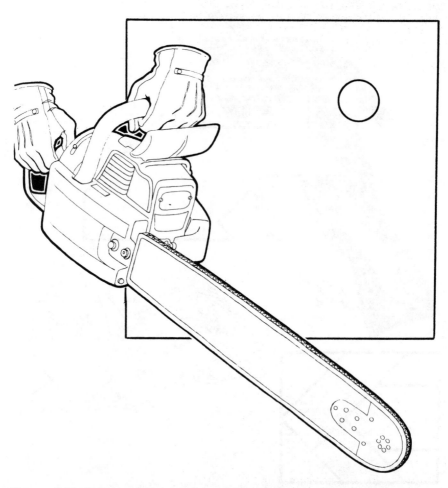

Buzz Saw Bailey dropped into the Grits-n-Bits coffee shop the other day and told everyone about a puzzle he had just heard about from a lumber salesman. The salesman showed Bailey a square piece of wood with a small hole drilled in it off-center. "The problem," he told Bailey, "is to figure out the least number of pieces the board would have to be cut up into so that when you reassembled the pieces the hole would then be in the center of the board." Can you figure out the answer?

# The Most Challenging "Word" Puzzle

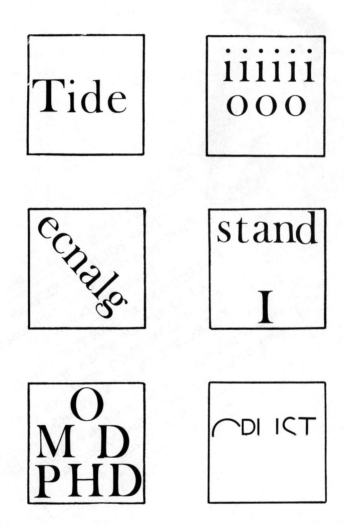

These six "word pictures" all stand for some object or expression. Four out of six is a passing grade on this one.

# The Most Challenging "Perception" Puzzle

TEST YOUR AWARENESS
First read the sentence enclosed in the box below.

FINISHED FILES ARE THE RESULT OF YEARS OF SCIENTIFIC STUDY COMBINED WITH THE EXPERIENCE OF MANY YEARS.

Now count the F's in the sentence. Count them only once and do not go back and count them again.

The above puzzle is printed on the back of a business card used by the G & C Auto Body Shop of Passaic, New Jersey. It's an interesting test in perception, a skill that their clients sometimes lack. Let's see how you score on this test.

# The Most Challenging "Spider" Puzzle

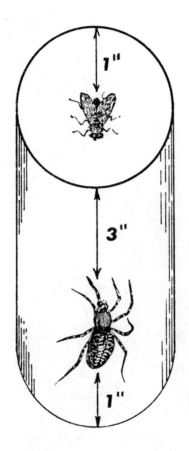

Don't let this problem bug you. In the illustration a glass cylinder is four inches high and six inches in circumference. On the outside of the cylinder is a spider one inch from the bottom, and a fly is on the inside of the cylinder one inch from the top. The spider, on seeing the fly, takes the shortest possible route over the cylinder and pounces on the fly. What route does the spider travel and how many inches does he walk?

# The Most Challenging "Earth" Puzzle

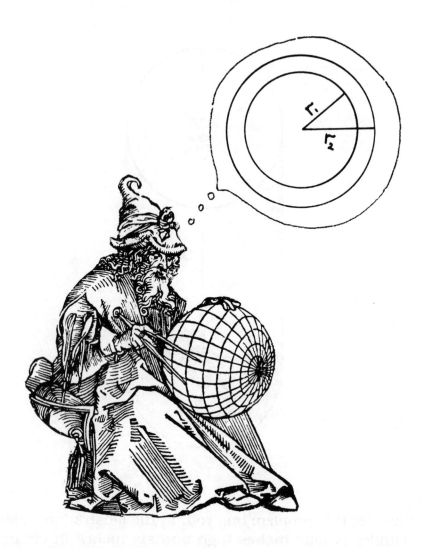

The ancient wise man here is working on the old "Steel Band" problem. He put a steel band around the earth at the equator, then cut the band and added ten feet to it. Some magical force now holds the band an equal distance away from the earth. What is this distance? (Assume that the radius of the earth is 4,000 miles and use 3.14 for pi.)

# The Most Challenging "Missing Letter" Puzzle

PRSVRYPRFCTMN

VRKPTHSPRCPTSTN

The above inscription appears just over the Ten Commandments in the chancel of a small church in Wales. The addition of a single letter, repeated at various intervals, makes it not only intelligible but appropriate to the situation. What is the missing letter and where does it go in the inscription?

# The Most Challenging "Clown" Puzzle

Here are three clowns, John, Dick and Roger. During the winter months each of them has two different vocations. Their six jobs are: truck driver, writer, trumpeter, golf player, computer technician and barber. Given the following six clues, find out the vocations of the three clowns.

- The truck driver flirted with the golf player's sister.
- The trumpeter and the computer technician went horseback riding with John.
- The truck driver laughed at the trumpeter because of his big feet.
- Dick received a box of chocolates from the computer technician.
- The golf player bought a used car from the writer.
- Roger was faster than both Dick and the golf player at eating pizza.

# The Most Challenging "Counting" Puzzle

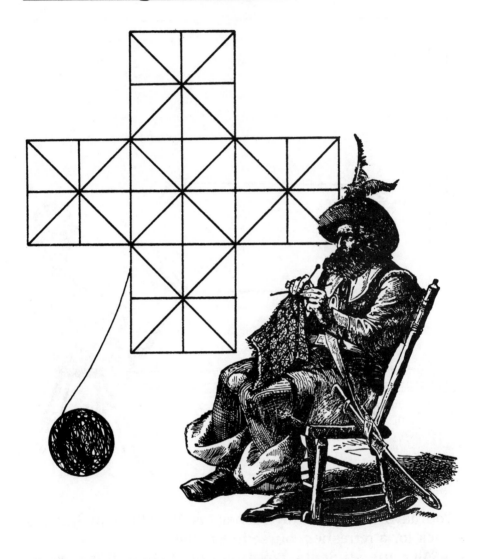

Our bold buccaneer is just a-sittin' and a-rockin', waiting for the doldrums to pass so that he can fly his new "puzzle kite." This kite challenges you to figure out how many different-sized squares and triangles are contained in its design. You are allowed only one chance to arrive at the correct totals.

# The Most Challenging "Mystery Word" Puzzle

Your favorite substitute teacher, Ms. Priscilla Sunshine, is back for a refresher course in English.

"All right, students, pay attention. Behind this piece of cardboard is a common English word, in use today, that describes a person or a thing as being in no place under the sun, neither here nor there nor anywhere. Yet, if you only add a space between two of its letters, the person or object will be right here at this very moment. Can you tell me what this word is?"

# The Most Challenging "Nuptial" Puzzle

"When the day after tomorrow is yesterday; then 'today' will be as far from Sunday as that day was which was 'today' when the day before yesterday was tomorrow."

Obviously the score of this match is Love. The young lady has just asked her fiancé what day of the week he would like to be married on. To say the least, his answer is a little muddled. Can you determine what day of the week he has in mind?

# The Most Challenging "Golf" Puzzle

Dashing Dan the Duffer has become the most talked-about player at the Idle Hours Country Club. After years of scooping divots and slicing golf balls through the clubhouse, Dan has finally gotten his game together. No matter what club he uses, the ball travels only one of two distances. Dan has worked it out so that by combining these two shots, sometimes hitting two long shots and one short shot, for example, he can play the front nine of the course in 26 strokes. He always plays in a straight line from tee to cup, since his hooks and slices are a thing of the past. Occasionally he hits the ball past the green but he always chips back to hole out. It makes no difference to him because he is always able to sink the ball by hitting it one of two distances. Our problem is: What are the two distances that Dan uses in hitting his way to fame and fortune? Keep in mind that Dan's yardage for the first nine holes is 150 yards, 300 yards, 250 yards, 325 yards, 275 yards, 350 yards, 225 yards, 400 yards, and 425 yards.

# The Most Challenging "Pyramid" Puzzle

From the valley of the Nile comes this ancient and venerable problem. Above the altar in the diagram are six pyramids. The problem is to rearrange them so that they will be positioned as shown under the altar. The rules for effecting this change are as follows: You only have three moves; you must move two *adjacent* pyramids during each move; a move is considered turning a pyramid end for end; and each pyramid must remain in the same spot. May the power of the pyramid be with you!

# The Most Challenging "College Boy" Puzzle

Dear Dad;

$$SEND$$
$$+MORE$$
$$\overline{MONEY}$$

Love

Jr.

"Send more money," the cry of the impoverished college student—a cry that this time will be answered only if his father can decipher the message. Each letter of the message represents a digit—zero through nine. Some of the letters are used more than once. How much, in dollars and cents, does Junior need?

# The Most Challenging "Punctuation" Puzzle

"Quimby, you call yourself a proof-reader? Just look at this quotation from Professor Stoic's address last night! You left out all of the punctuation!"

## THAT THAT IS IS THAT THAT IS NOT IS NOT IS THAT IT THAT IS IT

Above is Professor Stoic's quotation without any punctuation. Can you bring order out of this academic chaos with the proper addition of a few commas, a period or two, and perhaps a question mark for emphasis?

# The Most Challenging "Soup Tureen" Puzzle

Aunt Edna always kept a large amount of money around her house for emergencies. The only trouble was that she never trusted paper money; so her hoard became quite bulky. She also hid her savings in the most unlikely of places—a silver soup tureen. When she counted her money she found the most extraordinary coincidence. She had exactly $700, divided equally into quarters, half-dollars, and silver dollars. Can you tell how many of each there were?

# The Most Challenging "Bell" Puzzle

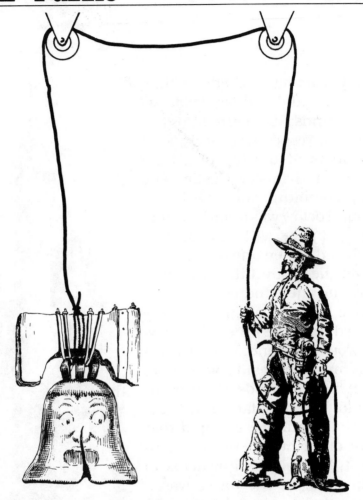

The Reverend I. N. Spire is back for a last try at stumping you. It seems the Reverend purchased a new bell for his church, and somehow he was able to talk the Durango Kid into helping him hang it. The bell and the Kid weighed the same. When the Kid started hauling on the rope a surprising thing happened. See if you can guess if . . .

- the bell went up while the Kid stayed down?
- the Kid went up while the bell stayed down?
- the Kid and the bell went up together?

# The Most Challenging "Castle" Puzzle

Many years ago, an elderly king, his son and daughter, weighing 195 pounds, 105 pounds, and 90 pounds, respectively, were kept prisoners at the top of a high tower in Grimsley Castle. The only communication with the ground below was a cord passing over a pulley with a basket at each end. When one basket rested on the ground the other was opposite the window. Naturally, if one basket was more heavily loaded than the other, the heavier would descend; but if the excess on either side was more than fifteen pounds, the descent would become dangerous, because it would be so rapid that none of the prisoners could control it. The only thing available to help them in the tower was a cannonball, weighing 75 pounds. Still, they managed to escape. How did they do it? (Our thanks go out to Professor Hoffmann, who wrote this puzzle over a hundred years ago in his great book, *Puzzles Old and New*.)

# The Most Challenging "Square" Puzzle

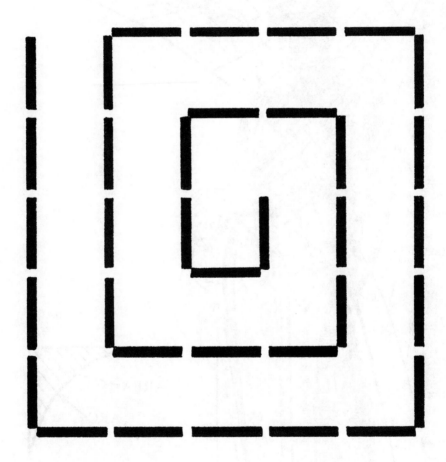

You're going to love fooling your friends with this one. Lay out 35 pencils in the spiral shown here. Now, challenge anyone to move four of the pencils to new positions so that three perfect squares are formed.

# The Most Challenging "Web" Puzzle

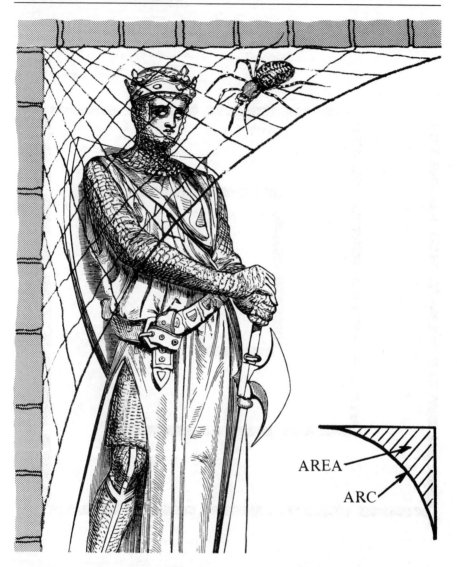

AREA

ARC

A statue stands in a gloomy alcove in Grimsley Castle. Partly blocking the entrance is a giant spider's web. The arc of the web is exactly one quarter of a circle and is twenty inches long. Given these facts, can you calculate the area covered by the web in square inches without getting caught in this problem?

# The Most Challenging "Bridge" Puzzle

Now, here's a good way to win a dinner the next time you're out with some friends. Put two glasses on the table a short distance apart and place a sheet of fairly stiff paper across the tops of the glasses. Next, state that you have the power to hypnotize the paper and make it strong enough to support a third glass placed in the middle of the paper. This puzzle is a good stumper, but give it a try before heading out to the restaurant.

# The Most Challenging "Bottle and Keg" Puzzle

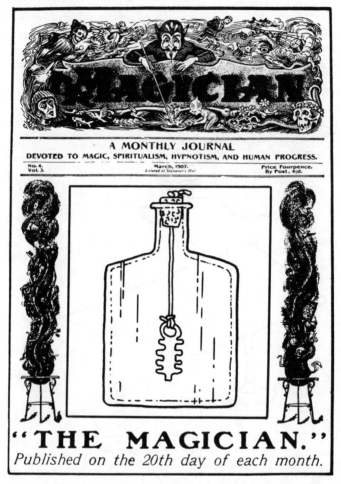

Framed in the cover of a fascinating old magic magazine is an equally fascinating old puzzle. Tie a key to the end of a piece of string; then pass the other end of the string through a hole that has been drilled in a piece of cork. After knotting the end of the string, lower the key into the bottle and place the cork firmly into the neck of the bottle. Your challenge, if you wish to accept it, is to remove the key from the string without touching the cork, the string, the bottle or the table that it is standing on. You're going to need a genie to help you solve this one.

# The Most Challenging "Horse" Puzzle

"I say, did you hear about the Tralawny will mix-up?"

"If it hadn't been for that lawyer chap, Trevor Torts, they'd still be at it!"

During the Annual Costume Hunting Breakfast at the Tallyho Club the following story was making the rounds:

When Squire Tralawny passed away, he left a will whereby he bequeathed his best jumping horses to his three sons, John, James, and William. The bequest was to be divided in the following manner: John, the eldest, was to receive half, James was to have a third, and William a ninth of the stable. When he died, however, it was found that the number of horses in the stable was seventeen, a number which was divisible neither by two, three, or nine. In their perplexity the three brothers consulted a clever lawyer, who hit on a scheme whereby the Squire's intentions were carried out to the satisfaction of all parties. How was it managed?

# The Most Challenging "Counterfeit Coin" Puzzle

This problem was used in the Annual Puzzle Club elimination contest.

On a table were ten hats numbered from one to ten. Inside each hat were ten gold coins. The coins all looked alike, but those in one of the hats were all counterfeit. The real coins weighed ten grams apiece, while each counterfeit coin weighed nine grams. To help the contestants solve the problem a scale was provided that gave weights in grams. However, the contestants could only use this scale once. They could, however, place as many coins into the scale as they wished for this one weighing. Given these facts, which hat contained the bogus bullion?

# The Most Challenging "Scholar" Puzzle

First Scholar: "Drat, I can't find the answer in any of these books. Please read that puzzle to me again."

Second Scholar: "Now, let me see. Oh, yes, here it is: 'Take away my first letter and I remain unchanged; take away my second letter and I remain unchanged; take away my third letter and I remain unchanged; take away all my letters and still I remain exactly the same.' "

First Scholar: "What in the world could the word be?"

# The Most Challenging "Shield" Puzzle

Our next problem comes from ancient Babylon. The shield is encircled by twelve black dots. The problem is to place eleven coins on eleven of these dots according to the following instructions: Starting at any dot, count six dots and place a coin on the sixth dot. Always count in a clockwise direction. Starting at another empty dot, count around the circle and place another coin on an empty dot. Continue this until all of the coins have been placed on different dots. When counting, treat a dot with a coin on it like an empty dot and count it along with the rest. Remember, you must always start counting at an empty dot.

# The Most Challenging "Door" Puzzle

While admiring a new door donated to his college, Willard Wordsworth was inspired to create a new puzzle. "Students," he challenged, "I want you to rearrange the letters in the two words *new door* to make one word." You have until the bell sounds to turn in your answer.

# The Most Challenging "Eight Word" Puzzle

crabcake     stupid

laughing     hijack

calmness    first

canopy     deft

What do the above eight words have in common?

# The Most Challenging "Mental" Puzzle

Punch is expressing himself rather freely concerning his thoughts on this puzzle. He had to add up all of the numbers from one to 100 in his head. After working ten minutes on the problem he gave up, complaining that he kept losing track of which number he had added last. What Punch didn't know was that there is a simple solution to this problem that would allow him to solve it in twenty seconds or less. Can you discover what this solution is?

# The Most Challenging "Hand" Puzzle

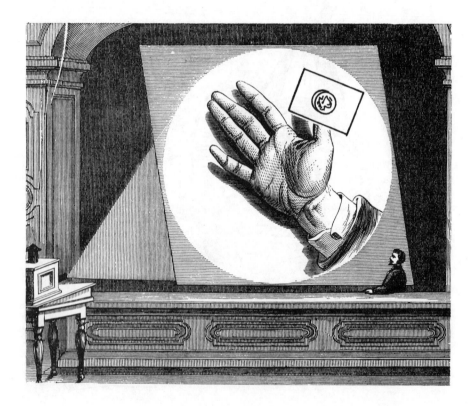

Balance a playing card horizontally on the top of your right thumb. Now lay a coin (a half dollar or a quarter) on it so that both are steady. Now comes the hard part. Remove the card without touching the coin. The coin should remain balanced on the thumb. You'll get a real hand if you can solve this the first time out.

# The
# **World's**
# Most Incredible
# Puzzles

# World's Most Incredible "Dress" Puzzle

Mrs. White, Mrs. Black and Mrs. Grey were chatting in the garden. One was wearing a white dress, one a black dress and the third a grey dress. Mrs. Grey looked around and said, "We're all wearing dresses that are the same color as our names but none of us is wearing a dress that is the same color as her name!"

"What difference does that make?" asked the lady wearing the black dress.

With these sparse clues can you tell what color dress each of the three ladies had on?

# World's Most Incredible "Carpentry" Puzzle

That old cut-up, Hiram Ballpeene, had everyone stumped down at the lumberyard the other day. He brought in an irregular sheet of plywood and challenged the millworkers to cut it into three pieces that could then be reassembled to form the top of a two-foot-square table. Let's see if you can rip out the answer in jig time.

# World's Most Incredible "Real Estate" Puzzle

Sidney, a local real estate maven, has boxed himself into a corner again. He bought an irregularly shaped piece of property he now wishes to subdivide into eight building sites all the same size and shape. Can you show him where he should lay out the property boundaries so he can start showing these choice lots to prospective customers?

# World's Most Incredible "Match" Puzzle

Many years ago, when smoking was the sophisticated thing to do, everyone carried matches and knew at least half a dozen match puzzles or games. Pictured above are twelve matches arranged in a square. This square encloses an area of nine square units. The side of these units are the length of a match. Can you rearrange these twelve matches so that they enclose an area of four square units? None of the matches can, of course, overlap.

# World's Most Incredible "Find-the-Items" Puzzle

Here's an easy spelling test for you. In the above grid of twenty letters are hidden the names of twenty items found around the house. When spelling an item start at any letter and move one letter at a time horizontally, vertically or diagonally until a word is spelled. During the spelling of any one word you cannot enter any box more than one time. If you can find more than the twenty words that we give, then you're eligible for a double gold star.

# World's Most Incredible "Archaeology" Puzzle

"We'll be in all the history books for this find, Petrie! The fabled Theban Tablet of Tiles has been unearthed at last!"

"Quite right, Hawkings! You are to be congratulated. Now let's solve the puzzle. According to the papyrus, 'To know perfection is to know the total number of squares, both great and small, in the Tablet of Tiles.'"

How many squares can the reader find?

# World's Most Incredible "Toothpick" Puzzle

"Here's an interesting problem, Mayor Fairweather. I've arranged these 24 toothpicks so they form nine small squares. See if you can remove five of them so you'll be left with six small squares."

Susan is entertaining Mayor Fairweather at the puzzle club today. Tea, sandwiches, and toothpick puzzles seem to be the main items on the menu. There's always room for one more at these afternoon sessions, so why don't you pull up a chair and give the mayor some help? He usually comes in second in this type of contest.

# World's Most Incredible "Treasure" Puzzle

Diver Duncan hit the jackpot the other day when he located the strong room in the wreck he was working on. The first four bags he brought up contained 60, 30, 20, and 15 gold coins, respectively. After he counted the coins in the remaining two bags he noted that the number of coins in each of the six bags corresponded to a specific progression. Knowing this, can you figure out how many coins were in bags five and six?

# World's Most Incredible "Medieval" Puzzle

Growing up in a castle wasn't all jousting and fighting. A certain amount of school work was also called for. Here we see Brother Venerable putting the lads through their paces with a substitute numbers problem. In this multiplication exercise certain of the figures have been replaced with asterisks. Let's see if you can put the problem back together again.

# World's Most Incredible "Butcher" Puzzle

Herman Rumplemeir, our local butcher, has grown in stature and girth since coming to work here some 20 years ago. Some interesting facts concerning Herman are:

At age 20 his waist size was 92 cm and his weight was 77 kilo.

At age 30 his waist size was 96 cm and his weight was 82 kilo.

At age 35 his waist size was 104 cm and his weight was 93 kilo.

At age 40 his waist size is 114 cm. What does he weigh?

# World's Most Incredible "Easy 'Z' " Puzzle

That Egyptian miracle worker, Joad Hereb, is about to perform his "Easy 'Z' " mystery. Before your very eyes he will cause this figure to split into three pieces which will then spin through the air and come back together again in the form of a perfect square. Can you determine where the cuts will be made and how the three pieces will be regrouped to form this square?

# World's Most Incredible "Toy" Puzzle

Calvin Collectible hit the jackpot the other day when he came across a trove of old steel mechanical toys. Included were dump trucks, steam shovels and farm tractors. Let's make a puzzle of his find. He bought the following four lots of toys:

> The first lot had one tractor, 3 shovels and 7 trucks and sold for $140.
> The second lot had 1 tractor, 4 shovels and 10 trucks and sold for $170.
> The third lot had 10 tractors, 15 shovels and 25 trucks.
> The fourth lot had 1 tractor, 1 shovel and 1 truck.

The problem is to figure out how much Calvin paid for lots number three and four.

# World's Most Incredible "Magic Coins" Puzzle

The man of mystery has laid out six magic coins. The first three are tails up and the last three are rabbit up. In three moves you are to change the order to tails, rabbit tails, rabbit, tails, rabbit. In each move you must turn over two adjacent coins.

# World's Most Incredible "Chicken" Puzzle

Chickens must be about the smartest of the barnyard animals, judging by the number of times they appear in puzzles. The other day Cy Corncrib, after losing another game of checkers to Pop Bentley, asked him the following question: If a chicken and a half lays an egg and a half in a day and a half, how many eggs can 6 chickens lay in 6 days? Pop is still working on that one. How many eggs do you think these chickens can lay?

# World's Most Incredible "Weight" Puzzle

"Right, sir! I'll tell Mr. Hackenbush as soon as he comes in. The total weight of boxes 1 and 2 is 12 pounds. Boxes 2 and 3 weigh 13½ pounds, boxes 3 and 4 total 11½ pounds, and boxes 4 and 5 total 8 pounds. Also, boxes 1, 3 and 5 total 16 pounds. You want him to figure out what each box weighs and to call you back right away. Have no fear, sir! I've got all the details right here in my head!"

I'd love to hear what Bascomb will remember when Mr. Hackenbush arrives. In the meantime, can you figure out what each box weighs?

# World's Most Incredible "Numero Uno" Puzzle

"To commemorate our great victory over the Spanish Armada, which, if you'll excuse the expression, made me Numero Uno in Europe, I've composed the following official puzzle: Create two numbers composed only of ones, which, when added or multiplied together, will give the same result. I pray that none of you will lose your heads trying to solve this one."

# World's Most Incredible "Printing" Puzzle

Philo Ramsgate has gone into the printing business and his first customer has ordered 10,000 calendars from him. However, the customer insists that the names of the months be printed in an exotic three-dimensional typeface that will cost Philo a bundle. Each letter costs $5.00. What are the fewest number of letters Philo will have to buy in order to print, in full, the twelve months of the year?

# World's Most Incredible "Addition" Puzzle

$$111$$
$$333$$
$$555$$
$$777$$
$$999$$
$$\overline{2{,}775}$$

Here we see Charlie Chin, the famous juggling puzzler, about to solve an addition problem submitted by a member of the audience. Charlie has to cross out six digits in the above five three-digit numbers so that when they are once again added together the total will be 1,111. (When a digit is crossed out consider that it is replaced by a zero.) Charlie will solve it in 30 seconds. Can you?

# World's Most Incredible "Square" Puzzle

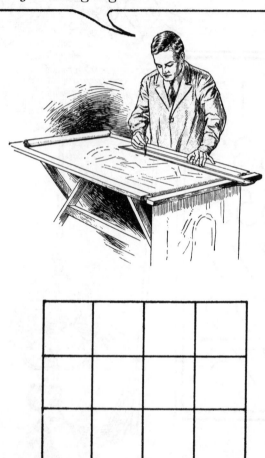

"Razzmatazz! I think I've got it! I'll have my picture on the cover of Drafting Digest!"

It looks as though Waldo Quiller has solved the famous Lines and Squares puzzle. The object is to draw a figure with exactly 100 squares in it with the *fewest number* of straight lines. In the above example you'll find 20 squares. Twelve are one unit, six are four units, and two are nine units. Solve this one and you'll be up for Square-of-the-Month.

# World's Most Incredible "Witch" Puzzle

One Halloween night a hapless, slightly tipsy farmer was captured by a malevolent witch who took him to a crumbling old church. "You are allowed to make one statement to save yourself!," she crooned. "If it is true I will boil you in oil. If it is false I'll feed you to my bats!" The farmer's befuddled brain cleared in an instant and he made a statement that caused the witch to curse him and set him free. What did the farmer say?

# World's Most Incredible "Counterfeit Coin" Puzzle

During the Crusades an English knight was captured and brought before the mighty Saladin. He was informed that he and his horse could go free if he paid a ransom of 100,000 pieces of gold.

"Great Saladin," spoke the knight, "I labor here at a disadvantage. In my country a prisoner is given a chance to do battle with his wits when he is captured. If he can correctly answer a puzzle put to him by his captors he is allowed to go free. If he fails the ransom is doubled!"

"So be it then," replied Saladin. "Here is your question: You are given twelve gold coins and a simple balance scale. One of the coins is counterfeit, but it is not known whether it is lighter or heavier than the other coins. You must find it, using only three weighings with the scale. You have until morning to solve this problem!"

So does the reader.

# World's Most Incredible "Abe Lincoln" Puzzle

"All right, gentlemen, I feel lucky tonight. Who wants a piece of the action? Here's a brand-new five-dollar bill. I'll let anyone hold this bill above his head and then release it so it floats down to the floor. If it lands with Abe Lincoln's face up you'll pay me $5.00. If it doesn't I'll pay you $10.00. Who'll take my bet?"

J. Wellington Moneybags is back in town and up to his old tricks. It's best to steer clear of this wager since Wellington only bets on sure things. However, it would be nice to know how he intends to fleece his flock. Can you figure it out?

# World's Most Incredible "Scholar" Puzzle

First Scholar: "Confound it, Mossback, I can't find any word in the dictionary that contains three double letters in a row. It's maddening!"

Second Scholar: "Quite right, Ploddington. I've found plenty of words with two double letters in a row, like balloon or woolly, but none with three!"

First Scholar: "The club's accountant, Paul Pinchpenny, assures me that there is such a word but he won't tell me what it is. I think he should be fired!"

(There's a clue to the answer in the above conversation.)

# World's Most Incredible "Route" Puzzle

America has always had a warm spot in its heart for the gifted eccentric. Otto Von Sprocket, pictured above, is a prime example. During the Golden Age of Bicycling Otto was the chief engineer at the High Flyer Bike Works. Every morning Otto would leave his home at point **A** on our map and proceed to the bike works at point **B**. Otto liked to vary his journey by going a different route each day. Can you figure out how many different routes there are between his home and the plant? He always travelled upwards and to the right.

# World's Most Incredible "Sears Hat" Puzzle

> "Well, pardner, back where I come from if the range boss don't wear a Sears Texan Chief hat he don't get no respect!"

**No. 33R2352 Texan Chief Cowboys' High Crown Mexican Style Sombrero Hat,** 5-inch brim and 6½-inch crown; fine leather sweat band; 1-inch silk ribbon band or tassel cord braided band, if desired. Flat, never flop brim with raw edge. One of the very best as well as the most popular sombreros ever made from best quality clear nutria fur. Full of real goodness and will give excellent satisfaction. Color, belly nutria. Sizes, 6⅜ to 7¼. Price, each......**$4.25**
Price, without fancy cord band.................

Shades of Rodney Dangerfield! That sure is a handsome hat Sears sold back in 1902. However, in the ad the type-setter left out the price of the hat without the fancy cord band. Now, if the hat alone cost $3.75 more than the fancy cord band, how much would the fancy cord cost and how much would the hat cost without the cord?

# World's Most Incredible "Bridge" Puzzle

The three men pictured above are named Claude, Horace, and Selwyn and they are married to the three ladies whose names are Deirdre, Erika, and Imogene, though not necessarily in that order. They are all enjoying a night out at the club. Let's see if you can guess who is married to whom.

Claude's wife and Erika's husband are bridge partners and they are playing Deirdre and Imogene's husband. None of the men are partners with their own wives. Finally, Horace doesn't play cards at all.

# World's Most Incredible "Superstition" Puzzle

This is a good puzzle for those who are superstitious around Halloween time. Mr. Pumpkin has given you thirteen threes to work with. Arrange these numbers to form an equation equal to 100. You have until the harvest moon is full.

# World's Most Incredible "Birthday" Puzzle

Mr. Gotrocks is momentarily suffering from an attack of existential Angst. I'm sure it will quickly pass. However, from the clues in his statement can you figure out when his birthday is?

# World's Most Incredible "Tree" Puzzle

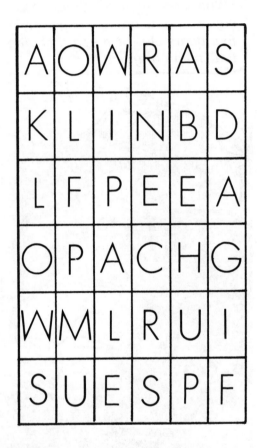

The Deforester Brothers are this state's best tree surgeons. They've saved more of our state's forests than all our senators put together. A list of all the types of trees they've worked on is contained in the above puzzle. To find each tree start at any letter and move one square at a time in any direction. Do not use any square more than once for any given name. Do not skip over any letters. All the letters must be adjacent. You can move horizontally, vertically, or diagonally. There are at least seventeen trees in the diagram.

# World's Most Incredible "Radio" Puzzle

"It's time to play 'Name Those Letters!' All our questions can be answered by using one or more letters of the alphabet. We'll give you the answer to the first question and then you're on your own!"

1. Name of a beverage. T (tea)
2. Name of jealousy.
3. Name of a place in England.
4. Name of too much of something.
5. Name of a composition.
6. Name of a tent.
7. Name of an image.
8. Name of a badly dressed person.
9. Name of something void.
10. Name of part of a house.
11. Name of a foe.
12. Name of a sad poem.

The questions from an early quiz program are coming through loud and clear on this beautiful old Lyradion radio. Each correct answer was worth a dollar. Let's see how much you would have made.

# World's Most Incredible "Mind Reading" Puzzle

"All right, Madame Zorrina, the next test is extremely hard. This gentleman is thinking of a unique number. When spelled out, the letters in the number are in alphabetical order. The number is between one and one thousand. I must have absolute silence from the audience, please!"

"The gentleman has very powerful brain waves! Yes, I see a number forming through the clouds of skepticism emanating from those around him! Wait, the mists are clearing! The number is . . . !"

In all of her years on the vaudeville circuit Madame Zorrina never failed to deliver the goods. Let's see if you're as good at snatching messages from the ether as she was. Close your eyes, lean back in your chair and see if you too can see the number that the gentleman in the audience is thinking of.

# World's Most Incredible "Indian" Puzzle

Shown here is the Puzzling Pooh Bah of Punjab making his entrance into last year's Puzzle Convention. His entry is pictured on the banner. First, lay out 16 matches in the form of 4 squares. Next, remove 4 matches and shift 3 others so that you have the answer to the question "What are matches made of?"

# World's Most Incredible "Prohibition" Puzzle

During Prohibition Swifty O'Brian was the fastest booze runner on Chicago's North Side. Here we see Swifty delivering twenty cases of Big Benny's finest hooch to four of his select clients. The drops went like this:

> Hanratty's received two more cases than the Dutchman's Cafe.
>
> Edna's Hide-a-Way received six less cases than Sal's Saloon.
>
> Sal's Saloon received two more cases than Hanratty's.
>
> The Dutchman's Cafe received two more cases than Edna's Hide-a-Way.

How many cases did each of these watering holes receive?

# World's Most Incredible "Halloween" Puzzle

When I heard that the fun-loving Armbruster clan was getting together for a Halloween party I figured that they would have to hire a hall. Arlo told me that the party would consist of two grandfathers, two grandmothers, three fathers, three mothers, three sons, three daughters, two mothers-in-law, two fathers-in-law, one son-in-law, one daughter-in-law, two brothers and two sisters. He said no, the party would be at his house since the whole family consisted of just 10 people. Can you figure out how this is possible?

# World's Most Incredible "Santa Claus" Puzzle

Even the animal helpers in Santa's workshop get time off for a pep rally as the great day draws near. Here they're working on a tricky math problem. To solve it you must substitute the numbers 1 through 9 for the nine different letters used in the math expression. You must end up with a correct subtraction problem. The same number is given to each occurrence of the same letter.

# World's Most Incredible "Subtraction" Puzzle

Great Victorian Puzzles                    Page 432

*"The puzzler is required to subtract 45 from 45 in such a manner that there shall be 45 left."* What an *extraordinary* problem. I'm sure that this must be a misprint!

Aunt Hattie looks the picture of Victorian comfort using her new Holloway Reading Stand that Grandpa gave her for Christmas. Propped on the book-rest is a copy of Professor Hoffmann's 1890s masterpiece, *Puzzles Old and New*. What do you make of the professor's interesting problem in subtraction?

# World's Most Incredible "Computer" Puzzle

"Well, Professor Henri, I certainly hope that your new computer can help me out. My students think me out of step because I can't seem to solve what they consider to be an absurdly simple problem. They challenged me to find the smallest number that when divided by 2, 3, 4, 5, or 6 will always leave a remainder of 1, and, when divided by 7, will leave no remainder at all. Can you help me?"

"But certainly, mon ami! I merely have to enter in the parameters of your little problem and voilà, out prints the answer! Here it is now! The number is . . . !"

# World's Most Incredible "Word" Puzzle

*"Fool, this is your last chance. If you don't give me the answer to that puzzle you will no longer have a head for figures. For the last time, what are those two eight-letter English words that each contain the first six letters of the alphabet? One, two . . . !"*

*"I'd rather be in Philadelphia than give you the answers. However, I'll give you two hints. One of the words has to do with printing and the other word pertains to survey information. Now, how about a last cigarette? I know that they haven't been invented yet, but I can wait!"*

# World's Most Incredible "Beer" Puzzle

"Oh, Brunhilda, life is so wonderful. Just imagine, before I met you it used to take me 20 days to drink a barrel of beer!"

"I know, Otto my love. But now with me at your elbow the two of us can polish off that same barrel in only 14 days. Life is good!"

Obviously a marriage made in Bavaria. However, an interesting question arises from the above bit of conversation. If Otto wasn't by her elbow at all times, how long would it take Brunhilda to drink a barrel of beer all by herself?

# World's Most Incredible "Pyramid" Puzzle

The above artist is going to be in a peck of trouble. The five-pointed star he painted depicts five straight roads and ten pyramids. Each road has four pyramids on it. Each pyramid can be directly approached from the desert. What the pharoah wanted was a design using five straight roads with four pyramids on each, but with two of these pyramids located within the design, so anyone coming in from the desert would have to cross one of the outer roads to get to them. What design should he use to keep from being sealed up when the tomb is closed?

# World's Most Incredible "Geometry" Puzzle

The gentleman above is trying to discover the smallest number of squares the above drawing can be cut into. Cutting along all the lines yields 169 squares, the greatest number. For example, one square might be six by six (36 small squares), another four by four (16 small squares), and a third two by two (4 small squares). More than one square can be the same size, but they can't all be the same size. *Hint:* our solution has less than 20 squares of varying sizes.

# World's Most Incredible "Poker Chip" Puzzle

Back in the 1920s a delightful line of books provided an endless source of cheap entertainment. For only ten cents a copy you could learn all about magic, puzzles, chess and boxing. Here's an interesting puzzle from one of these books.

On a large sheet of paper draw the above ten-box diagram. Place four white poker chips and four red poker chips on squares one through eight. Alternate the colors as shown. Now, moving two adjacent chips at a time to any two empty squares, change the order of the chips to that shown below. You must do this in only four moves.

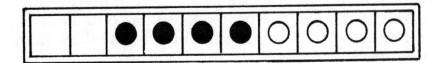

# World's Most Incredible "Betting" Puzzle

"When the deck is cold, and the odds run out,
    and you're feeling mighty low,
Here's a bet that without a doubt,
    Will make your bankroll grow!"

A good bet is hard to find, but the following one is sure to work if the other party has never seen it before. Take a deck of cards and arrange it so every other card is red from start to finish. Next, cut the deck into two piles. Make sure that the bottom card of one pile is red and the bottom card of the other is black. Riffle shuffle both halves together thoroughly and square up the deck. Now for the fun. State that you will remove cards from the top of the pile two at a time and that you will make the following bet: If the two cards are both the same color you will pay out two dollars; however, if the pair has one red card and one black card you are to receive one dollar.

With such a wager what's the least amount of money you could expect to make every time you ran through the whole deck?

398

# World's Most Incredible "Shooting" Puzzle

Squire Pickumoff is shown here regaling the locals with tales of his hunting prowess and boasting of the superiority of his new Black Forest shotgun. Unfortunately for his favorite hunting dog, Rusty, the squire's aim didn't live up to his boasting. Rusty is now half a tail shorter. The squire's plight can be summed up in the following puzzle poem.

"He _____ to be _____ as a wonderful shot.

He potted his dog and _____ was his lot."

Can you fill in the three missing words? The interesting thing about these words is that they are all made up of the same seven letters.

# World's Most Incredible "Drink Stirrer" Puzzler

The fastest waiters down at Wolfgang's Haus of Suds are the Adalbert twins, Ike and Mike. Besides dispensing suds and spuds the boys keep the revellers entertained with a selection of puzzles. The drink stirrer problem below shows an equation using Roman numerals. As stated, the equation is wrong, but if you shift just one of the stirrers to a new position it will be correct. The next round is on you if you fail this test.

# World's Most Incredible "Golf" Puzzle

Golf is a very old game indeed. Here we see a young nobleman playing a round of miniature golf in the Borghese Gardens in Rome. The year is 1729 and all his luck has been bad. If, at the end of the front nine, the lad had not lost twice plus half of what he had left after playing eighteen holes, and had he not then lost an additional 80 ducats on the back nine, he would have finished the round with the original 500 ducats he started with. Can you tell how many ducats he did have when he finished the round?

# World's Most Incredible "Vintage Car" Puzzle

Two old car buffs, "Duster" Bigalow and Harlow High-wheeler, are shown here discussing the merits of Harlow's latest acquisition, a reconditioned 1904 Packard Model L.

"That's a grand addition to your collection," said Duster. "Just how many vintage cars do you now have in your collection?"

"Let's see if you can figure it out," replied Harlow. "All but two of my cars are Packards, all but two are Brewster Town cars, and all but two are Duesenbergs. I'll bet you an oil change you can't come up with the answer in five minutes."

How many cars do you think Harlow owns?

# The
# **World's**
# Most Perplexing
# Puzzles

# World's Most Perplexing "Math Signs" Puzzle

"Put them on the desk, Bill. The answer must be in one of those books!"

Farleigh is at his wit's end trying to solve this old chestnut: Write down the digits 1 through 9 in the order shown above. Insert two minus signs and one plus sign between certain of the digits so that the result will be a mathematical expression equal to 100.

# World's Most Perplexing "Bolt" Puzzle

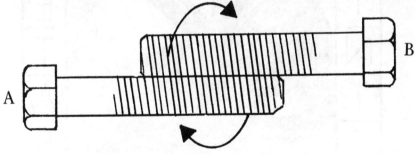

Down at the Burlington Bolts and Nuts factory no apprentice becomes a full-fledged foundryman without correctly answering the famous Bolt Puzzle! Each apprentice must take two large bolts that are exactly alike and place them together so the threads mesh, as shown below. The apprentice must then move bolt A around the bolt B, as indicated by the arrows, holding the bolts tightly so they do not rotate while this is being done. The question to be answered is: Will the heads of the bolts move closer together, move farther apart, or remain the same distance from one another?

# World's Most Perplexing "Tin Man" Puzzle

Pictured above is that symbol of early American sales-manship, the tin man. The motto of this industrious mer-chandiser is hidden in the above frame of letters. To find it, start at any letter and go around the frame twice, read-ing every other letter as you go. This could also be the motto of America's senior citizens.

# World's Most Perplexing "Treasure" Puzzle

In 1639 an English ship returning from a trip to the Holy Land sank off the coast of North Africa. Among the items lost was a treasure chest belonging to the bishop of Bristol. This chest could only by opened by setting the three dials on its side to positions that would spell out a three-letter English word appropriate to its owner. See if you can decipher the lock's secret before the octopus dispatches yonder diver and turns his attentions to you!

# World's Most Perplexing "Chocolate" Puzzle

*"Look at this huge piece of chocolate, Mama! Papa says we can have some just as soon as we solve his famous 'Squares of Salzburg' candy puzzle!"*

In the Squares of Salzburg puzzle the problem is to take a giant slab of chocolate made up of twenty two-inch squares, and to cut it into nine pieces that can then be rearranged to form four perfect squares all exactly the same size. I have a feeling that this puzzle will disappear long before it is solved.

# World's Most Perplexing "Animal" Puzzle

It's Saturday night at the Pigeon Côte Club and the betting gentry are hot to trot. How many of the following "collective nouns" would you win a dollar on?

1) A doylt of _____.
2) A gaggle of _____.
3) A rout of _____.
4) A troop of _____.
5) A leap of _____.
6) A skulk of _____.
7) A sloth of _____.
8) A muster of _____.

# World's Most Perplexing "Match" Puzzle

Edgar Puffington's pipe is so foul-smelling, his boss makes him work in the shipping bay. Edgar gets even by winning large matchstick bets with his boss every payday. Last week he challenged his boss with the 24 matches arranged as shown above. The pattern forms nine squares. The puzzle is to remove eight of these matches in such a way as to leave three squares.

# World's Most Perplexing "Line" Puzzle

"Ladies and gentlemen, we are happy to present Jocko, the simian Shakespearean sketcher and portrait painter extraordinaire! His drawings of the Bard sell for hundreds of bananas each. The amazing Jocko drew the above puzzle portrait using one continuous line. At no point does the line cross over itself. Can you duplicate this amazing artistic feat?"

# World's Most Perplexing "Magic Square" Puzzle

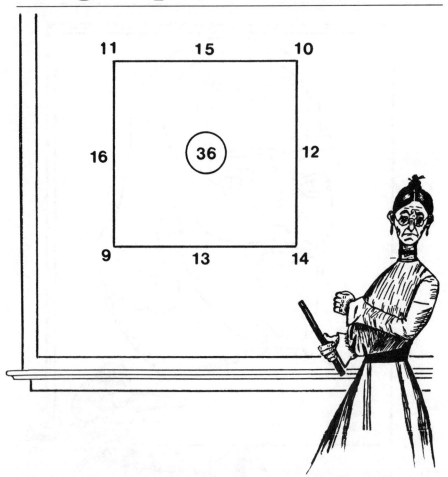

That nonpareil of substitute teachers, Ms. Priscilla Sunshine, will conduct today's math class. Listen up!

"Your regular teacher, Mr. Tracy, informs me that you need some extra practice in solving magic squares. On the blackboard I've arranged the numbers 9 through 16 around the sides of a square in such a manner that the sum of the three numbers on any one side is 36. Your problem is to rearrange these eight numbers so that the sum of the three numbers on any one side will be 37.

"While you're solving that one, I'll put some more up on the other board!"

# World's Most Perplexing "What, When, and Why" Puzzles

"What makes an empty match box superior to any other?"

"When is a wall like a fish?"

"Why did Babe Ruth make so much money?"

"What is the difference between a mountain and a pill?"

"When is a window like a star?"

"Why is a hen sitting on a fence like a penny?"

"What state is round at both ends and tall in the middle?"

The Sawmill Valley "What, When, and Why Septet" is shown here warming up for their turn at the annual Northwest Riddle Contest at the Sourdough County Fair back in 1903. How many of these melodic mysteries can you decipher?

# World's Most Perplexing "Fireworks" Puzzle

**No. 6416. Laughing Uncle.**
When lit, goes off with a bang, throwing out a large quantity of entertaining parlor jokes.
Each ........................10 cents

**Tower of Gold.-5cents** When lit, it goes off with a loud bang, throwing out a large quantity miniature gold and silver coins,

**No. 6327 E. Joke Bottle Corks.**
Each................1 cent

**Comical Nut Cracker. ........ 25 cent**
Throws out jokes, riddles, etc.,

At the turn of the century Grandpa Townsend liked to celebrate a birthday with what was then thought to be harmless indoor fireworks. For one party he spent $2.42 for a variety of items. He bought the same number of 1¢ and 5¢ items. Also, the total sums spent on the 10¢ and 25¢ items were both the same. Can you figure out how many of each type were purchased and how much was spent on each type?

# World's Most Perplexing "Aces and Kings" Puzzle

*"Alakazam, let the other cards scram! Your card, madame, is . . . the five of clubs!*

*"And now for an amusing card puzzle I call 'Aces and Kings.' Here, sir, are the four aces and four kings from a deck of cards. I challenge you to arrange them in such an order that when you alternately deal them face-up onto the table they will be in the order king, ace, king, ace, king, ace and king, ace. The deal must go as follows: Hold the pack of eight cards face-down. Transfer the top card to the bottom of the pack and turn the next card over and place it face-up on the the table. Continue in this manner until all eight cards are on the table.*

*"If you solve this problem by the end of my act you'll get to assist me in the sensational 'French Guillotine Mystery.' "*

Ned "King of Kards" Fairbanks has provided our readers with an interesting challenge. Let's see if you can discover the secret before the blade falls.

# World's Most Perplexing "Book" Puzzle

First Scholar: "It clearly states in the unabridged edition of Henri Decremps' *La Magie Blanche Dévoilée* (Natural Magic Disclosed) that it is possible to concentrate your breath to such a degree that you can actually knock fairly heavy objects over with it. As an example he tells of how the magician Pinetti placed a large book on top of a massive dictionary and then proceeded to topple both with a few puffs of his breath."

Second Scholar: "There has to be more to it than that. Perhaps he used a plate lifter!"

Can the reader help these two savants out by discovering the secret to this well-kept mystery?

# World's Most Perplexing "Checker" Puzzle

Pop Bentley's perfect record against Cy Corncrib is still intact. Pop just beat Cy for the umpteenth time with one of his patented slam-bang endings. Pop was playing the black pieces and it was his turn. The white pieces were moving up the board, while the black were moving down. What series of moves did Pop use to dispatch Cy so quickly?

# World's Most Perplexing "Toothpick" Puzzle

# World's Most Perplexing "Sandwich" Puzzle

"My dear Camilla, haven't you finished making those sandwiches yet? How many have you made? The last foursome is approaching the eighteenth green now. My reputation as host for this tournament is on the line!"

"Oh, keep your shirt on, Norbert. If you had helped me with the asparagus sandwiches I'd have been finished an hour ago. If you really want to know how many sandwiches are made I'll give you a hint. If you divide the total number of sandwiches by 2, 3, 4, 5, or 6 you would find that you always have a remainder. However, if you divide the total by 11 you will get no remainder. What you are looking for is the smallest total that will satisfy these conditions. Now here they come. Start pouring the sarsaparilla."

# World's Most Perplexing "Racing" Puzzle

| Atlantic City—Sixth Race | | | | | | |
|---|---|---|---|---|---|---|
| Horses | 1 | 2 | 3 | 4 | 5 | Fin |
| Eight Ball | 6 | 2 | 3 | 5 | 4 | 1 |
| Hay Burner | 3 | 6 | 1 | 4 | 5 | 2 |
| Slow Start | 5 | 1 | 6 | 2 | 4 | 3 |
| No Luck | 5 | 6 | 1 | 2 | 3 | 4 |
| Swayback | 4 | 1 | 3 | 6 | 2 | 5 |
| Last In | 2 | 5 | 3 | 1 | 4 | 6 |

LAYING WAGERS ON THE RACES AT THE OCEAN HOTEL

It's the summer of 1903 and the high-rollers are busy deciding which horses to bet on for the next race. In the sixth race six horses competed in a six-furlong affair that ended as shown on the above tote board. One improver of the breed, an inveterate puzzler, noted that an interesting puzzle would be to rearrange the positions of the horses in the above columns so the numbers 1 through 6 would appear only once in every row and column, making a neat numeric magic square. What are the odds you can solve it in ten minutes flat?

420

# World's Most Perplexing "Synonym" Puzzle

"Quick, driver, to the main branch of the public library, and don't spare the whip! I'm late for the annual New York City Synonym Contest!"

We're happy to report that the above gentleman made it to the contest on time and won first prize in the "Five-Letter Word" contest. He had to find a five-letter synonym beginning with the letter "Q" for each of the following words:

| | | | |
|---|---|---|---|
| 1) cover | 6) line | 11) pen | 16) subdue |
| 2) doubt | 7) measure | 12) scruple | 17) suppress |
| 3) entirely | 8) monarch | 13) search | 18) swallow |
| 4) fraud | 9) nimble | 14) secluded | 19) tremble |
| 5) game bird | 10) particle | 15) share | 20) whip |

# World's Most Perplexing "Grand Prize" Puzzle

THE "WATERBURY"
GRAND PRIZE

Problem No.99

12        6
345   789

"Look, chums," crowed Winthrop Swellhead, "a Waterbury watch! I won this for solving problem 99. The numbers 1 through 9 were placed above or below a line according to some scheme. I had to determine where the next number, 10, was to go. The answer was mere child's play!"

# World's Most Perplexing "Watch" Puzzle

The Clancy brothers were the crackerjack clean-up crew in the old Flatiron Building in New York City. In appreciation for their punctuality the owners gave each of them a Callander watch. Then the trouble began. While Brian's watch kept perfect time, Barry's lost a minute a day and Patrick's gained a minute a day. If the fellows set their watches to the correct time at noon the day they received them and never reset them after that, how many days would pass before the three watches would again all show the correct time at noon?

# World's Most Perplexing "Rearranging" Puzzle

TCLTUACA
RZIBRTIA
OULHNULO

TENAWCOP
YVRIKEKAJ
GESPRIANO

ORNONAG
SSRFACONCAIN
NKGNGHOO

TRHMUPTOOS
LENUMEOBR
BNACSAALAC

The U.S.S. *Extravagantic* celebrated its maiden voyage in 1922 by taking a three-month cruise around the world. The lucky passengers visited dozens of famous cities along the way. We've scrambled the names of twelve of them to give you the opportunity to join in the fun. Let's see if you can unscramble them before it's time to disembark.

# World's Most Perplexing "Millennium" Puzzle

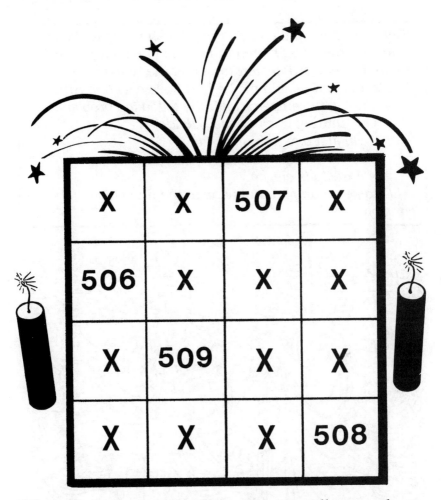

| | | | |
|---|---|---|---|
| X | X | 507 | X |
| 506 | X | X | X |
| X | 509 | X | X |
| X | X | X | 508 |

Although the second millennium is still several years away we would like to be among the first to start the celebrating with a special "Millennium Magic Square" puzzle. We've set up a magic square that's designed to total 2000 in any direction, horizontally, vertically, and diagonally corner to corner. We've entered four of the numbers for you. The remaining twelve three-digit numbers, 492 through 503, inclusive, are for you to enter. You have until January 1, 2000, to finish the square.

# World's Most Perplexing "Ancient" Puzzle

"Before taking up the matter of point-shaving in the last Olympic Games, let's break the tension with a puzzle I heard in the agora yesterday. I met the Roman, Gaius Perplexus, and he told me he had been exiled to Athens for stumping the emperor with the following problem:

　　'One third of twelve if you divide,
　　　　By just one fifth of seven,
　　　The true result (it has been tried)
　　　　Exactly is eleven.'

"I'll give an amphora of wine to the first citizen who can solve it!"

426

# World's Most Perplexing "Insect" Puzzle

When things slow down in the winter, the folks in Bugville pass the time of day solving "Insect Spelling Bee's." The one they're working on now requires the player to use the sixteen letters on the billboard to spell the names of eight different insects. Each letter can only be used once in a name. Don't get stung winging this one!

# World's Most Perplexing "Triangle" Puzzle

"Rosalinde, where in the world did that strange ornament on top of yonder tower come from?"

"Why, Sir Guy of Grimsby brought it back from the Crusades. The design is made by welding eighteen rods together forming nine triangles. There's a puzzle associated with it. It's possible to remove three of the rods and be left with seven triangles. If you can figure it out I'll let you wear my handkerchief in the joust tomorrow."

Can you help the young man out?

# World's Most Perplexing "Dog House" Puzzle

Our dog Jackie is pictured here showing off her new house to her friends. For our puzzle we've outlined the house using ten matchsticks. Her friends like it all right but think it should be turned 90 degrees so it faces the road. Can you accomplish this by moving two of the matches to new positions?

# World's Most Perplexing "Chickenman" Puzzle

"My head and tail both equal are,
   My middle slender as a bee.
Whether I stand on head or heel
   Is quite the same to you or me.
But if my head should be cut off,
   The matter's true, though passing strange
Directly I to nothing change."

Challenging the reader to a battle of wits is the dreaded Chickenman. Free at last from the Tree of 10,000 Thorns, he's lean and mean and mighty hungry. Industrial pollution caused the thorns to fall off the tree and now Chickenman is looking for his first square meal in 700 years. Answer his poetic question and he'll pass you by. Fail and it's pass-the-seasoning time.

# World's Most Perplexing "Christmas" Puzzle

Christmas in the good old days! Mother around the tree with her children. Father snoozing in his favorite chair. This is a special day for three of their children because they were also born on Christmas Day. Let's see if you can figure out their ages. Today Barton is as old as the combined ages of Wendel and Susan. Last Christmas Wendel was twice as old as Susan. Finally, two years from now, Barton will be twice as old as Susan.

Can you dope out their ages before the turkey and fixings are brought to the table?

# World's Most Perplexing "Magic Kettle" Puzzle

"A farmer brought two cages of animals to market. One contained rabbits and the other contained pheasants. When asked how many of each he had, the farmer replied:

'The total number of animals in these two cages have thirty-five heads and ninety-four feet. Knowing that, you should be able to answer your own question!'"

Pictured here is that famous Victorian entertainer, Puzzling Prendergast, the prince of parlor prestidigitators, and his talking tea kettle. It has never been determined just how Prendergast made the kettle talk, but ventriloquism has been hinted at. However, his problems were always first rate. Can you solve the above potted problem?

# World's Most Perplexing "Santa" Puzzle

Here's an excellent puzzle for your next Christmas party. In the above square we have two pictures of Santa Claus. Run off a dozen copies of the square and hand them out to your guests. Tell them that in order to solve the Santa puzzle they must first cut the square into four parts and then reassemble the pieces into two separate squares, each square containing one complete Santa. A candy cane to the first one who solves it!

# World's Most Perplexing "Pentagram" Puzzle

This early nineteenth-century performer certainly had a colorful act. However, it seems his rather thin assistant had doubts concerning his abilities. In the Star of Pythagoras, pictured above, the puzzler must rearrange the ten numbers in the circles so the four numbers along any of the five lines of the pentagram will add up to 24. How would you do it?

# World's Most Perplexing "Solid Shape" Puzzle

"Now students, pay attention. Before we study the supernatural powers of the Infinite Sided Solid of Fra Sebastian, let us review the surface properties of some simple shapes. Please give me the names of the solids that:

1) Have only one surface.    4) Have only four surfaces.
2) Have only two surfaces.   5) Have only five surfaces.
3) Have only three surfaces.  6) Have only six surfaces."

You have 60 seconds to complete this test.

# World's Most Perplexing "Musical" Puzzle

It was opening night, and the Wunderkinder of Seattle, Washington, Olaf and Katrina Gustafsonn, were about to bring the house down when the last seven notes of their Concerto for Spotted Owl came out upside down. Can you save the day and turn the seven notes right side up in three moves? During each move you must turn any three notes upside down.

# World's Most Perplexing "Color" Puzzle

*"Oh, Ramon, what will happen to our careers when color comes to the movies?"*

*"Our pasty complexions will doom us to selected black-and-white short subjects, my dear!"*

Ramon and Rita's fear of technical advancements brings to mind a colorful test. The following ten statements each define a word whose first few letters spell a color. Ten out of ten will earn you a screen test.

    1) On the ocean. (*White*cap)
    2) A first starter
    3) Found in pies
    4) Some find it tasty
    5) A type of building
    6) Lacking in sense
    7) The ape man
    8) Best in the shade
    9) An unpleasant sight
    10) A strong liquid

# World's Most Perplexing "Apple" Puzzle

> *"Farmer Sy Corncrib brought a basket of apples into his kitchen and had his six sons line up. The basket contained six apples. After he divided them equally among his sons one apple was left in the basket. He did not cut or smash up any of the apples. How did he do it?"*
>
> *"Land 'o Goshen! What a persnickety problem! I'll be up until nine o'clock trying to solve this one!"*

Given enough time and her Holloway Reading Stand, there wasn't any puzzle that Maude Marionberry couldn't solve. How do you think Sy did it?

# World's Most Perplexing "Word Square" Puzzle

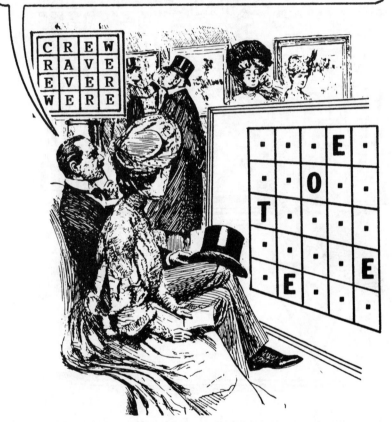

> "That, my dear, is this year's winner in the 'Word Square' painting contest. To solve it you must use the same five words both horizontally and vertically. The answer is in the back of your program!"

The following hints concerning the definitions of the five words should help the reader solve this interesting little problem:

1) Filled
2) To make up
3) A salutation
4) Follow in order
5) To hinder

# World's Most Perplexing "Sphinx" Puzzle

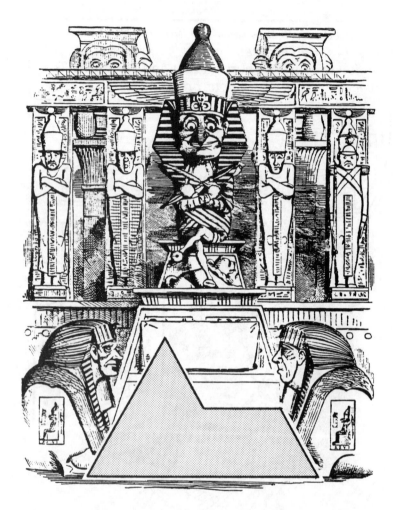

Looking back in history we find the world's first great puzzler, Stumpumost II. He has a brand-new problem titled "The Second Riddle of the Sphinx" to stump his courtiers with. The solver must divide the above minimalist drawing of a sphinx into four equal, identically shaped pieces. The pieces must also have the same shape as the original drawing of the Sphinx. Let's see if you can dig up the answer.

# World's Most Perplexing "Radio" Puzzle

"Radio Dog! Fetch the Royal Executioner!"

*"Ali Babel here with another round of your favorite riddle show, 'What's the Difference?' To start off:*
> *'What's the difference between our king and a rejected lover?'*
> *'What's the difference between our king and a flea?'*
> *'What's the difference between a hungry man and our king?'"*

When early radio came to the Middle East a lot of people lost their heads over it. The above short-lived program is a perfect example. Do you know the answers to Ali's kingly riddles?

# World's Most Perplexing "Detective" Puzzle

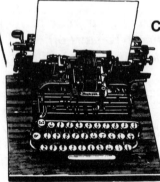

When the new hundred-dollar bill printing plates disappeared from the U.S. mint, word went out to the world's ten top detectives. Their names above are encoded using the secret vowel code. Only the vowels in their names are printed. The first is Charlie Chan. Can you decipher the remaining nine?

# World's Most Perplexing "Anagrams" Puzzles

*"Look, dear, this painting is by your favorite artist, 'I Paint Modern.' "*

The above charming drawing illustrates a flying trip through an extensive art museum. The gentleman at the top, pointing out a particular painting to his companion, has playfully transformed the artist's name into an anagram. In an anagram, you take the letters in a word or name, and rearrange them to form other names or words that, ideally, have something in common with the original word. The answer to the one here is "Piet Mondrian." Try your skills at unscrambling the examples below:

1) To love ruin = ?
2) Great help = ?
3) Govern, clever lad! = ?
4) Hated for ill = ?
5) Flit on, cheering angel! = ?
6) Old West action = ?
7) Name for ship = ?

# World's Most Perplexing "Hopping" Puzzle

"All right, gents, belly up to the starting line. The race course runs straight ahead to the old oak tree. When you reach it you are to turn around and head back to the starting line. The first one to cross it wins the race. On your mark, get set, start hopping!"

The course measured twelve feet from the starting line to the old oak tree, so the total length of the race was twenty-four feet. According to the morning line, the grasshopper could cover ten inches during a single hop while the little frog could only cover six inches per hop. However, since the frog could hop five times for every three hops of the grasshopper, he stayed neck in neck with him down the course. Despite being so evenly matched, when they reached the finish line one of them crossed it ahead of the other. Who took home the trophy?

# World's Most Perplexing "Christmas Stocking" Puzzle

Let's see, now, this year we have two sizes of stocking for the children. We have the "I've been good" size and the "I've been very good" size! Why, bless me, I see a puzzle here. The number of toys in the large stocking is equal to the number in the small stocking reversed. And the difference between the amounts in each is one-eleventh the sum of the two amounts. My, my!

How many toys are in each stocking?

# World's Most Perplexing "Riddles" Puzzles

*"Which letter is like a Roman emperor?"*

*"Which candles burn longer—wax or tallow?"*

*"Who was the most successful physician in the Bible?"*

*"What is eaten at breakfast or lunch, but usually drunk only at dinner?"*

*"What kind of grain is usually sown at night?"*

The above streetcar is heading out of town to the "1927 International Puzzle Fair" being held at Olympic Park, New Jersey. The riders are all entered in the riddle contest. Hop on board and try your luck!

# World's Most Perplexing "Nails" Puzzle

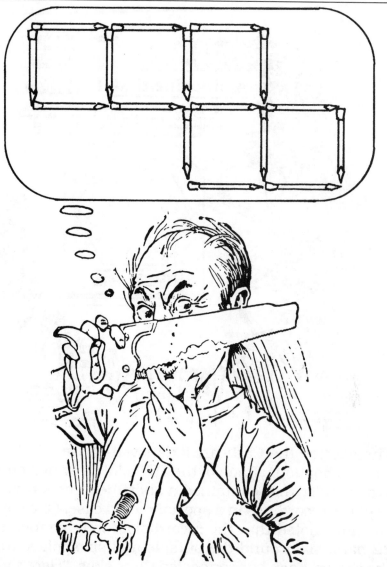

Old Charlie "Crosscut" Callaway, proprietor of our local lumberyard, is having a hard time concentrating on his morning shave. The boys in the warehouse bet him he couldn't move four nails in the above setup to new positions to make six squares instead of five. See if you can hammer out the answer before starting time.

# World's Most Perplexing "Echophone" Puzzle

The one toy the Cathcart kids loved above all else was their Echophone. Each of the 19 children owned one record cylinder that contained a short bedtime story. They kept the recordings in a special record case. One day Uncle Mohr noted that the record slots were connected by 12 bars, six around the outside and six spokes around the center. Each bar connected three slots. "Here's a puzzle," he said. "See if you can place the 19 numbered records in the slots in such a manner that the sum of any three record values along a bar will add up to 23."

The reader is invited to make a copy of the record case and play along with Uncle Mohr.

# World's Most Perplexing "Picture" Puzzle

Back on page 70 we introduced you to word square puzzles. Here's a second one for you to work on. Lay out a grid with four letters across and four letters down. Hints concerning the four words needed to solve the puzzle are in the above picture of a circuit rider minister in the Old West preaching to his flock.

# World's Most Perplexing "Addition" Puzzle

*"Don't turn around! You numbskulls have had five minutes to write down the correct solution on the blackboard to that simple problem! I give you five more seconds!"*

Professor Nebelwerfer is about to live up to his name (it means rocket launcher). In five seconds the Inkerman twins will lift off the floor. The Herr Professor has rather a unique way of showing his displeasure with dunderheads. The problem that has caused consternation for Hans and Fedor is as follows: Arrange five odd digits in such a way that they add up to 20. The same odd digit can be used more than once. You also have five minutes to solve this one.

# World's Most Perplexing "Diner" Puzzle

Come and join us at our favorite diner in Bloomfield, New Jersey. Hash House Harriet is calling out an order using the colorful mode of speech employed in this type of eatery. We've arranged the sentence to form an interesting puzzle for you to solve. If you replace each letter with a number, using the same number for the same letter wherever it appears, you can make a correct mathematical expression out of her order. Also, can you figure out what the order is for?

# World's Most Perplexing "Puzzle Poker" Puzzle

*"Sabilla, I'll bet you $100 you can't solve this triangle card puzzle in less than five minutes!"*

*"Really, Zoë, when will you ever learn! I'll see that $100 and raise you $200 more!"*

In "Puzzle Poker" the players wager on each other's ability to solve pasteboard problems. Using the cards ace through nine of diamonds, Zoë has dealt out a card triangle on the table. The problem for Sabilla is to rearrange the cards so that the total number of pips of any four cards that make up the three sides of the triangle will add up to 23. The value of each corner card will appear in two sides.

To take the pot from these ladies the reader will have to solve the puzzle in less than four minutes!

# World's Most Perplexing "Maze" Puzzle

The above maze is probably the most famous one constructed in the 19th century. Created by Lewis Carroll to amuse his brothers and sisters, it is extremely devious. The paths go in and out, over and under, and contain many dead-ends. Can you get to the center of the maze in time to save Mr. Dumpty from falling?

# World's Most Perplexing "Sock Sale" Puzzle

The time is 1902 and Davenport Department Store is having its great Holiday Sock Sale! The one collaring the hapless sales clerk with her umbrella is Aunt Hattie. For only $8.00 Hattie was able to purchase the last 20 pairs of socks in the store. She paid $1.60 a pair for some very nice long winter socks, 20¢ a pair for calf-high socks, and 10¢ a pair for children's short socks. How many pairs of each type of socks did Aunt Hattie buy?

Judging by the above picture, little has changed over the years when it comes to shopping at Christmastime.

# World's Most Perplexing "Enigma" Puzzle

"*My first you will be,*
   *If you're good and upright.*
*My second you'll see*
   *In a sharp, frosty night.*
*Together combined,*
   *I'm a virtue that's great,*
*That should govern each mind,*
   *And preside in each state*
'*Now, mosey on up to the bar and name your poison. If the defendant can solve the riddle I just propounded I'll let him off with time served and a round of drinks for the court! Miss it, and spend 30 days in the lockup!*'"

Here we see Judge Roy Bean, the "only law west of the Pecos," about to try Pegleg Patterson for a breach of the law. The answer to this riddle has something to do with Roy's profession.

# World's Most Perplexing "Dictionary" Puzzle

For those of you who enjoy word puzzles we present the old dictionary quiz. Above are illustrations taken from a very old dictionary. Below are listed seventeen words, twelve of which describe the illustrated items. Can you match them up?

A) Generatrix
B) Dirk
C) Shroud
D) Ballista
E) Aboma

F) Obelisk
G) Coupe
H) Arbalest
I) Oubliette

J) Colophon
K) Shako
L) Tetrapylon
M) Scarab

N) Moulage
O) Deadeyes
P) Hippogriff
Q) Pediment

# World's Most Perplexing "Lunch Tray" Puzzle

GLEN RIDGE  CALDWELL  VER

DO NOT Stack Trays

C.B.T.

Back in high school "Muscles" Moran made extra money by taking the other kids' empty trays back to the kitchen. He charged them a nickel a tray and was famed for the number of trays he could carry at one time. One day he returned 99 trays in only two trips. When asked how many he carried on each of the trips, he replied, "Two-thirds the number of trays I carried on my first trip equals four-fifths the number of trays I carried on my second trip. Now, you figure it out!"

# World's Most Perplexing
## "Surveyor" Puzzle

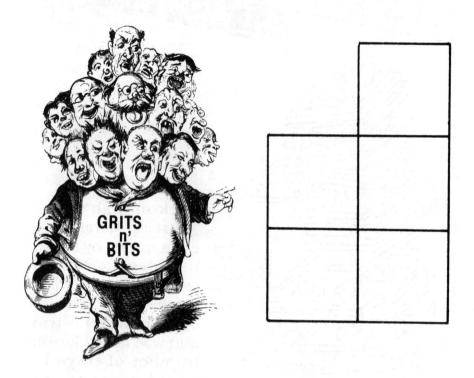

A surveyor stopped by the Grits-N-Bits coffee shop the other day and told about a job he had just finished. Two farmers had bought five square acres of land that had divided their farms and had asked him to lay out a straight fence that would divide their purchase into two equal parcels of land. After much thought, the surveyor came up with the answer. The only trouble is that he left town before telling anyone how he did it. Can you tell the folks at the Grits-N-Bits how it was done?

# The
# **World's**
# Toughest
# Puzzles

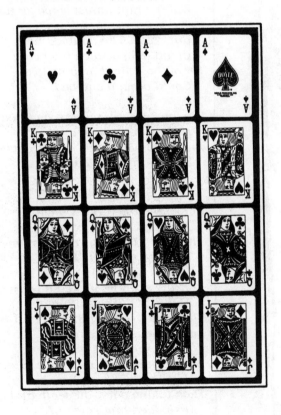

# The World's Toughest "Poem" Puzzle

Ten weary footsore travellers
  All in a woeful plight,
Sought shelter in a wayside inn
  One dark and stormy night.

"Nine beds—no more," the landlord said
  "Have I to offer you;
To each of eight a single room,
  But the ninth must serve for two."

A din arose. The troubled host
  Could only scratch his head;
For of those tired men no two
  Could occupy one bed.

The puzzled host was soon at ease—
  He was a clever man—
And so to please his guests devised
  This most ingenious plan

### A B C D E F G H I

In room marked **A** two men were placed;
  The third he lodged in **B**
The fourth to **C** was then assigned;
  The fifth retired to **D**.

In **E** the sixth he tucked away
  And in **F** the seventh man;
The eighth and ninth in **G** and **H**
  And then to **A** he ran.

Wherein the host, as I have said,
  Had laid two travellers by,
Then taking one—the tenth and last—
  He lodged him safe in **I**.

Nine single rooms—a room for each—
  Were made to serve for ten,
And this it is that puzzles me,
  And many wiser men.

# The World's Toughest "Coin" Puzzle

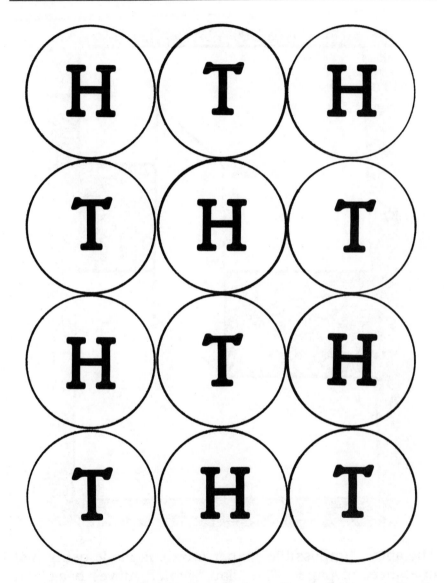

Lay out 12 coins on the table as shown here with six heads and six tails showing. Note that each of the four rows of coins contains a mix of both heads and tails. Now, by touching only one of these coins make the four horizontal rows either all heads or all tails.

# The World's Toughest "Paper" Puzzle

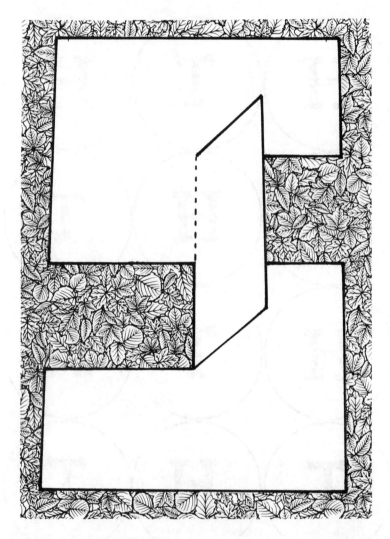

The above "impossible" paper puzzle is made using just one sheet of paper. The "flap," which moves back and forth, is part of the sheet, and it has not been cut out and glued back down. The area of the flap is exactly the same as the area of the two cut out sections of the paper. Yet the illustration is plainly an impossibility. So how was this paper puzzle created?

# The World's Toughest "Change" Puzzle

> Please, Mr. Wellheeled, could you go over that puzzle once again before the trolley arrives? Rodger does so like a good problem!

> Of course, Mrs. Crustworthy, it goes like this: Mr. Smith holds his closed fist out to Mr. Jones and says, "In this hand I am holding two coins. The sum of these coins comes to exactly 55 cents. One of the coins is not a nickel. Can you tell me the value of each of the coins?" I'll wager 55 cents that Rodger can't solve that one in less than five minutes!

Can you beat out Rodger and claim an award from Mr. Wellheeled?

# The World's Toughest "Archaeology" Puzzle

'WHAT WALKS ON FOUR LEGS IN THE MORNING, TWO LEGS IN THE AFTERNOON AND THREE LEGS IN THE EVENING'?

Those intrepid archaeologists, Hawkings and Petrie, have dug up another relic from the past. Let's listen in:

"At last, Petrie, we've discovered that sensational monument from the past, the famous 'Riddle of The Sphinx.' It must be all of 3500 years old!"

"What do you mean, *we*," sputtered Petrie, "leave me out of this! I hardly think that the puzzlers of the Pyramids wrote in English!"

The monument is a fake, of course, but the riddle is a good one. See if you can solve it while Hawkings and Petrie check the lads downstream.

# The World's Toughest "Bell Ringer's" Puzzle

Brother Sebastian and Brother Thaddeus are on clock tower duty. From the look of things I'd say that they're in for a hectic night. Normally when the bell is in working order they are fairly consistent in their work. For example, it takes them exactly 25 seconds to ring out 5 o'clock. Given these facts, can you tell how long it takes them to ring out 10 o'clock?

# The World's Toughest "Talisman" Puzzle

Pictured here is the talisman of that famous gambler J. Wellington Moneybags. Unfortunately the printer put the numbers in the wrong places, causing the charm to lose its power. To restore its strength you must rearrange the numbers one through nine so that the total of four numbers along any one side will be 17. The numbers at the corners will, of course, be included in the totals of the adjacent sides.

# The World's Toughest "Stocking" Puzzle

SIR·ROJER·DE·ROMILY·ROSE
HAD·AT·LEAST·SIXTY-FIVE—
SUITS·OF·CLOTHES
HIS·CRAVATS·OF·ALL·STYLES
MEASURED·MILES·UPON·MILES
WHILE·HIS·RUFFLES·
·AND·FRILLS

GOODNESS KNOWS!

Although Sir Rojer played the part of a fop he is reputed to have been an excellent swordsman. Early one morning, while dressing for one of the many duels that he fought during his checkered career, he went looking for a pair of matching stockings. In the bottom drawer of his dresser he knew that he had ten pair of white stockings and ten pair of grey stockings. However, the light from the single candle atop his dresser was too dim for him to discern white from grey. Can you determine what the least number of single stockings would have to be removed from the drawer so that he would be sure of having one pair of matching stockings to put on when he got outside in the light?

# The World's Toughest "Measuring" Puzzle

Many years ago, so the tale goes, two good old boys, Billy Bones and Pester Pew, got in an argument down at the Bucket O'Blood grog shop. It seems that Billy came in with an empty five-gallon cask and asked Pester to put four gallons of his finest rotgut rum in it. Unfortunately the only measure in the house was an old three-gallon pewter jug. Try as they might Pester and Billy just couldn't figure out a way to measure out exactly four gallons from the rum vat using these two receptacles and as you can see, their frustration soon evolved into mayhem. If you had been there, could you have solved their problem?

# The World's Toughest "Alice" Puzzle

Alice, on her way to the Mad Hatter's Tea Party, came to a fork in the path that she was following. Luckily, Tweedledum and Tweedledee were there to help her out.

"The Walrus told me that one branch of this path would lead me to the Mad Hatter's house and that the other would take me to the den of the Jabberwock, a place I certainly don't want to go to. He said that you boys know the right path to take. He also warned me that one of you always tells the truth, and that the other one always lies. He also says that I can only ask of you one question." Alice then phrased her question in such a way that she was sure to get a correct answer regardless of which brother she asked. Can you figure out what question she put to the boys to get the right directions?

# The World's Toughest "Sea Horse" Puzzle

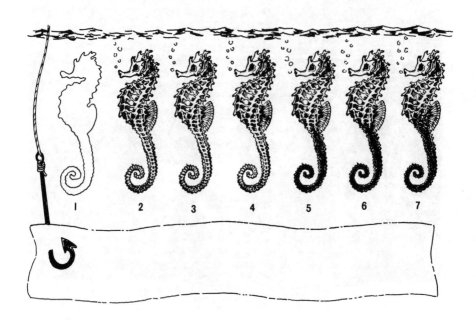

Six playful sea horses are lined up to play a little game. The first three have light-colored tails while the last three have dark-colored tails. What they want to do is to change positions in ten moves or less. Now a sea horse can move backwards or forward to the next adjacent position if it is empty and can swim over one or two other sea horses to get to a vacant position. When they're finished the first three positions should have three dark-tailed sea horses, the next three should have three light-tailed ones and the seventh position should be empty.

The problem looks easy but watch out, you might get hooked by it.

# The World's Toughest "Relation" Puzzle

"Well, what do you think of it, Daphne? I commissioned William Farquar himself to paint it. Do you think it's a good likeness? It moves me to verse.
Sisters and brothers have I none,
But that man's father was my father's son."

The beaming gentleman above is certainly happy about his newly purchased work of art. However, the big question is, who is the person in the picture? What is the relationship between the art connoisseur here and the subject of his masterpiece?

# The World's Toughest "Watch" Puzzle

The little old watchmaker has dropped by to test your skills of precision and orderliness. He has arrayed nine examples of his noble profession, and his challenge is to arrange these timepieces into ten rows with three watches in each row. You'll get a big hand if you can sweep through this puzzle in less than 15 minutes.

# The World's Toughest "Contest" Puzzle

PUZZLE No. 77

Professor Doubtinger is seen here examining the winning entry to puzzle number 77 during last year's International Puzzle Contest. The Professor was making sure that the lines do not cross at any point in the solution. To check the Professor, draw the figure shown here using one continuous line. At no point can the line cross itself nor can you lift the pencil from the paper. You also cannot fold the paper at any point.

# The World's Toughest "Target" Puzzle

Family fun at the turn of the century leads us to an interesting puzzle. Alexander and his sister Sybilla both put three of their rubber-tipped arrows in the same circles of the target and came up with a combined score of 96 points. Can you figure out which circles the arrows ended up in?

# The World's Toughest "Counterfeit" Puzzle

Trusting Ned Armstrong, the owner of Ned's Wonderful World of Sports, made his first sale the other day to a somewhat suspicious looking gentleman. The customer purchased a package of golf balls for $12 and paid Ned with a $20 bill. Ned was all out of singles so he went next door to the bakery to change it; then he gave the customer his purchase and $8 in change. Ten minutes later the baker came in complaining that Ned had given him a counterfeit bill. Ned took back the bogus twenty and gave the baker a $20 bill from the register. Now, the big question in Ned's mind was just how much money had he lost on his first sale? Keep in mind that the markup on a package of golf balls is 100 percent.

# The World's Toughest "Orchard" Puzzle

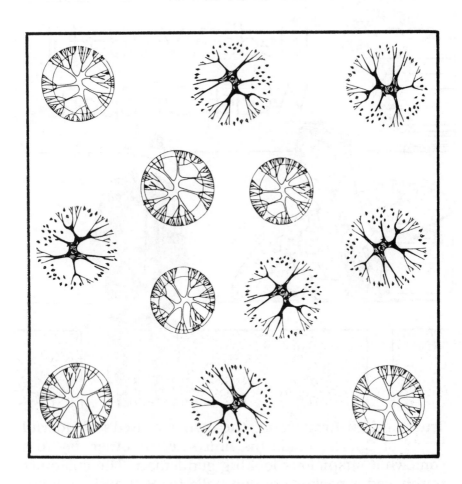

When that famous agriculturist, Farmer Brown, died, he specified that his holdings were to be equally divided among his four sons. He specifically stated that his orchard, which contained 12 prize fruit trees, was to be divided in such a manner that each portion was to be of the same size and shape and was to contain three of the trees. How did the sons fence off the orchard to comply with their father's wishes?

# The World's Toughest "Button" Puzzle

At the turn of the century no button was better than a Barton button, and here is one of their speedy delivery vans making its rounds. It was noted, even back then, that the pattern of buttons painted on the side of the van could be made into a puzzle. The ten buttons are in three rows with four buttons in each row (one horizontal row and two vertical rows). By moving only two of the buttons to new positions you can create four rows with four buttons in each row. See if you can fasten onto the solution within ten minutes.

# The World's Toughest "IQ" Puzzle

Here's a real IQ tester. Pictured above are six random (perhaps) patterns made up of circles, triangles and squares. The test is to determine what the next three patterns in the series will be. On your mark, get set, start drawing!

# The World's Toughest "Robbery Plans" Puzzle

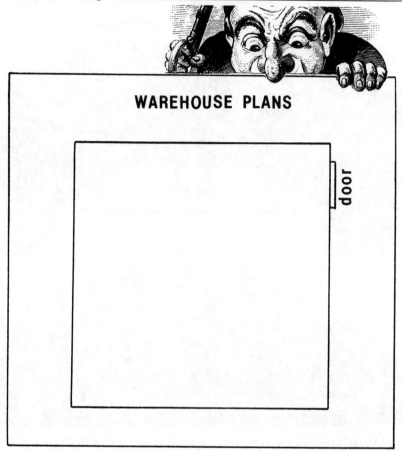

**WAREHOUSE PLANS**

door

Warehouse Willy, that infamous safecracker, was also the cheapest crook in the business. To save money he bought a cut-rate set of floor plans that didn't show where any of the rooms were in a warehouse he intended to rob. The seller told him that the entire building was square and that the main room had a door to the outside. Inside, the warehouse floor plan is divided into six square rooms. Four of the smaller rooms have doors opening into the main room. The fifth small room contained the safe. The seller told Willie that all he had to do to complete the floor plan was to draw four straight lines across the square shown in the above plan. Where do the lines go?

# The World's Toughest "Chess" Puzzle

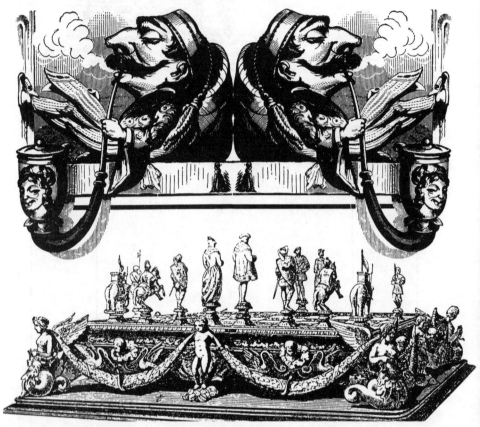

The Puff Brothers are not speaking to each other since Bertram won a chess bet from Augustus. Up until last Friday Bertram had never beaten Augustus at chess. Here's how he challenged his brother on that fateful day:

"Augustus, I'll bet you a tin of your favorite tobacco that I can simultaneously play two chess games with you and either win one of the games or draw both of them. The only stipulations I make are that we alternate our moves on two separate chessboards and that on one board I play black while on the other board I play white. Finally, to show you how confident I am, I will give you the honor of going first. Are you game for a game?"

How did Bertram puff his way to victory?

# The World's Toughest "Farmer" Puzzle

Squire Murdock was a gentleman farmer of some renown around these parts. He was also something of an eccentric. Here he's studying the plans for a new enclosure for his nine prized heifers. He told his men that they had to build four fenced-in enclosures to hold the cows, but each enclosure must contain an uneven number of cows. Can you figure out how the men solved this cantankerous problem?

# The World's Toughest "Scholars" Puzzle

Professor, I think you'll find that this is a devilishly hard word puzzle to solve. Give me a word that contains five consonants in a row.

"That is a tough one, professor, but you'll have to line up to get the answer to my latest problem, namely, what word contains five vowels in a row?"

# The World's Toughest "Answerless" Puzzle

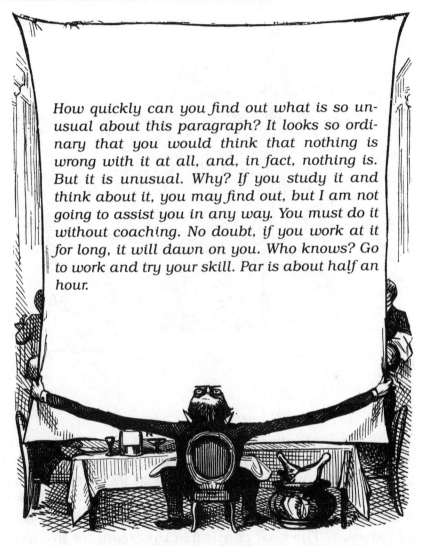

*How quickly can you find out what is so unusual about this paragraph? It looks so ordinary that you would think that nothing is wrong with it at all, and, in fact, nothing is. But it is unusual. Why? If you study it and think about it, you may find out, but I am not going to assist you in any way. You must do it without coaching. No doubt, if you work at it for long, it will dawn on you. Who knows? Go to work and try your skill. Par is about half an hour.*

Quimby Sureye, the editor of a local puzzle magazine, is at his wit's end. The above puzzle was submitted without an answer, and Quimby's been trying to solve it for over a week. Day and night, wherever he goes, Quimby's been studying it without success. Can you solve this perplexing problem and bring tranquility back into Quimby's life?

# The World's Toughest "River" Puzzle

Ezra Walton, skipper of the Speedy Water Taxi Service, was transporting Herbie Bakewell up river to his new business location. As soon as the boat left the dock Herbie fell asleep. After the boat had traveled one mile Herbie's hat blew off into the water and started floating back downstream. The boat continued upstream for five more minutes before Herbie woke up and discovered that his hat was missing. Herbie then made Ezra turn around and head back downstream. They finally caught up with the hat just as it reached their original starting point. The sailing speed of Ezra's boat was constant whether going upstream or downstream. With these facts to work with can you figure out how fast the river was flowing?

# The World's Toughest "Hidden Sentence" Puzzle

**PUZZLE #1**

$\dfrac{\text{STAND}}{\text{I}}$  $\dfrac{\text{TAKE}}{\text{YOU}}$  $\dfrac{\text{MINE}}{2}$  $\dfrac{\text{STANDING.}}{\text{MY}}$

**PUZZLE #2**

10  20  04  18  0

Tommy and Rusty are shown here rushing two new puzzles over to the editor of the *World Puzzle Gazette* newspaper. Each of the puzzles is really a mathematical expression that encodes a grammatically complete English sentence. Can you break the codes and tell what message is to be found on each sign?

# The World's Toughest "Jumping" Puzzle

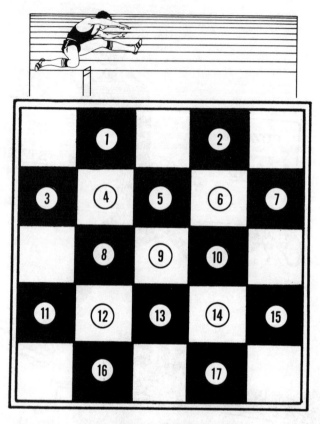

Let's see if you can hurdle to victory on this. Lay out a small checkerboard as shown above and place a checker on every square that has a number in it. The problem is, starting with the checker in square 9, remove all of the checkers from the board, save one, and have this last checker end up where you started in square 9. You can jump one checker over another checker in any direction, sideways, up and down, or diagonally. Whenever you jump over a checker you must remove it from the board. However, as in checkers, the square beyond the checker you are jumping over must be empty. A continuous series of jumps, using one checker, will count as one move. Solve the puzzle in just four moves.

# The World's Toughest "Rearranging Bee" Puzzle

KLASAA
LHATDAIN
INDIRTDA

ACGIUNAAR
RUSLAITAA
RISACFOAUHT

ADEKMRN
GRBAAILU
HPEITIAO

DAUROHNS
HFNNAASTGAI
SHININECLTEET

Get set for a "rearranging bee" puzzler! Listed around the globe above are the names of eleven different countries and one of the United States of America. For our test we've scrambled the letters in each name. It's up to you to rearrange them correctly. Ten out of twelve will confirm that you are indeed a seasoned traveller.

# The World's Toughest "Circle" Puzzle

Professor Melbourne is contemplating an ancient puzzle brought to class by one of his students. The problem: Take the numbers 1 through 12 and place them in the twelve circles depicted in the diagram. The catch is that the sum of the numbers in the outer circle must be twice as large as the sum of the numbers in the inner circle; and the four inner numbers must be in consecutive order.

# The World's Toughest "Boarding House" Puzzle

Mr. Williams, Mr. Barnet and Mr. Edwards all live in Ma Boscombs boarding house. One is a baker, one a taxi driver and one a fireman. Which is which is for you to figure out. Here are five clues to help:

1. Mr. Williams and Mr. Barnet play chess every night.
2. Mr. Barnet and Mr. Edwards go to baseball games together.
3. The taxi driver collects coins, the fireman lead soldiers, and the baker stamps.
4. The taxi driver has never seen a ball game.
5. Mr. Edwards has never heard of approvals.

# The World's Toughest "Utility" Puzzle

**WATER**

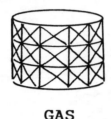

**GAS**

**ELECTRICITY**

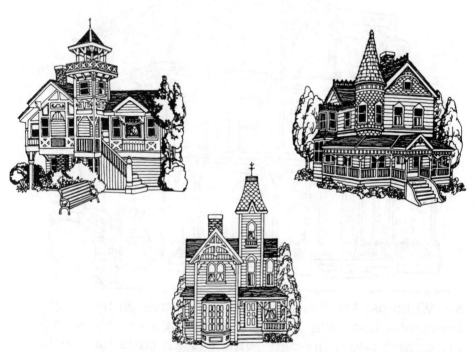

Back when they built the above three houses they had some pretty stiff building codes. When it came to connecting the water, gas and underground electric lines to each house the builder was told that none of the lines could cross under, through or over any of the other lines. It took him over a week to figure out how he could do it and stay within the letter of the law. How did he dig himself out of this municipal predicament?

490

# The World's Toughest "Speed" Puzzle

Mad Man Moriarty, an early motoring madcap, is shown here negotiating the hazardous road down from atop of Old Baldy Mountain. When all's well with his vintage vehicle Moriarty can leave his home in Hooterville, climb up one side of Old Baldy at a steady 10 miles per hour and descend, on the other side, at an equally steady 20 miles an hour. If Moriarty turned around and came right back to Hooterville what would his average speed for the round-trip be?

# The World's Toughest "Transpositional" Puzzle

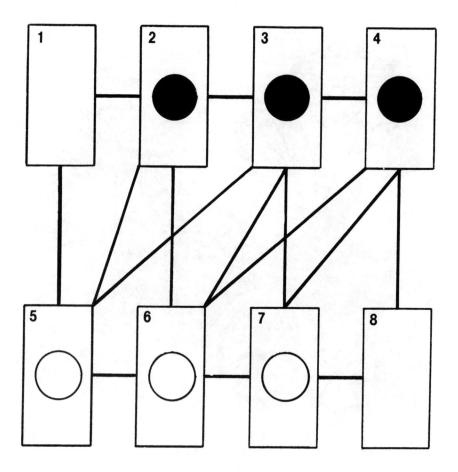

Here's one of those transpositional puzzles that we all love (?) so well. First place three pennies on the black spots in boxes 2, 3, and 4; then place three dimes on the white spots in boxes 5, 6, and 7. Now make them change places in just seven moves, moving the coins from one box to another along the heavy lines that connect them and only moving a coin to an empty box.

# The World's Toughest "Brick Wall" Puzzle

The other day Humpty Dumpty called in a mason and asked him to build two brick walls in his garden. Both walls were to be the same height and distance. (The length of **ab** is equal to **cd**). The mason said that he would have to charge more for wall **cd** since it stood on a hill and would need more materials to construct.

"Nonsense," said Mr. Dumpty, "it should cost less since you will need fewer bricks and mortar to build it!"

Who do you think is right? Is this a case for Trevor Torts, practising attorney?

# The World's Toughest "Trolley" Puzzle

Amos Fastchange, a conductor on the old Metropolitan Trolley Line, used to entertain his passengers with puzzles during their travels. His favorite one went something like this.

"In my hand I'm holding the largest sum of money, in good ol' American coins, that you can have at one time without being able to give change for a dollar, a half-dollar, a quarter, a dime or a nickel. None of these coins is a silver dollar. Let's see if you can calculate this amount before we get to the next stop."

# The World's Toughest "What Am I" Puzzle

> Twice ten are six of us,
> Six are but three of us,
> Nine are but four of us;
>     What can we possibly be?
> Would you know more of us,
> Twelve are but six of us,
>     Five are but four, do you see?

The famous Three Bavarian Bafflers have put their favorite puzzle to song. Can you discern what the mysterious items referred to in this platinum record could possibly be?

# The World's Toughest "Easter Egg" Puzzle

*Wow! There's a swell toy inside this Easter Egg!*

Jimmy, the Honest Newsboy, asked the store owner if he could buy just the toy and not the egg. The pastry maker told him that the price of the stuffed egg was $4.50 and that the cost of the egg alone was $4 more than the cost of the toy inside. How much did Jimmy have to pay for the toy?

# The
# World's
# Trickiest Puzzles

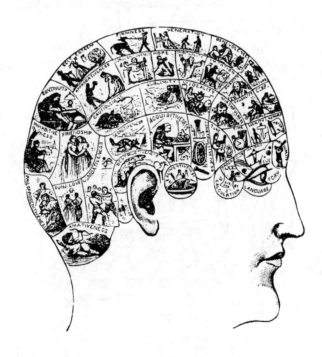

# World's Trickiest "Checkers" Puzzle

Mr. Fogg is a hard man to beat. At their last game the senator thought he had a sure win but Fogg made short work of him. It was Fogg's move and he was playing the black checkers. White was moving up the board while black was moving down. What were Fogg's winning moves?

# World's Trickiest "Dragon" Puzzle

"So I had these three knights trapped inside Old Misery Cave. I had them pinned up against the wall with my tail and I said, 'I'm Cedric, the guardian dragon of St. Basil's treasure. Answer the following three questions correctly and the gold is yours. Fail, and you'll never leave this cave alive.

1. What song do you get when you cross the Ape Man with a zebra?
2. How do you make a hippopotamus float?
3. In the following series of numbers what number comes next: 1, 4, 3 . . . ?'

"Now, you in the poorly fitting suit of armor, what's your answer to the first question?"

"Gosh, Grandpa, what happened next? Did you roast them? Did you toast them?"

# World's Trickiest "Restaurant" Puzzle

*"I've had it! First the Benson twins, as usual, skipped out on paying their share of the bill, and now I'm treated to a chicken gumbo shower. This club has seen the last of Frederick Highcollar."*

Every Monday the Good Samaritan Club would meet for lunch. Before the check arrived the Benson twins would always be called away on business. On the day that Freddy took his bath, the remaining diners were presented with a bill for $80.00. It was their custom to divide the bill up equally among those present. To cover the Benson twins' share, each member had to pay an additional $2.00. How many people originally sat down to lunch?

# World's Trickiest "Kite" Puzzle

It's relaxation time down at the Puzzle Club and Mr. Okito, the resident expert on Japanese puzzles, is showing off his latest creation. Can you beat the other "experts" to the solution? How many different-size equilateral triangles are in the kite's construction?

# World's Trickiest "Sledding" Puzzle

Harry and Harriet barely missed meeting up with the Brody Bunch while participating in the West Orange Downhill Sled Races. Over a measured one-mile course Harry's new sled made the run two and a half times faster than the Brodys' older bobsled. Harry and Harriet beat them out by six minutes. Given these scant facts, can the reader figure out how long it took each contestant to run the one-mile course?

# World's Trickiest "Stick" Puzzle

Over the years the above problem seems to have been a sure attention getter. All you need are 36 ice cream sticks and a lot of patience. Lay out the sticks, as shown above, so that they form thirteen squares. Now, remove eight sticks so you're left with just six squares.

# World's Trickiest "Riddle" Puzzles

*"What was the greatest feat of strength?"*

*"Who is bigger, Mr. Bigger, or his baby?"*

*"When is a boat like a heap of snow?"*

*"Why is an old one-dollar watch like a river?"*

During the "Riddle Ball," at the Palm House in 1896, whenever the music stopped you asked your partner a riddle.

# World's Trickiest "Golf Tees" Puzzle

*"Ever since Andrew MacDivot made that golf tee bet with me last week I can't concentrate on my game. At this rate, I'll never win another club tournament!"*

Nelda Niblick, the lofty amateur women's champion of the Idle Hours Country Club, has been put off her game by one of Andrew MacDivot's famous 19th-hole wagers. He bet Nelda a new set of irons that she couldn't arrange 24 golf tees in such a manner that they would form four perfect squares. Can you help her beat MacDivot at his own game before tee-off time?

# World's Trickiest "Word Square" Puzzle

*"Beware, problem solvers! It is I, the Masked Puzzler, and I'm back to challenge you with one of the world's oldest word puzzles. Pictured on my mask is a six-letter word square. The same six words appear both horizontally and vertically. To cloud your minds so you can't see the answer, I've scrambled the letters in each of the words. However, I'm not without a modicum of mercy. Below are helpful hints regarding the meaning of each word."*

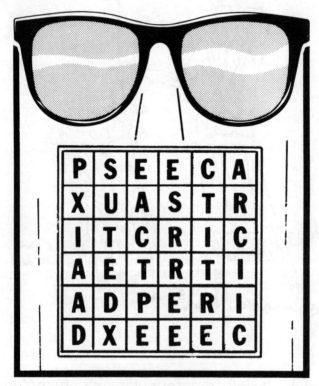

1. What a famous magician did.
2. An extra load to bear.
3. He who sits in judgment.
4. The best clothing.
5. Having something in common.
6. To outdo all others. (Old spelling)

# World's Trickiest "Puzzle Spy" Puzzle

Also at the exhibition was the infamous J. Pinkerton Snoopington, seller of puzzle secrets. With his patented invention, the Snooper Phone, he could eavesdrop on puzzle officials as they were making up contest questions. Let's listen in, too. ". . .Then we're all agreed: Question number 25 is, 'What word is formed if we add the same three letters to the front and the back of the letters ---ERGRO---? The word thus formed is familiar to everyone living in London."

Let the record show that Snoopington was thrown out of the country before he could peddle his info. Do you know the answer to this purloined question?

# World's Trickiest "Cloth" Puzzle

"Try to stay awake, Barton. Old Feziwig will fire you if he sees you dozing on the job!"

"I can't help it. I was up all night trying to solve the cloth puzzle our draper challenged me with yesterday!"

Barton Bolt is having his problems. The store's draper bet him he couldn't take a square piece of cloth of any size and cut it into several pieces that could then be used to form three smaller squares of material. The draper said Barton could make only two straight cuts across the cloth. Finally, one of these squares was to be formed by sewing two of the pieces together along one edge of the material.

Can you weave a solution to Barton's problem?

# World's Trickiest "Betting" Puzzle

"That was a fine meal, Arbuthnot. Well worth the $111.00 the bill comes to. Why don't we have a wager to determine who gets to pay for it? I'll bet you the cost of our two dinners that you can't calculate in your head in 15 seconds what two-thirds of three-fourths of the bill comes to!"

"You're on, Wendell. Start timing me now!"

The reader is also on the clock.

# World's Trickiest "Bar Room" Puzzle

FLAMING COMET
$1.15

Many a strange concoction was served up in the Gold Rush saloons of the Old West. Here we see a mixologist dispensing a flaming libation called a "Flaming Comet." After one you're seeing stars. Newcomers were given a chance to get one free if they could come up with the $1.15 using only six coins. The hitch was that with these coins you *couldn't* make change for a dollar, a half dollar, a quarter, a dime or a nickel. You have until the flames die down to solve this one, pardner!

# World's Trickiest "Rebus" Puzzle

"Well, Farquhar, here is the jumping-off place for our special agents. The last coded message we received was: 'Captain BBBB arrived in the DWDEDSDTD today with his CCCC.' Have you heard anything more about their whereabouts?"

"Well, Liverston, the agent apparently never made contact with the enemy. My agent down there smuggled out the following message last night: 'Captain BBBB mission a bust. NAR EH HE RAN across the island, like EDalienEN, finding 023456789.' "

Can you decipher the above coded messages being discussed by these two turn-of-the-century secret service agents?

# World's Trickiest "Weighing" Puzzle

"This is really a neat puzzle that your father, Professor Kane, challenged us to solve. We have to find out which one of these nine lead weights was incorrectly made. Eight of them each weighs exactly 16 ounces, while the ninth one weighs only 15¾ ounces!"

"That's right, Mike, and we're only allowed to use this scale when looking for the short weight. The problem would be easy if we could weigh two of them at a time until we found the light one, but Dad said we had to do it in just two weighings. I think now's the time for one of your patented hunches!"

# World's Trickiest "Fishing" Puzzle

Four of the guests at Ma Boscomb's boarding house—
Calvin, Wylie, Emmet, and Quentin—went fishing down
at Moran's Creek. Altogether they caught 10 fish. When
they gave their catch to Ma to put in her freezer she noticed that:

1. Calvin had caught more than Quentin.
2. Wylie and Emmet gave her as many fish as Calvin
   and Quentin.
3. Calvin and Wylie had caught fewer fish than Emmet and Quentin.

Given these facts can you figure out how many fish
each of the boarders caught that day?

# World's Trickiest "Poor Sport" Puzzle

"I beat you again, Lionel, and I'll always beat you, whether it's in cards, chess, or any other of life's endeavors that may find us pitted against one another!"

"Confound it, Jeffreys, they ought to invent an ____iperspir____ to combat your offensive personality. The only thing that you really excel in is being the world's greatest ____men____!"

In the above acerbic exchange Jeffreys finally got the better of Lionel by challenging him to play an old word game. The two partially completed words in his rejoinder are missing the same three letters at the beginning and end. The letters are also in the same order. Each word has a different set of letters to find.

# World's Trickiest "What" Puzzles

When the Watts gave one of their famous riddle dinner parties you were expected to come with at least a half dozen "What" questions to help enliven the festivities.

# World's Trickiest "Toy Train" Puzzle

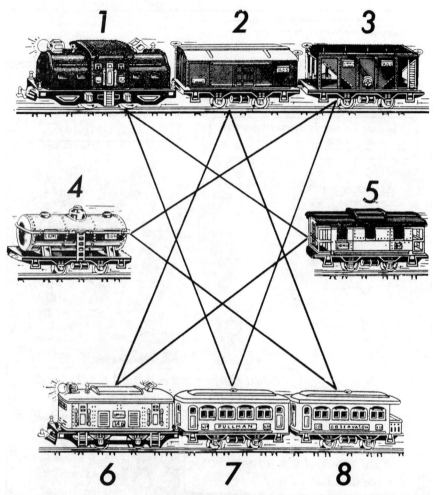

Pictured here are eight old Lionel toy train locomotives and cars. We've linked them together with six lengths of track so we can present the reader with an interesting problem in car switching. First, place two dimes on cars 1 and 3, and then place two pennies on cars 6 and 8. Moving one coin at a time along the tracks, make the coins change places. At no time can any two of these coins be on the same car at the same time. You have to solve this puzzle using no more than 16 moves.

# World's Trickiest "Quilting" Puzzle

This is another delightful problem by that great turn-of-the-century puzzler, Sam Loyd.

"The children have worked all of their names into a wonderful patch quilt, which they are going to present to their teacher. Commence wherever you please and go from square to square, and see how many names you can discover. You can move vertically, horizontally, or diagonally around the quilt. However, each letter can only be used once in any one name. In our picture if you start at the letter *N*, and follow the line, you will spell out the name NANCY. See if you can find all of the other kids' names in her class."

# World's Trickiest "Maze" Puzzle

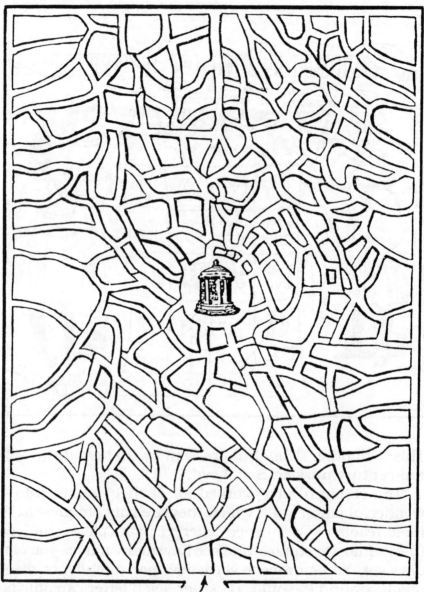

This puzzle, while not being very hard to solve, is certainly a curiosity. We found it in an 1857 copy of *The Magician's Own Book*. After entering the maze try to reach "Rosamond's Bower" in less than 60 seconds.

# World's Trickiest "Candle" Puzzle

"I wish Mr. Wainscoat, our sexton, wouldn't tempt me with these puzzles on Saturday night. I'll never finish my sermon for tomorrow if this one proves to be difficult. And how in the world was he able to fuse these candles together, anyway?"

Reverend I.N. Spire is faced with a dilemma. The sexton wagered him lunch that after laying out 12 candles in the shape of a church and tower he couldn't then shift five of the candles to new positions that would leave him with three squares of equal size. I have a feeling the parishioners are in for a short sermon on Sunday.

# World's Trickiest "Square" Puzzle

"Well, Monsieur Count de Numburrs, how did you do with the previous 'Triangle' puzzle? I bet it took you 60 minutes, instead of 60 seconds, to solve it. Here's another problem to test your skills with: 'How many squares will you find on an ordinary chessboard? You can have up to 60 days to figure it out.'"

"As usual, my dear Count de Pomade, your wit is as light as an English plum pudding. Even Fifi here knows that there are 64 squares on a chessboard. No, wait a minute. There are 65, or is it 70, or maybe 75? Anyhow, your question is stupid and I refuse to answer it!"

The reader has six minutes to find the answer.

520

# World's Trickiest "Vowel" Puzzle

"Well, Freddy, did you get the book editor's job down at the Helenium Press?"

"I'm afraid not, Drucilla. Even my old school tie carried no weight after I flunked their 'Split the Vowels' test. Imagine losing out on a swell job like that because of faulty eye/hand coordination!"

During the test, Freddy was given a sheet of paper that had been divided into 25 squares. The squares contained the vowels A, E, I, O, and U repeated five times. The applicant had to cut this sheet into five pieces, each of which would contain a set of these five vowels.

Care to try your luck at getting the position that Freddy missed?

# World's Trickiest "Motoring" Puzzle

"Barstow, we're at the Raritan River and I'm famished! How far have we come since leaving Maplewood?"

"We've come half the distance from where we are now to Point Pleasant Beach, where we're going to have lunch at Dave's Seafood Shanty!"

Here we see Aunt Hattie out for a drive in her 1903 Benz Parsifal. She's headed for Atlantic City with her husband, Barstow, and their driver, Uncle Mohr. Later on, after lunch, a weary Aunt Hattie once again asked her husband where they were. "Well, Barstow, we've reached Forked River. How much further is it to Atlantic City?"

"Hattie, my answer to that is the same as the one that I gave to you at the Raritan River 76 miles ago!"

"Really, Barstow, if I'd known that the distance between Maplewood and Atlantic City was so far I'd have gone to Lake Hopatcong instead!"

From the above information can the reader calculate the total distance that Hattie had to travel to reach the fabled boardwalk at Atlantic City?

# World's Trickiest "Archaeology" Puzzle

*"Well, Petrie, what do you think of my hunch now? I told you that if we dug here we'd find the Tablet of the Scribes!"*

*"Quite right, Hawkings. If memory serves me correctly, the fledgling scribe had to place the above seven hieroglyphic symbols seven times within the Grid of Harmony. No individual symbol was to appear more than once in any one horizontal row or vertical column. Furthermore, they could not be repeated in either of the two great diagonals."*

(The reader can take this test by using the letters "A" through "G" instead of trying to draw the symbols.)

# World's Trickiest "Fencing" Puzzle

"Land sake, Emma, do you know what Zebediah is up to now? He wants to divide the fruit orchard with four straight fences so he can graze the horses there!"

"And that's not all! He says the four fences will create eleven enclosures and each enclosure will contain one apple tree. I know the fences can cross each other, but I can't figure out where they go. After these pies are done let's see if we can solve this problem!"

The reader is invited to grab a post hole digger and meet us down at the orchard.

# World's Trickiest "WWII" Puzzle

"Babbington, I've just discovered the most amazing coincidence concerning World War II. If you add up the birth dates, ages in 1944, dates of taking power, and years in office of the five main leaders of the Western world, the sums of the numbers in 1944 are all the same!"

"If you're right, that's the greatest coincidence of all time! But surely there must be a rational explanation for this oddity?"

| | Churchill | Roosevelt | Stalin | Hitler | Mussolini |
|---|---|---|---|---|---|
| Year of birth | 1874 | 1882 | 1879 | 1889 | 1883 |
| Age in 1944 | 70 | 62 | 65 | 55 | 61 |
| Took office | 1940 | 1933 | 1924 | 1933 | 1922 |
| Years in office | 4 | 11 | 20 | 11 | 22 |
| Total | 3,888 | 3,888 | 3,888 | 3,888 | 3,888 |

Can the reader explain this coincidence?

# World's Trickiest "License" Puzzle

"Look, Mike, here comes Dr. Stall. He sure loves that old 1909 Ford Model T that belonged to his father!"

"I know. When my dad saw it yesterday he remarked on the license plate. He said that if you added two more 'ones' to the plate you could change the number on it into a person. Can you figure out how to do that one, Biff?"

# World's Trickiest "Mad Scientist" Puzzle

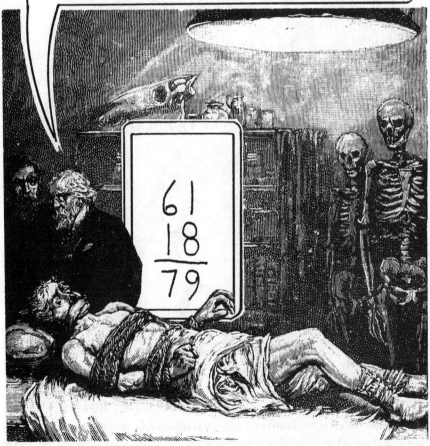

"This, Victor, is Claude Smythe, the cur that humiliated me before the faculty of Carfax University last night. In an attempt to discredit my theories, he openly challenged me to solve the trivial mathematical puzzle chalked on the board here behind me. To solve it, you must rearrange the four figures in the math problem so they equal 100. You can add plus or minus signs if you wish. I still haven't solved it, but who cares now? Soon Smythe will join my army of living skeletons. Victor, prepare my instruments. There's honest work to be done!"

How could Professor Bentbrain have turned the tables on Smythe and solved this problem at the meeting?

# World's Trickiest "Tea" Puzzle

Pictured above is Mr. Foo Ling Yu, the owner of the Spicy Tea Export Company. Mr. Yu was a great puzzler and enjoyed stumping the foreign agents who came to see him. He claimed that with a simple balance scale and four different iron weights he could weigh out any amount of tea in whole pounds, from one pound to 40 pounds. Can you determine the weight of each of these four weights and how Mr. Yu used them?

528

# World's Trickiest "Hurdles" Puzzle

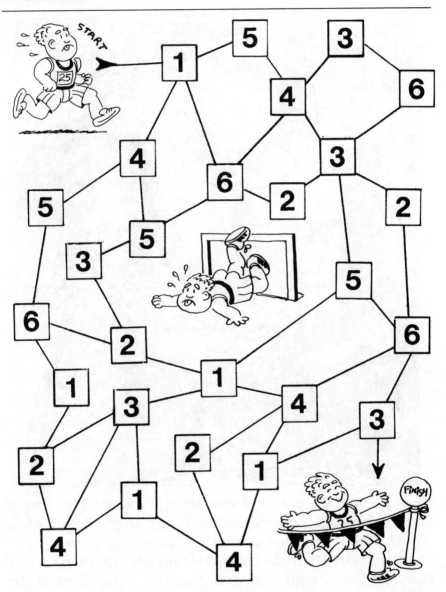

Welcome to the "Hurdle Maze" competition. To solve this event the runner must find the shortest route to the finish line over an even number of hurdles. The sum of the numbers on the hurdles jumped must be the greatest amount possible. Each square box represents a hurdle.

# World's Trickiest "Gambling" Puzzle

Here we see an eastern dude being relieved of his spare change by that famous railroad cardsharp Poker Alice Ivers. When the pigeon tired of losing at poker, Alice would lay out 13 cards in a circle and bet him even money that she could beat him in a game of "Ring Around the Rosie." In this game each player, in turn, could remove from the circle one card or two cards next to one another. The player who picked up the last card was the winner. What was Alice's winning strategy in this so-called even-money game of chance?

# World's Trickiest "Checkerboard" Puzzle

Pop Bentley, owner of the "We Got It General Store!", came up with a new puzzle to beat Cy Corncrib with. He glued nine white checkers and a black king to a checkerboard and cut the board into eight pieces. He then challenged Cy to rearrange the eight pieces so that the king would be able to jump all nine white pieces in a single move. You have until planting time to solve this one.

# World's Trickiest "Stone Carver" Puzzle

"Well, Popol, we're the only ones in our team to show up on the last day of this project. Do you know it's taken us as many months to finish this Calendar Stone as there are workers in our team!"

"You're right, Kuku. If we had had six more workers in our team we could have finished it in one month!"

From the information given in the above conversation can you figure out how many workers there were in the team?

# World's Trickiest "Egg" Puzzle

Albert, the unchallenged prince of butlers, has done it again. For the second year in a row he is being honored by the Puzzle Club for submitting the winning gastronomic puzzle. His problem was: "How would you boil a fifteen-minute egg if you had only two sand timers, one that ran for 11 minutes and another that ran for 7 minutes, to time it with?" Once again Albert received a standing ovation and a glass of the bubbly for this one. The reader is invited to join the party and crack the problem before dessert is served.

# World's Trickiest "Star" Puzzle

The mentalist, pictured here in another era, is about to solve the famous "Star of Salamanca" coin puzzle. The object is to place a coin on any empty numbered circle and then, moving along one of the lines, to pass over the next circle, and to then lay the coin on the next empty circle. Continue along in this fashion until all the circles, numbered 1 through 9, have been covered by coins.

# World's Trickiest "Underwater" Puzzle

"No, Miranda, her age is not 38. You must try harder. Remember, five years ago Mrs. Bellows was five times older than her daughter, Cecily. Now she is only three times as old as Cecily. What is Mrs. Bellows' age today?"

"38 years old?"

This has to be one of the strangest acts in the history of entertainment. Billed as Professor Nemo and Miranda, the Underwater Puzzlette, they toured North America and Europe answering every puzzle put to them from the audience. As Miranda could only surface between questions, she had to find the correct answers quickly and bubble them to the professor or face a watery end. Can you help her ascertain Mrs. Bellows' current age?

# World's Trickiest "Quibble" Puzzle

Mike and his friends are researching a problem in the Puzzle Club library. Let's see if we can give them a hand.

# World's Trickiest "Farm" Puzzle

"Ebenezer, I'll trade you six pigs for a horse. You'll then have twice as many animals as I'll have."

"Hold on, Zebediah. I'll trade you 14 sheep for a horse. You'll then have three times as many animals as I'll have."

"I have a better idea. Absalom, I'll trade you four cows for a horse. You'll then have six times as many animals as I'll have."

Listening to these three horse traders, you should have enough information to figure out how many animals each of them now owns.

# World's Trickiest "Card" Puzzle

"These four face-down cards contain all four suits and the values Ace, King, Queen, and Jack. Here are five clues that will help you figure out what each card is:

1. The Ace is to the right of the Spade.
2. The Diamond is to the left of the Queen.
3. The Club is to the right of the Queen.
4. The Heart is to the left of the Jack.
5. The Spade is to the right of the Jack.

Mike Miller, along with Linda Kane and Biff Bennington, is shown here relaxing in the Puzzle Club's game room. Mike is challenging them to discover the values of the face-down cards he's just dealt out. The reader is invited to play along. For the sake of clarity, assume that the clues pertain to the cards as they face the reader.

# World's Trickiest "Anagram" Puzzles

"Are you ready to order from Me a No Study, Sir?"

"Yes, Henri, tonight I'll start off with Man Take Loss and finish up with A Race Track, or I Sin."

"I'll start with a Dad Saw Floral and follow that with But Marge Has Tripe."

Fred and Alice are celebrating his promotion with a night out at the famous Anagram Club, where all the dishes are written as anagrams on the menu. Can you decode their orders? (Anagrams are words or groups of words where the letters have been mixed up to form new words. For example, the word "meals" could be made into the word "Salem.")

# World's Trickiest "Train" Puzzle

No. 463.     NEW YORK, OCTOBER 18, 1907.     Price 5 Cents.

FRED FEARNOT AND RAILROAD JACK
OR, AFTER THE TRAIN WRECKERS
By HAL STANDISH

Fred Fearnot, hero of the dime novel, needs your help fast! Fred and his friends have captured the Train Wreckers Gang. Now he has to save the afternoon passenger train. He's too far away to flag down the work train just coming out of Dead Man's Tunnel. However, the daily passenger train is just entering the other end of the tunnel and is travelling at 75 miles per hour. The tunnel is one-half mile long. It will take 6 seconds for the train to completely enter the tunnel. If Fred runs his fastest he can reach the tunnel's exit in 27 seconds. Will this be fast enough for him to flag down either the engineer or the brakeman in the caboose?

# World's Trickiest "Word Pyramid" Puzzle

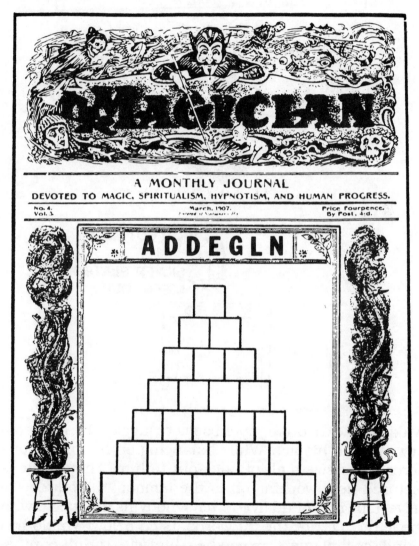

The year is 1907 and Will Goldston, editor of *Magician*, a monthly journal, is challenging his readers to solve a "Word Pyramid" puzzle. Using the seven letters A D D E G L N, you must form seven words, starting with a one-letter word at the top of the pyramid. Each subsequent word, going down, must use all of the letters in the preceding word plus one new letter.

# World's Trickiest "Q" Puzzle

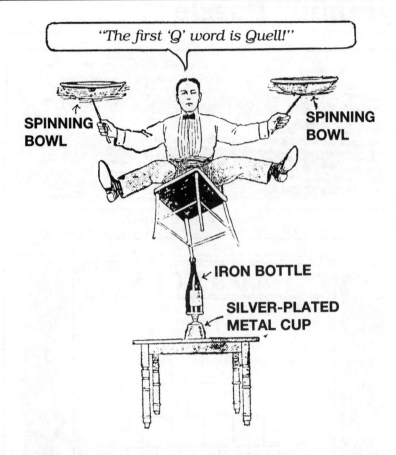

Waldo Quackenbush, noted society juggler, has added a new twist to his act. While balancing on his precarious perch he answers all puzzles put to him. The one he is pictured here working on is the famous "Q" puzzle. To solve it, he must find five-letter synonyms that begin with the letter "Q," for the 20 words listed below. Waldo has found the first one. Can you help him with the other nineteen?

| | | | |
|---|---|---|---|
| 1. subdue | 6. nimble | 11. swallow | 16. secluded |
| 2. pen | 7. repeat | 12. scruple | 17. tremble |
| 3. measure | 8. doubt | 13. seeming | 18. monarch |
| 4. share | 9. game bird | 14. entirely | 19. twist |
| 5. line | 10. singular | 15. search | 20. oddities |

# World's Trickiest "Poem" Puzzle

"Really, Lionel, I'm most disappointed. You should have solved my little puzzle in a thrice. Now stop your pouting and listen carefully to every word I say:

The beginning of eternity,
The end of time and space,
The beginning of every end,
The end of every place."

Now, what is this little poem all about?

# World's Trickiest "Fours" Puzzle

Professor Flunkum's students know that if they chalk an interesting problem on the wall outside his study window he's apt to get so caught up in it that he'll miss his classes. Right now he's trying to figure out how to arrange five fours and one plus sign so the result equals 55. If you figure it out, don't tell the professor. His students are hard on snitches.

# World's Trickiest "Store" Puzzle

> *"Let's see now. I have a dollar to spend and I think I'll purchase an assortment of colored thread. First, give me some two-cent blue spools. Next, I'll take ten times as many one-cent red spools as I took blue spools. Finally, I'll take the balance of my money in five-cent green spools. And please hurry! My carriage is double-parked at the curb!"*

**THE LITTLE STOREKEEPER'S OUTFIT, WITH CASH CARRIER**

It's Christmas time in 1902 and the Bartholomew kids have received a Franklin Play Store set complete with toy money, products to sell and an overhead cash carrier. Neville is in charge of making change while Bascomb waits on his sister, Fleurette. Back in those days a dollar went a long way, no pun intended. Can you figure out just how many spools of each type of thread were purchased during the above transaction?

# World's Trickiest "Subtraction" Puzzle

"Now who wrote this subtraction problem on the mirror? I know it's wrong, but the Mad Hatter insists I'm looking at it the wrong way. He says that if I study it from the correct angle it will be perfectly correct. I know he's in this mirror somewhere but I just can't find him. This just gets curiouser and curiouser."

Can you help Alice find the solution to this problem so she'll be one up on the Mad Hatter?

# World's Trickiest "Contest" Riddles

"What is full of holes and still holds water?"

"Where did Noah keep his bees?"

"What has five eyes, but cannot see?"

"When is a doctor most annoyed?"

The time is May, 1926. The place is the offices of England's premier magic magazine, *The Magic Wand*, and the editor, George Johnson, and his friends are having a riddle contest. Let's listen in!

# World's Trickiest "Party" Puzzle

A group of partygoers on their way to a puzzle and joke soiree stopped off at the local magic store to purchase some game prizes. Each purchased one item. Each item cost the same price, which was between $1.00 and $4.00, and the price contained an even number of cents. The total amount spent by the group, before taxes, was $20.30. How many people were in the group and how much did each item cost?

# Super Brainy
# Puzzles of
## The
# World

# Super Brainy "Quotation" Puzzle

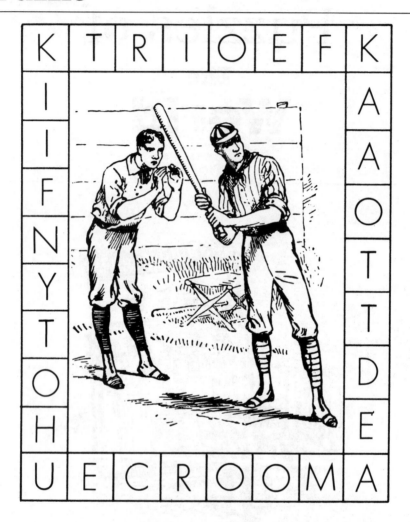

Down through the years baseball has given us many colorful characters. One of those, who was as adroit with a quotation as with a bat, was Yogi Berra. One of his most famous quotes is hidden in the above frame of letters. To read it, find the correct starting letter and then go around the frame twice, reading every other letter as you go. Now, batter up, or should I say, puzzler up?

# Super Brainy "Checkers" Puzzle

Pop Bentley, the sage of cracker barrel checkers, is about to trounce Cy Corncrib for the umpteenth time. Pop is playing the white checkers and it's his move. The black checkers are moving down the board. Can you figure out the set of moves that Pop will use to win yet another dime from Cy?

# Super Brainy "Concert" Puzzle

*"What do you think of his execution, Bertie?"*

*"I'm in favor of it."*

*"Now don't be cross, dear. I know that Professor Rinaldi is not your cup of tea, but you don't have to turn your back on him. Here's a puzzle for you to work on while he works his way through Debussy's 'Clair de Lune.' See if you can find a five-letter word that means "to strike someone hard with a fan" if he falls asleep again. The thing about this word is that the five letters that it's composed of can also be rearranged to form four other words. Here's a hint: one of these words refers to a type of insect. Now, be a good boy and solve it while I enjoy the rest of the recital."*

# Super Brainy "Liars" Puzzle

"Now Henry, I know you tell lies."

"Nonsense, Thelma. Jeffrey is the one here who tells lies."

"Confound it, you're both liars. I'm innocent of all charges. Just for that, Schnappsie and I are going home!"

I don't know who lied about what, but I do know that only one of this trio is telling the truth. Is it Henry, Thelma, or Jeffrey?

# Super Brainy "Fax" Puzzle

VEAGNE

LHTMOCOKS

ARWCOC

NAOMRSINA

IOPVLELOR

GRTSSORUAB

FSDRSODULE

MKILECIR

The home office for the Farlow Soft Drink company has just faxed Norbert Gladhander the travel schedule for his upcoming European sales trip. Unfortunately the message has become garbled after bouncing off one too many satellites. Can you unscramble the names of the eight cities on his itinerary list before flight time?

# Super Brainy "Money" Puzzle

"I received your letter today, Selwyn, and I'm a little confused about the puzzle in it. You say that Uncle Andrew has a drawer in his desk that he calls his cash drawer. You state that the drawer is divided into nine compartments with three compartments to a side and that he keeps his loose change in the center compartment. In your puzzle you say that at one time he had placed forty $1.00 bills in the eight outside compartments in such a way that the total amount of cash in the three compartments along any one side of the drawer totaled $15.00. Am I right so far?"

"Absolutely, Hattie. Andrew had five singles in each of the eight compartments. He then removed all the bills from the drawer, added sixteen new $1.00 bills to the total, and then placed them all back in the same eight compartments in such a manner that the total amount of cash in the three compartments, along any one side of the drawer, still totaled $15.00. Can you tell me how he did that?"

# Super Brainy "Watch" Puzzle

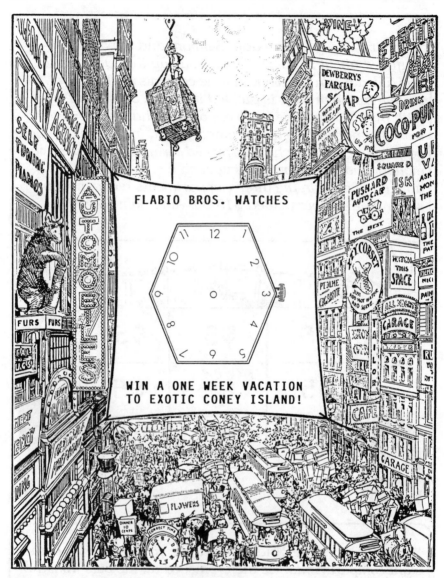

To solve the Fabulous Flabio Watch Contest all you have to do is rearrange the numbers 1 through 12 on the six-sided watch face so the sum of the three numbers on each of the six sides totals 22. If more than one person wins, the Flabio Brothers will declare a "Going Out Of Business Sale."

# Super Brainy "Line" Puzzle

"There's my new puzzle kite, Mike. Isn't it a beaut! To solve the puzzle you have to make a drawing of the kite using one continuous line. At no point can the line cross over itself. I was up all last night building it. I'm going to enter it in the school puzzle contest tomorrow."

The reader is invited to solve Biff's winning puzzle.

# Super Brainy "Counterfeit" Puzzle

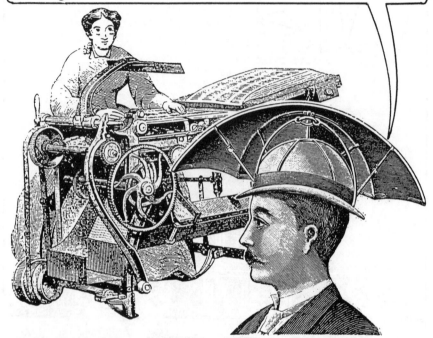

"The game's up, Madame Duplicator. Umbrella Man is your undoing!"

Private investigator Harry "the Hat" Hulbertson, A.K.A. Umbrella Man, is shown here breaking up the largest counterfeiting ring in New York City during the 1890s. The cutaway drawing of Harry's hat shows the umbrella apparatus that allowed him to leap through skylights and land unharmed below. When asked by reporters how much phony cash was found in the room Harry, who loved a good puzzle, replied:

"We took the bills that Madame Duplicator had printed and stacked them on the table by denomination. We found that we had ten times as many $5.00 bills as $1.00 bills. We also had twice as many phony $50.00 bills as $10.00 bills. The total amount of phony money found was $1,500. Now, gentleman, you tell me how many of each type of bill was liberated from the premises."

# Super Brainy "Hidden Cities" Puzzle

Palex and Rialto were the early trotting kings

Like a weary traveler, I entered the town.

Hidden in the description at the bottom of each picture is the locality of the incident depicted. You have 30 seconds to find each of the cities.

# Super Brainy "Word Pyramid" Puzzle

Blocks and Puzzles are the order of the day this Christmas at the Gundersons' house. Uncle Olaf has stacked his present in the form of a Word Pyramid. The problem is to restack the blocks so they form eight words, starting with the letter "R" at the top. Each subsequent word, going down the pyramid, must use all the letters in the preceding word plus one new letter.

# Super Brainy "Voting" Puzzle

"And in conclusion, my friends, I leave you with the following thoughts as you prepare to go to the polls tomorrow. Vote early, vote often!"

The above speech sounds like New Jersey ward politics in the old days. (I was born and raised there, so I can say that.) All of which brings us to an interesting line puzzle. Above is pictured a box on a ballot with an "X" in it. Your problem is to draw this box, with the "X," using one continuous line. Also, the line cannot cross itself at any point. Solve this one and you're a winner!

# Super Brainy "Blackboard" Puzzle

"This is ridiculous! They want me to add two positive numbers to 19 and end up with a sum less than 20."

Little Gloria has just received an Educational Puzzle Blackboard for her birthday and she is not amused. After all, how can you add two positive numbers to a positive 19 and expect to get a result that is less than 20. I think that this is a trick question. What do you think?

# Super Brainy "Hexagon" Puzzle

In ancient times, during the Festival of Squat, people took time off from pyramid building and sat around playing games and doing puzzles. The priests at Abu Simbel would bring out the giant shield of the puzzle god, Stumpumost, and display it against the statues of Ramses II. Inside the hexagonal shield were the Nine Stars of Wisdom. To solve the problem of the shield the puzzler had to draw nine straight lines of equal length across the shield in such a way that each of the stars would be alone in its own oblong box. Successfully solving the problem meant an invitation to the palace. Failure earned the contestant an invitation to participate in a crocodile race. Would the reader care to compete?

# Super Brainy "Miller's" Puzzle

Timothy the miller, a man of some education, delighted in puzzling his neighbors. Each fall he would post a puzzle on his mill worth one free grinding of 10 bags of grain to the first farmer who could solve it. The problem here is to move four of the sacks of grain to new positions so you are left with five rows, each row containing four sacks. No loafing on this one.

# Super Brainy "Butter Knife" Puzzle

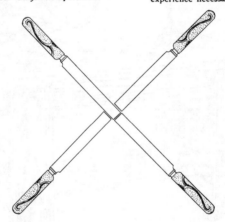

Valadon Wormwood, a successful graduate of Professor Grey's Silver Plating Academy, is shown here overhauling Ma Bascomb's silverware. Valadon is also known as a clever bettor. The other day, down at Kelly's Oasis, he lay four butter knives down on the bar in the form of a cross.

"I'll wager any man here that I can form a square by moving one of these knives. Any takers?" How did Valadon win his bet?

# Super Brainy "Platter" Puzzles

> *"Cut off my head and I shall still be found,*
> *Though somewhat shorter, still the same in sound.*
> *Cut off my tail, I still remain the same;*
> *Bereft of both, I will not change my name,*
> *Not even if you deprive me of my middle.*
> *Now, lest as me you would considered be,*
> *I pray you quickly to find out this riddle."*

We're listening to an old time "Puzzle Platter" from the early days of sound recording. In this puzzle when you "behead" a word you drop the first letter. When you "curtail" a word you drop the last letter. An office building, at Christmas time, has something to do with the answer to this poetic problem.

# Super Brainy "Cities" Puzzle

"What is a haunted house?"
"Who is the most famous ghost in the house?"
"What does an accountant concern himself with?"
"What is found at every wedding?"
"What city rises above the rest?"
"Who was the president of the Michigan Garden Club?"

While crossing the frozen north in his Atomic Ice Cruiser, Fred Reade and his party passed the long Arctic night by making up puzzles. The one they're working on here is an American Cities puzzle. The answer to each of the above questions is the name of a city.

# Super Brainy "Magic Square" Puzzle

*"Madame, you are now the greatest mathematician in all of France. I command you to construct a magic square for the New Year 1779. Just the last two digits of the year will suffice!"*

*"I hear and obey, O great Mesmer. The first four numbers are 26, 15, 28, and 27. Place them in squares 3, 5, 10, and 16."*

The year is 1779 and the fashionable hypnotist, Franz Anton Mesmer, is entertaining his aristocratic followers at a New Year's Eve party. Once a year he got to play the palace. In our picture his subject is well on her way to solving Anton's puzzle. The square must total 79 in every direction, horizontally, vertically, and diagonally, from corner to corner. The remaining twelve two-digit numbers, which the reader must fill in, include numbers between 11 and 29. No number may appear in the square more than once.

# Super Brainy "Billiard" Puzzle

> "Phillip, I've just noticed something that should give you pause for thought. The last six balls that I pocketed, in order, were the 11, 15, 9, 1, 7 and 2. While I run the rest of the table, see if you can figure out what is significant about this sequence."

The reader is invited to chalk up and play along with Phillip and Miss English.

# Super Brainy "Signs" Puzzle

$9 + 8 + 7 + 6 + 5 + 4 + 3 + 2 + 1 = 0$

CHANGE ONE PLUS SIGN TO A MULTIPLICATION SIGN ($\times$)

CHANGE FOUR PLUS SIGNS TO MINUS SIGNS ($-$)

ADD A SET OF PARENTHESES ( )

When the flu season starts, that ace of substitute teachers, Ms. Priscilla Sunshine, is not far behind.

"Well, students, I see by yesterday's test results that you can use some practice in the use of signs. With that in mind I've devised the following exercise. The above mathematical expression is incorrect. I want you to put it right by changing one plus sign to a multiplication sign; changing four of the plus signs to minus signs; and, finally, adding a set of parentheses. Since this is the last period, feel free to continue after the bell if you run into any trouble solving it."

# Super Brainy "Banking" Puzzle

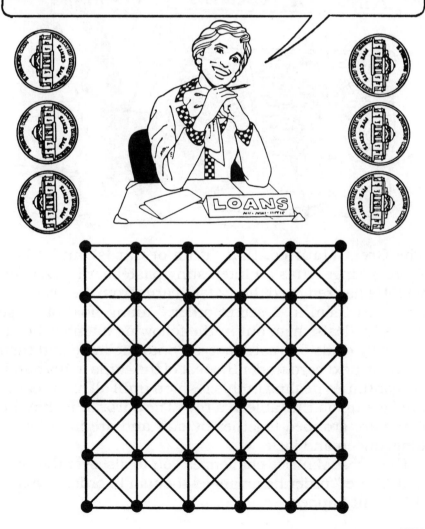

"Congratulations, Mr. Spendenborrow, you've passed all of our qualifications for obtaining a loan. There is, however, one final test of your ability to manage money. The Puzzler First National Bank has devised the following problem. You must take these six nickels and place them on the dots in the grid in such a manner that no two nickels will be on the same line horizontally, vertically or diagonally. You have 10 minutes to do it."

# Super Brainy "Card" Puzzle

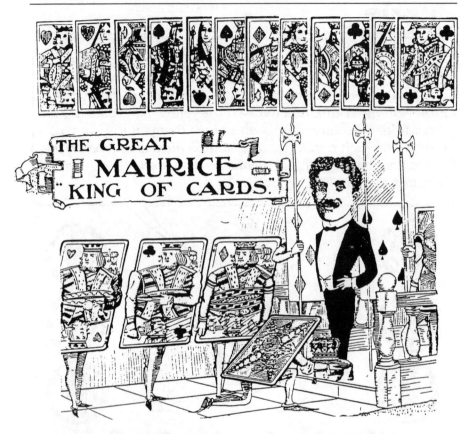

The Great Maurice, that "King of Cards" and "Card Among Kings," has an interesting pasteboard puzzle for you. He has removed the 12 face cards from the deck and arranged them in a secret order. Taking hold of these cards he deals them out in the following manner: he alternately deals one card face-up onto the table and then puts the next card under the rest of the cards in his hand. He continues dealing in this fashion until all of the cards are face-up on the table in a row. The surprise is that the cards are grouped together by suit and are in order by king, queen and jack.

The Great Maurice challenges you to discover the original "secret" order he arranged them in in order to make this stunt happen.

# Super Brainy "Five Buck" Puzzle

"Well, now, this puzzle in the New York Bugle is certainly apropos.
    'My first is a number, my second another,
    And each, I assure you, will rhyme with the other.
    My first you will find is one-fifth of my second,
    And truly my whole a long period reckoned.
    Yet my first and my second (nay, think not I cozen),
    When added together will make but two dozen.
    Now, who am I, anyway?'
"If only my other problems were as easy to solve."

Sometimes money can talk. The above five-spot has an interesting problem for you to work on. There's a clue in the above picture if you can find it. Good luck.

# Super Brainy "Contest" Puzzle

"Hi, Linda! I just finished my Poem Puzzle. See if you can solve it!
   'Take a third of twelve
   Plus four-fifths of seven,
   Add them all together
   And come up with eleven.' "

ABC
X DE
FG HI

"That's a tough one, Mike! My contest puzzle is about numbers, too. You have to replace the nine letters in my sign with the digits 1 through 9 so you end up with a valid multiplication problem. Each digit can only be used once."

# Super Brainy "Limerick" Puzzle

> *"There once was an impetuous Castilian,*
> *Who made a bet with a wealthy Sicilian.*
> *Using eight ones and threes*
> *He won it with ease,*
> *When he arranged them to equal one million!"*

Limerick puzzles. What won't they think of next? Now let's see. If I'm reading the problem right, they are asking the reader to take eight digits, which must be either ones or threes, and to arrange them into a mathematical expression that will equal one million. Now where's a pencil and paper?

# Super Brainy "Roller Ship" Puzzle

Pictured here is the famous Chapman Roller Vessel. Built back in 1895, this ship moved through the water on two giant rollers each of which was powered by an electric locomotive running on a track inside. In its first year of active service on the Amazon River it ran between two ports. When it left port A going downstream it was able to travel at a speed of 20 miles per hour. When it reached port B it took on passengers and mail and went back upstream to port A. On the return trip the ship could only travel at a speed of 15 miles per hour, which meant that it took five hours longer to cover the same distance. Can you figure out how far port A was from port B?

# Super Brainy "Scholar" Puzzle

First Scholar: "Now, Mossback, let us go over the rules once again. To win this contest in the *Puzzle World Review* we have to find 10 contractions that, when the apostrophe is omitted, leave a word that is unrelated to the original contraction."

Second Scholar: "Quite right, Ploddington. In the example given in the rules the contraction 'we'll' (we will) becomes the word 'well' when the apostrophe is removed!"

First Scholar: "I've found three already. If we send out for pizza we can work through lunch and get our entry in under the wire."

(The reader is also invited to help the above savants in their quest for fame and fortune.)

# Super Brainy "Penmanship" Puzzle

Have Quills, Will Travel! The motto of Nellie Cook, an independent stenographer of another era. Ms. Cook was ready at a moment's notice to tackle any job of dictation. To hone her calligraphy skills she had a daily set of exercises that she faithfully performed. One of these exercises involved drawing the four perfect circles pictured above. Ms. Cook drew these circles using one continuous line that never crossed itself at any point, nor did the line ever double back on itself. A steady hand and a keen eye are needed to solve this example of puzzle penmanship. Quill pens are optional.

# Super Brainy "Alderman" Puzzle

"Congratulations, Mr. Gladhander! I understand that you're our new alderman!"

"That's right, Mr. Needlesworth. As usual the best man won. Of the 5,219 votes cast I received 22 more than Murphy, 30 more than Hoffmann, and 73 more than Dangerfield. At this rate who knows, someday I may be your mayor!"

While Mr. Needlesworth is working on Mr. Gladhander's new suit, the reader might try to figure out how many votes each of the four candidates received.

# Super Brainy "Word Square" Puzzle

# Super Brainy "Acronym" Puzzles

"Our new promotional testing pro-gram really has Treadmill worried."

"I'll give you a quarter for the acronym test answers!"

"Make it a dollar and I'll do the whole test for you!"

Test #3
Nursery Rhyme Acronyms

1) Okcwamos
2) Dddmsj
3) Twaowwlias
4) Pppapopp

When the Whipsnaid Trolley company toughened up their qualifications for advancement, certain members of the staff grew apprehensive. In the Acronym test section the first letters of the words that begin a given nursery rhyme are grouped together as a word. As an example: Hddtmrutc would be "Hickory, Dickory, Dock, The mouse ran up the clock." Can you discern the four nursery rhymes given in the test?

# Super Brainy "Automobile" Puzzle

"Hello, Mr. Mulroy, this is Mr. Armtwister down at Sam's Preowned Car Emporium. I just received a shipment of four slightly driven cars and I thought of you right away. . . . How old are they? Well, the oldest, an Essex Coach, is four years older than the second oldest, a Lincoln Victoria, which is four years older than the third oldest, a Duesenberg Convertible, which is four years older than the youngest, a Cord 812, which is half as old as the Essex Coach. Mr. Mulroy, are you still there?"

Back in 1948 Swifty Armtwister could really move the iron. From his description can you figure out how old each of these vintage cars was when he called up Mr. Mulroy?

# Super Brainy "Row" Puzzle

"All right, Durwood, now let me see if I've got this straight. I'm to arrange 12 checkers in seven rows in such a manner that there will be four checkers in each row. If I fail to solve it we'll go to see the Clydesdale Tractor Pulling contest down at Cy Corncrib's farm this afternoon. If I solve it we get to go to the band concert in the park. Can't I have more than five minutes to work on it?"

The reader is also limited to five minutes.

# Super Brainy "Auction" Puzzle

"Going, going, gone for $1,800 to Mr. Collectable!"

Calvin Collectable, eminent antique dealer, returned from an auction with an $1,800 settee and several second thoughts. "You know," he said to himself, "instead of this settee I could have bought one phonograph, three gravy boats, and three Toby mugs; or two phonographs and six Toby mugs; or four gravy boats and six Toby mugs. I must have been crazy to buy this moth-eaten old stick of furniture. I wonder if I can unload it on Ma Bascomb?"

From the above information can the reader discover the price of a single phonograph, gravy boat, and Toby mug?

# Super Brainy "Garden" Puzzle

The time, the 1920s; the event, an International Puzzle Convention; the place, the Boston garden of a Back Bay Brahmin's Venetian-style palazzo. The three puzzle connoisseurs shown here are contemplating a tile puzzle-board in the floor of the central atrium. The problem is to join the sixteen black circles using six connected straight lines. No circle can be touched by more than one line.

# Super Brainy "Breakfast" Puzzle

"Hey, Roderick! Did you lose your glasses when you made up that breakfast board?"

"Heck no! When I saw you jokers pull up, I decided to make a puzzle out of today's menu. I scrambled the letters in each of the eight items. You have until my boss, Karsten, arrives to unscramble them."

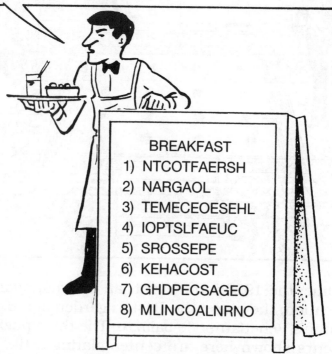

BREAKFAST
1) NTCOTFAERSH
2) NARGAOL
3) TEMECEOESEHL
4) IOPTSLFAEUC
5) SROSSEPE
6) KEHACOST
7) GHDPECSAGEO
8) MLINCOALNRNO

The next time you're in Seattle visit Julia's, in Wallingford, for the best breakfast and grilled potatoes in the Northwest.

# Super Brainy "Gold Claim" Puzzle

"Pa said if anything ever happened to him we should divide his gold claim up equally among the four of us!"

"That should be easy. The claim is on a perfectly square piece of land!"

"Hold on! Pa also said that each parcel of land must have a common border with each of the other three parcels!"

"And remember, Pa said that parcels touching at a common corner didn't count. It had to be a real border!"

How did these 49-ers fulfill their pa's wishes?

# Super Brainy "Puzzleman" Puzzle

"I don't get it. You say the puzzler has to take the 12 digits, 111, 333, 555, and 777, and form them into six numbers that, when added together, will give a sum of 20. That's a stupid puzzle. Nobody will spend the time necessary to figure it out. Now, why don't you create a nice 'Find-the-Word' puzzle?"

"Godfrey Daniel! Why didn't I become an accountant?"

A puzzleman's lot is not always a happy one. Still, his problem is not really a bad one. The reader is invited to try it out.

# Answers

*Some puzzles have more than one solution. Here are the most common ones.*

**"Window" Puzzle (page 6).** The shaded area is the part of the window that is painted blue.

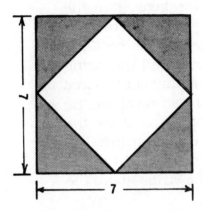

**"Soda Straw" Puzzle (page 6).** Tightly fold the straw about three inches from one end so that it forms a "V." Insert this end of the straw into the bottle and maneuver it around until it gets wedged in the bottle, as in the illustration. When this happens, you will be able to lift the bottle off the table.

**"Fish Tank" Puzzle (page 7).** Tip one end of the tank up into the air, letting the water spill out over the other side. Continue this until the water level runs from one bottom corner to the top of the opposite side. At this point, the tank will be exactly half full of water. It's a messy solution, but it works.

**"Coin" Puzzle (page 8).** The moves are: (1) 5 to 8, remove 7; (2) 2 to 5, remove 4; (3) 9 to 2, remove 6; (4) 10 to 6, remove 8; (5) 1 to 4, remove 2; (6) 3 to 7, remove 4; (7) 5 to 8, remove 7; (8) 6 to 10, remove 8.

**"Line" Puzzle (page 9).** The illustration shows how to draw the kite without crossing the lines at any point or going over any part of the line more than once.

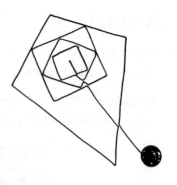

**"Book" Puzzle (page 10).** To break the string below the book, give the string a sharp downward jerk. You will be pulling against the inertia of the two-pound book, and the string should break before any of this force is transmitted to the string above the book. To break the string above the book, pull slowly on the string. The force exerted, plus the weight of the book, will cause the string above the book to snap first.

**"Ice-Cream-Stick" Puzzle (page 11).** Slide the stick on the "bottom" of the glass partway to the left. Then move the stick that is on the "right" side of the glass to the left of the glass stem. The glass is now upside down, and the cherry is on the outside.

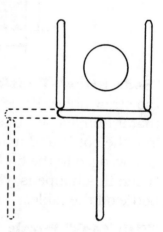

**"Toothpick" Puzzle (page 12).** Move the three toothpicks denoted by broken lines in the fish at the left (A) and replace them in the positions indicated by the broken lines in the fish on the right (B).

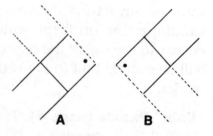

**"Rope" Puzzle (page 13).** Pass the loop of your rope through the loop which encircles one of your friend's wrists, slide it over the hand, and pass it back again through the loop. The ropes will now be separated.

**"Stamp" Puzzle (page 14).** Place two stamps, one on top of the other, in the middle of the cross. There are now "four" stamps in each line of the cross.

**"Hardware Shop" Puzzle (page 15).** The builder of the condos had forgotten to place their house numbers on each unit. Down at the hardware shop, they sell these numbers for $1.00 each. Since there are only nine units in the Friar Briar Estates, no condo will need more than one number. Therefore, four buyers will buy four numbers for a total sale of $4.00.

**"Dime" Puzzle (page 16).** Place your forefinger on the table opposite the dime, and scratch the cloth lightly. The dime will move slowly in the opposite direction. Soon it will come out from under the glass.

**"Arrowhead" Puzzle (page 17).** If you place the four arrowheads on the table as shown in the illustration, you will "see" a fifth arrowhead outlined in the middle. That answer should send a "quiver" up your spine.

**"Sugar" Puzzle (page 18).** This is a puzzle with a "catch" to it. Place one lump of sugar in cup one, two lumps in cup two, and three lumps in cup three. Finally, pick up cup three and place it in cup two. Now each cup has an "odd" number of sugar cubes in it.

**"Dollar Bill" Puzzle (page 19).** Though it looks easy to catch the dollar bill, it's impossible to do it more than once in ten tries. Your reflexes are just not fast enough.

**"Card" Puzzle (page 20).** The moves are as follow: (1) card 4 on card 1; (2) card 6 on card 9; (3) card 8 on card 3; (4) card 2 on card 7; and (5) card 5 on card 10.

**"Bookworm" Puzzle (page 21).** The total distance travelled is $2^1/_2$ inches. Since the bookworm starts at page one of volume 1, which is on the right side of the book, and heads towards volume 3, the first thing he will start chewing on will be the cover of volume 1. Once through this cover, he will chew through the back cover of volume 2, then on through 2 inches of pages, through the cover of volume 2, and, finally, through the back cover of volume 3, where he will come to the last page of the book, the finish line of our puzzle. This totals four covers and the contents of one volume, or $2^1/_2$ inches of delicious grazing.

**"Code" Puzzle (page 22).** First spy: "Did you get my photos of the enemy's new secret weapon?" Second spy: "Yes, you dolt! It turned out to be a plan for a new electric eggbeater."

To break the code, write the 26 letters of the alphabet, "A" through "Z," across the paper. Under them write the letters of the alphabet in reverse order, "Z" through "A." Find each letter, in the coded sentences, in the bottom reversed line of letters and substitute the letter above it in the first line. That's all there is to it.

ABCDEFGHIJKLMNOPQRSTUVWXYZ
ZYXWVUTSRQPONMLKJIHGFEDCBA

**"Geometry" Puzzle (page 23).** Line OD is the radius of the circle and is six inches long. Figure ABCO is a rectangle whose opposite corners touch the center of the circle and the edge of the circle. Therefore, a radius line OB would be six inches long. Since both diagonals of a rectangle will have the same length, line AC will be equal to line OB, or six inches in length.

**"Starship" Puzzle (page 24).** Take the following route: Starting at command center 2, go E, N, H, 3, J, N, M, 4, L, 3, G, 2, C, 1, B, N, K, 3, I, N, F, 2, D, N, A, 1.

**"Archery" Puzzle (page 25).** To score exactly 100, using six arrows, put them in the following target rings: 16, 16, 17, 17, 17, 17.

**"Button" Puzzle (page 26).** Here are the moves (W = white and R = red): (1) W2 to 3; (2) R4 to 2; (3) R5 to 4; (4) W3 to 5; (5) W1 to 3; (6) R2 to 1; (7) R4 to 2; and (8) W3 to 4.

**"Chain" Puzzle (page 27).** Since there are six sections of chain, the solution that comes to mind first is to open the end link on one chain and reclose it around the end link of another chain. Doing this five times would join all six sections together at a total cost of $6.25.

However, there is an even cheaper way to solve this puzzle. Take the chain with four links and have each link opened. This will cost 75¢ times 4, or $3.00. Use these four links to join the remaining five sections of chain together. Welding these four links shut will cost an additional $2.00. Our total cost for creating one chain, with 29 links, will be just $5.00.

**"Word" Puzzle (page 28).** The words are as follow: (1) Sidewalk, (2) Sitting Bull, (3) Hopscotch, (4) Fast Break, (5) Clipboard, and (6) Drop Kick.

**"Block" Puzzle (page 29).** The answers are as follow:

|   |   |   |
|---|---|---|
| (1) 3 sides painted blue | = | 8 cubes |
| (2) 2 sides painted blue | = | 12 cubes |
| (3) 1 side painted blue | = | 6 cubes |
| (4) no paint on any side | = | 1 cube |
| Total | = | 27 cubes |

**"Animal" Puzzle (page 30).** There are four lions and 31 ostriches. Here's how to figure it out: Since he counted 35 heads, there had to be a minimum of 70 legs. However, his total count of legs was 78, or eight legs more than the minimum. These eight extra legs must, therefore, belong to the lions. Dividing these eight legs by two, we get the number of four-legged animals. Therefore, the total number of lions in the preserve has to be four.

**"Mars" Puzzle (page 31).** Those 50,000 readers who wrote in and said "There is no possible way" were all correct, for that particular sentence is the answer to the puzzle.

**"Crossroads" Puzzle (page 32).** Napoleon had the pole replaced so that the board that had the name of the town that he had just come from was pointing back down the road he had used to get to the crossroads.

**"Coaster" Puzzle (page 33).** A to C show how to rearrange the coasters into a perfect circle.

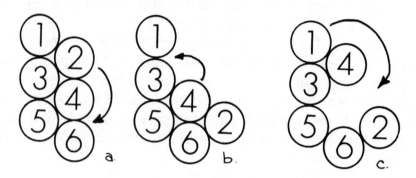

**"Age" Puzzle (page 34).** Have the person write down her shoe size (forget the $1/2$ sizes). Next, have her multiply the size by 2 and add 5 to the result. Then instruct her to multiply this sum by 50. Now add the "magic number" 1736 to the last product. Finally, have her subtract the year of her birth from the previous sum. Now, ask her what number she is left with. The last two digits of this number will be her age on her birthday this year. (*Note*: Every year, the magic number increases by 1. For example, 1986 = 1736; 1987 = 1737, etc.

**"Record" Puzzle (page 35).** On *any* record there is just one groove that spirals in towards the middle.

**"Circle" Puzzle (page 36).** Take the square of cardboard and place the tip of one corner against any spot on the inner rim of the circle. Now, at points A and B, where the sides of the cardboard cross the line of the circle, make two marks (see Fig. 1). Using the cardboard as a straightedge, draw a line across the circle from points A and B. Now, placing the tip of the cardboard at some other inner point on the rim of the circle, repeat the actions of step one, placing marks at points C and D (see Fig. 2). Finally, draw a straight line from C to D. The exact center of the circle is where line AB crosses line CD (see Fig. 3).

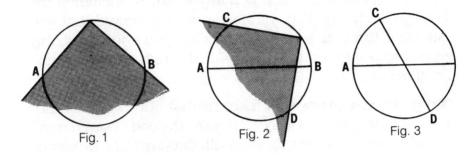

Fig. 1    Fig. 2    Fig. 3

**"Rune Stone" Puzzle (page 37).** The one thing that all the characters have in common is that they are numbers. Each number, 1 through 9, is chiselled along with its mirror image. If you cover the left half of each figure, you'll see that this is true. The missing number, of course, is six.

**"Truck" Puzzle (page 38).** This would only be true if the driver had on open-bed truck. With an enclosed truck, however, in order for a bird to remain in flight, its wings must push against the air with a force equal to its weight. This causes the air to press down on the bed of the truck with a force equal to the weight of the bird. Thus, the truck will weigh the same whether or not the birds are sitting or flying.

**"Bottle" Puzzle (page 39).** The paper strip is too long to jerk out from under the coins, although this is the method that has to be used to solve this type of problem. What you have to do is cut, or tear, the paper strip off one side about an inch from the stack of coins. Now, take hold of the strip on the other side of the bottle and hold it straight out, 90 degrees from the side of the bottle. With the forefinger of your other hand, strike the paper a sharp blow midway between your hand and the bottle. The paper will be snapped out from under the coins so quickly that inertia will keep them from falling off the bottle top.

**"X-Ray" Puzzle (page 40).** Press the paper tightly over the coin. Now, rub a soft-lead pencil over the portion of the paper directly above the coin. An outline, or "rubbing," of the coin will appear showing many features, including the date, quite clearly. You will have certainly proved that you can "see" through solid objects. Why, you could probably even read a date on a silver dollar through aluminum foil. Try this one out.

**"Frog" Puzzle (page 41).** It seems that our frog is ascending at the net rate of one foot a day. At the end of seven days, he's climbed seven feet up the wall. On day eight he climbs the final three feet, which brings him to the top edge of the wall, where, with a final "frogculian" kick, he plops over the rim, tired but happy. The answer, then, is eight days.

**"Pilsner Glass" Puzzle (page 42).** We will fill the large glass eight times using the small glass. When all the dimensions of a three-dimensional vessel are doubled, its volume is multiplied by a factor of eight. As an example, take a cube 1 foot by 1 foot by 1 foot. Its volume is one cubic foot. Double its dimensions, 2 feet by 2 feet by 2 feet, and you get a volume of eight cubic feet.

**"Policeman" Puzzle (page 43).** The illustration shows the route the policeman took.

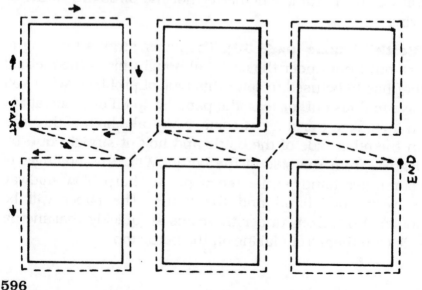

**"Jealous Husband" Puzzle (page 44).** Let's label the husbands A, B, and C and their wives a, b, and c. The crossing would be made as follows:

1. a and b cross over, and b brings back the boat.
2. b and c cross over, and c returns alone.
3. c lands and remains with her husband, while A and B cross over. A lands and B and b return to the other side.
4. B and C cross over, leaving b and c at the starting point.
5. a takes back the boat and b crosses over with her.
6. a lands and b goes back for c.
7. b and c cross over and all are reunited. Happy ending!

**"Bicycle" Puzzle (page 45).** Betty rode the bike for one hour and covered eight miles. She then left the bike by the side of the road and walked the remaining eight miles, in two hours, to her aunt's house. After walking for two hours, Nadine arrived at the bicycle, and an hour later she pedalled up to the front door of her aunt's house at the same moment Betty arrived. The total time needed to cover the last 16 miles was three hours.

**"Deductive" Puzzle (page 46).** What we have to determine is: Does every blue-backed card on the table have a king on its other side? We certainly have to turn over card 1 because it has a blue back. We're not interested in red-backed cards, so we'll skip card 2. Number three is a king, but it doesn't matter whether its back is blue or red, so we'll skip it too. Finally, we have to turn card 4 over. If card 1 is a king and card 4 is red-backed, the answer is yes. However, if card 1 is not a king, or card 4 has a blue back, then the answer is "no."

**"Tennis" Puzzle (page 47).** Since it takes one match to eliminate one couple from play, and we have 128 couples, it would take 127 matches to eliminate all but the winning team.

**"Nail" Puzzle (page 48).** As you can see, in this arrangement each nail touches every other nail.

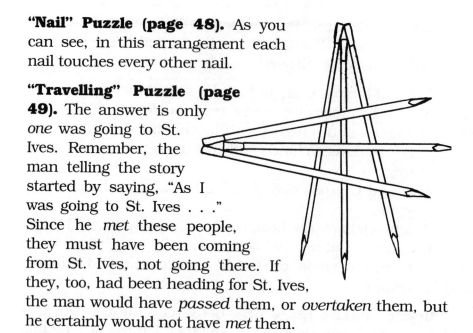

**"Travelling" Puzzle (page 49).** The answer is only *one* was going to St. Ives. Remember, the man telling the story started by saying, "As I was going to St. Ives . . ." Since he *met* these people, they must have been coming from St. Ives, not going there. If they, too, had been heading for St. Ives, the man would have *passed* them, or *overtaken* them, but he certainly would not have *met* them.

**"Antique" Puzzle (page 50).** The difference between 90 percent of book value and 125 percent of book value is 35 percent. Since 35 percent is worth $105, 1 percent would be worth $3. Therefore, the original book value has to be $300.

**"Fly" Puzzle (page 51).** Now, most people will decide that the shortest route for our travelling fly to take would be a straight line directly from point A to point D, and then along the edge to point B. Using the Pythagorean Theorem, we calculate that line AD is 2.8284 inches long. (The Pythagorean Theorem states that the length of the longest side of a right triangle is equal to the square root of the sum of the squares of the other two sides of the triangle.)

Now, add to this measurement of 2.8284 inches another 2 inches for line DB and we get a total distance of 4.8284 inches. If, however, we plot a course AC to a point midway along the top edge of the cube, we get a line that is 2.2361 inches long. Also, line CB is 2.2361 inches long. Therefore, we get a total length of 4.4722 inches, a distance considerably shorter than the first "obvious" course.

**"Racing" Puzzle (page 52).** The farmer's solution was for each racer to get into his opponent's buggy. Remember, the original wager specifically stated that "the *first buggy* that crosses the finish line will lose."

**"Cookie" Puzzle (page 53).** Poor Ariadne started with 15 cookies. Lorella received 7¹/₂ + ¹/₂, or 8 cookies, leaving 7. Melva received 3¹/₂ + ¹/₂, or 4 cookies, leaving 3. Laureen received 1¹/₂ + ¹/₂, or 2 cookies, leaving 1. Finally, Margot was given ¹/₂ + ¹/₂, or 1 cookie, leaving Ariadne with zilch. Oh, well, there's always next month's mail delivery.

**"Horn" Puzzle (page 54).** Groucho came up with an ingenious solution. He had the shop wrapper find a large box that measured three feet by four feet. He took the bulb off the horn and packed it into the box on a diagonal from corner to corner. (The length of the diagonal was five feet.) After having the box wrapped up, he now had a package that measured three feet in width by four feet long. The post office had to accept it. The "Case of the Incredible Shrinking Horn" has been solved.

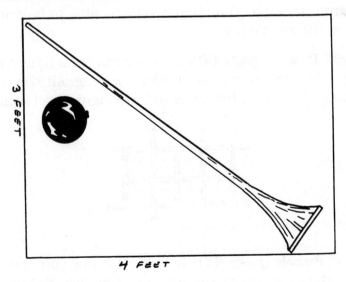

**"Wallet" Puzzle (page 55).** Mr. Gotrocks had one $50 bill, one $5 bill, and four $2 bills.

**"Egyptian" Puzzle (page 56).**

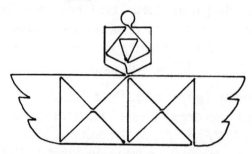

**"Checkers" Puzzle (page 58).** Black to move and win: 27 to 24, 28 to 19, 26 to 23, 19 to 26, and 30 to 16.

**"Plate" Puzzle (page 59).** First, cut the two corks in half lengthwise. Next, force the tines of each fork into a half cork, as pictured at right. Make sure that the angle created by each fork and cork is less than 90 degrees. Now place the four corks around the edge of the plate. The  forks should be up against the plate edge. This will keep the forks from rocking. You should now be able to balance the plate on the needle point easily.

**"Match" Puzzle (page 60).** This is certainly a different way to solve this type of match puzzle. The diagram shows how to arrange the 15 matchsticks to form eight small squares.

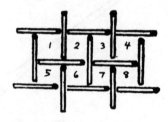

**"Chess" Puzzle (page 61).** To solve this one you have to go outside the nine corner squares, but this doesn't invalidate the solution. You still visit each of the nine corner squares during the four moves of the queen. Try this one at your next chess club meeting.

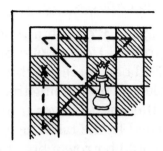

**"Old Salt" Puzzle (page 62).** Old Billy came into port on a Tuesday. In the first place, since the Binnacle Pet Lodge was closed on Thursday and Friday, we have to rule out those days. Next, we can rule out Saturday because the barber shop was closed. Since Billy came home with more money than he went to town with, we can suppose that he cashed his paycheck. We know that he was paid on Thursday, but since the next two days have been eliminated, it stands to reason that he came to town the following Tuesday when the bank was next open. This is also the day when both the barber shop and the Pet Lodge were open.

**"Name" Puzzle (page 63).** Mr. Neederwaller's friend was a lady, not a gentleman, and her name was, of course, Eleanor.

**"Family" Puzzle (page 64).** Grandpa had quite a turnout for his birthday party: The following members, including himself, were present: two brothers and two sisters, their mother and father, and both their mother's and father's parents—the children's two grandfathers and two grandmothers. Ten family members in all.

**"Safe" Puzzle (page 65).** Knuckles made off with 60 pennies, 39 dimes, and one half dollar.

**"Prophesy" Puzzle (page 66).** High Pockets has the advantage of going second. No matter what date Jeffords picks, all High Pockets has to do is select the next higher and the next lower dates and he will be closer to the date on almost any coin Jeffords removes from his pocket. The only way High Pockets can lose is if Jeffords correctly guesses the date on the coin he removes.

**"Cigarette" Puzzle (page 67).** From nine of the ten butts Ned made three cigarettes. He had one butt left over. After enjoying his weeds, Ned had three new butts. From these he made his fourth smoke. After finishing that one Ned had two butts left, counting the one left over from the original 10. What to do? Ned turned to the table next to his and asked the party there if he could borrow a butt from their ashtray. He now had three butts, from which he made his fifth cigarette. Once he had finished smoking this farewell cigarette, he returned the butt to the party he had borrowed it from (why they'd want it back is beyond me) and went home.

**"Poker Chip" Puzzle (page 68).** The two rows intersect at one corner. The corner chip has a second chip on top of it. In this way, one row has three chips in it and the other has four.

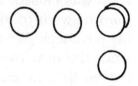

**"Cork" Puzzle (page 69).** The secret lies in the position of the hands as they are brought together. The uninitiated brings them together with the palms of both

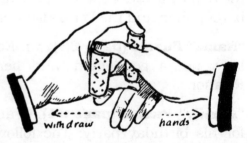

turned toward the body, with the consequence we have described. To solve the puzzle, turn the palm of the *right hand inward*, and that of the *left hand outward*, in the act of seizing the corks. They will then not get in each other's way, but may be separated without the least difficulty. (From that wonderful 1890s book, "Puzzles Old and New," by Professor Hoffmann.)

**"Wagering" Puzzle (page 70).** The first win goes like this: The only obvious move for Black is to move from square 19 to 24. White then moves 29 to 25. Black continues by moving 24 to 28. White then moves 30 to 26. Black has to jump 21 to 30 and is made a king. White then moves 31 to 27. Black then has to double-jump 30 to 23 to 32, clearing the last of the white checkers off the board and ending the game before the black checker, from square 19, could make it to the king row.

For bet number two, where you're now playing the black checkers, you make the first move 21 to 25. White then has to jump this checker either going 29 to 22 or 30 to 21. You then move the black checker on 19 to 24. It is now impossible for the white checkers to stop you from eventually moving this checker to the king row and winning your second bet. It's easy when you know how.

**"Planetary" Puzzle (page 71).** The planets are: Mercury, Venus, Earth, Mars, Jupiter, Saturn, Uranus, Neptune, and Pluto. The star, of course, is the sun. The illustration shows how to find Venus.

**"Horned Lizard" Puzzle (page 72).** This is an easy puzzle. The lizard transversed two legs of a right triangle. When the points of a right triangle touch the sides of a circle the long side, or hypotenuse, of the triangle will be equal to the diameter of the circle. The diameter, therefore, is 100 inches. Remember, the square of the hypotenuse equals the sum of the squares of the two sides of the triangle. (3660 + 6400 = 10,000. The square root of 10,000 is 100 inches.)

**"Number" Puzzle (page 73).** The answer is:

$$
\begin{array}{r}
147 \\
25\overline{)3675} \\
25\phantom{00} \\
\overline{117\phantom{0}} \\
100\phantom{0} \\
\overline{175} \\
175
\end{array}
$$

Here's how it's solved: (1) Since the first product is the same as the divisor, the first number of the quotient must be 1. (2) In the second subtraction the letter *E* must be 0 since the letters *FC* are brought down. (3) The letters *FEE* stand for 100. This is the product of *AB* times the second letter, *D*, in the quotient. The divisor does not contain a zero. The only two-digit number when multiplied by a one-digit number that could give a product of 100 is the number 25. So, the divisor is 25 and the second number of the quotient is 4. (4) In the first subtraction, 25 from *GH* gave 11. Therefore, *GH* must be 36. (5) Finally, the last number for *C* must be 7, 8, or 9. If you try each one you'll soon see that only number 7 fits the bill. That wasn't too hard. You're next at the lift.

**"Poker" Puzzle (page 74).** The money was divided as follows: Melvin had $94.25; Harvey had $74.25; Bruce had $41.25; and Rollo had $23.25.

**"Toy Train" Puzzle (page 75).** He bought the following 20 cars for $20: three passenger cars at $4.00 each ($12); fifteen freight cars at $0.50 each ($7.50); two coal cars at $0.25 each ($0.50). This comes to $12 + $7.50 + $0.50 = $20.00.

**"Punishment" Puzzle (page 76).** The answer is to use a whole number with a fraction such as $3^3/_3$, which is equal to 4, an even number. Some other examples are: $9^9/_9$, which equals 10, and $7^7/_7$, which equals 8. Batter up!

**"Play Store" Puzzle (page 77).** Strawberry jam costs $0.50 a jar and peach jam costs $0.40 a jar. In the original purchase, three jars of strawberry came to $1.50 and four jars of peach came to $1.60, for a total of $3.10, the amount specified in the problem.

**"Word" Puzzle (page 78).** When he mused ". . . *there* is a five-letter word . . ." he had the answer. The word *THERE* contains: *THE*, *HE*, *HER*, *HERE*, and *ERE*. I hope Malcolm isn't too exhausted working that one out.

**"Bullet Hole" Puzzle (page 79).** After the smoke cleared, did you have the following answer?

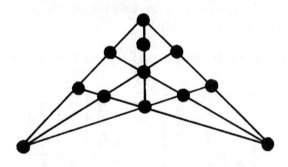

**"Car Sale" Puzzle (page 80).** Since Daphne's hero was dropping the previous price by 20 percent every time he changed it, the final selling price had to be $563.20.

**"Playing Card" Puzzle (page 81).** If all the bets are down, I'll show you the seven similarities: (1) There are 52 playing cards and 52 weeks in a year. (2) There are 13 cards in each suit and 13 weeks in each season. (3) There are 4 suits and 4 seasons. (4) There are 12 court (face) cards and 12 months in the year. (5) The red cards stand for day and the black cards, night. (6) If you total up the value of all the cards, counting jacks as 11, queens as 12, and kings as 13, the sum will be 364. Add 1 to this for the joker and you have the number of days in a year. (7) Also of interest: The number of letters in the names of the cards (one, two, three, four, five, six, seven, eight, nine, ten, jack, queen, and king) equals 52, the number of weeks in a year.

**"Hoop Gun" Puzzle (page 82).** Ned scored as follows: 14 hoops in the 10 slot for a score of 140; 8 hoops in the 20 slot for a score of 160; 2 hoops in the 50 slot for a score of 100; 1 hoop in the 100 slot for a score of 100. 140 + 160 + 100 + 100 = 500.

**"Royal" Puzzle (page 83).** The setup of the cards, face down, top to bottom, is as follows: king, king, queen, king, king, queen, queen, queen.

**"Rebus" Puzzles (page 84).** Rebus #1—"They say that I am a *LIONESS* among women!" (LI on S). Rebus #2—"I've seen a lot of *ANEMONE* down at our pond!" (An M on E). Rebus #3—"Marry me and we will be as snug as *TWO PEAS IN A POD!*" (Two P's in a POD).

**"Computer" Puzzle (page 85).** There are at least two solutions to this puzzle:

| 2 | 1 | 9 |
|---|---|---|
| 4 | 3 | 8 |
| 6 | 5 | 7 |

| 3 | 2 | 7 |
|---|---|---|
| 6 | 5 | 4 |
| 9 | 8 | 1 |

**"Kissing" Puzzle (page 86).** Caleb solved the problem by using Roman numerals. The number 29 is XXIX. Caleb said he would take one away from 29. In this case he removed the I. This, of course, left him with XXX, which is 30. I think this problem isn't worth more than a peck on the cheek.

**"Rope Ladder" Puzzle (page 87).** Since the ship rides up and down with the tide, there will still be 50 rungs above the water at high tide. Did any landlubbers get wet on that puzzle?

**"Bottle" Puzzle (page 88).** The captain, of course, was Noah. He had a large ship with animals from around the world, none of which were for sale. Since there was no land, he didn't care which way the wind blew; all ports were below water. What he wanted most was to find land to ground his ship on.

**"Ballot" Puzzle (page 89).** Wolfram figured that the queen would pull a fast one on him, so he did the following: He removed one of the slips from the crown, tore it into small pieces and put them in his pocket. He removed the other piece of paper, opened it up and passed it around for all to see. Since this paper had "Get Lost" written on it, everyone assumed Wolfram's first selection had "Stay" written on it. The queen, of course, could not admit that she had cheated, so Wolfram was able to remain in the palace and serve with distinction for many more years.

**"Addition" Puzzle (page 90).** The answer to this bearish problem is:

$$1 + 2 + 3 + 4 + 5 + 6 + 7 + (8 \times 9) = 100$$

**"Vacation" Puzzle (page 91).** The sequence of letters *SHONIX* are the only ones in the alphabet that can be read the same upside down. Therefore, the remaining letter that could be added to this group is *Z*.

**"Magic Store" Puzzle (page 92).** As the amount of each share corresponded with their length of service, it is plain that the housemaid received one share, the parlour maid three, and the cook six, for a total of ten shares. The value of a single share was one-tenth of $700, or $70, which was the portion of the housemaid. The parlour maid received $210 and the cook $420.

**"Substitution" Puzzle (page 93).** The answer is:

$$
\begin{array}{r}
17 \\
\times\ 4 \\
\hline
68 \\
+\ 25 \\
\hline
93 \\
\end{array}
$$

**"Bubble" Puzzle (page 94).** The proof is: Start with 10, add another 10, then add 5, which is half of the original amount, and finally add 7. This comes to: $10 + 10 + 5 + 7 = 32$. The answer is ten bubbles. Judging from the picture of the party, I'd say that he probably used the balcony to set that record.

**"Camera" Puzzle (page 95).** The distribution came out as follows: Farrington received $94^1/_4$ cameras, Smollet $74^1/_4$ cameras, Pennington $41^1/_4$ cameras, and Barlow $23^1/_4$ cameras. How can you have a quarter of a camera, you ask? What they did was to take the least valuable of the cameras, disassemble it and divide up the pieces among themselves for spare parts.

**"Transposition" Puzzle (page 96).** The moves are: 2 to 3, 8 to 5, 10 to 7, 3 to 9, 5 to 2, 7 to 4, 9 to 6, 4 to 10, 6 to 8, 1 to 6, 2 to 4, 6 to 5, 4 to 3, 10 to 9, 5 to 7, 3 to 2, 9 to 1, and 7 to 10.

**"Carnival Wheel" Puzzle (page 97).**

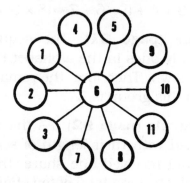

**"Tips" Puzzle (page 98).** Pat started out with $50 and Mike with $30.

**"Beehive" Puzzle (page 99).** There are many, many ways to solve this one. If you managed to find one of them, it's time to cell-ibrate!

**"Castle" Puzzle (page 100).** There are several routes you could take. One of them is: f, b, a, u, t, p, o, n, c, d, e, j, k, l, m, q, r, s, h, g, f.

**"Marbles" Puzzle (page 101).** The number of marbles Dutch had left is one-fifth the total of all the marbles both boys started with, or two-fifths Dutch's original amount. Dutch's original number, when increased by 20, is six-fifths, and 20 is one-fifth of the original amount. Therefore, each boy started with 100 marbles. When the game was over Dutch had 40 marbles and Spike had 160 marbles.

**"Balloon" Puzzle (page 102).** You can arrange the numbers in several ways. Here's how we did it: One arm is 3, 6, 9, 7, 2; the other arm is 5, 4, 9, 8, 1. The 9, of course, appears in both arms.

**"Wine" Puzzle (page 103).** At the start, barrel A contained 66 pints of wine and barrel B contained 30 pints of wine.

**"Domino" Puzzle (page 104).**

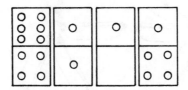

**"Primate" Puzzle (page 105).** They are five gorillas, 25 apes, and 70 lemurs.

**"After Dinner" Puzzle (page 106).** This puzzle is the work of England's greatest puzzle creator, Henry Dudeney, Figure A shows the original triangle and the five pieces that it is to be cut into. Piece 1 is the first of the four smaller triangles. Figures B, C, and D show how the other three triangles are formed from some of the pieces. A very interesting puzzle.

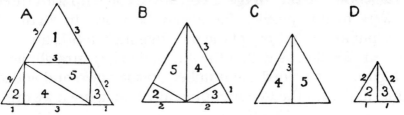

**"Tinsmith" Puzzle (page 107).**

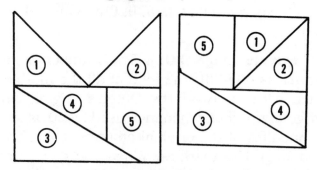

**"Hot Dog" Puzzle (page 108).** The drawing here explains all. Do you want your prize with kraut or piccalilli?

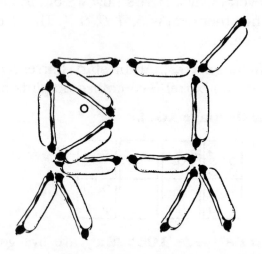

**"Chemistry" Puzzle (page 109).** Jimmy is not about to burn any holes in his mother's carpet, nor will he have any trouble finding uses for *HIJKLMNO*. Jimmy is just having fun with his mother. The compound should be read *H* to *O*, or $H_2O$, or water, since the compound's name is comprised of the letters in the alphabet from *H* through *O*.

**"Vitascope" Puzzle (page 110).** We've come up with three answers to this puzzle. There may be more. In Figure 1 we've put an "S" in front of the nine making it a *SIX*, an even number. We didn't say that the line had to be a straight line. In Figure 2 we turned the number upside down and added a line, making it the Roman numeral 12. In figure 3 we drew a straight line through the middle of the number. This makes the top half a Roman numeral 4, and, if you turn the paper upside down, the bottom half a Roman numeral 6.

SIX        XII        +X-

**Fig. 1**      **Fig. 2**      **Fig. 3**

**"What" Puzzles (page 111).** The answers are: (1) A joke. (2) An old deck of cards. (3) A donkey. (4) A baseball team. (5) Tulips. (6) Those who cannot write. (7) Hailing Taxis.

**"Triangle" Puzzle (page 112).** Just remove the bars indicated by the broken lines. You'll be left with four small triangles and one large one. I never said the triangles had to be the same size.

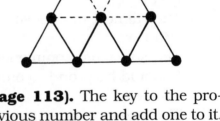

**"Thinking Cap" Puzzle (page 113).** The key to the progression is to double the previous number and add one to it. Thus, 2 times 5 plus 1 equals 11, 2 times 11 plus 1 equals 23, 2 times 23 plus 1 equals 47, the answer.

**"Spelling" Puzzle (page 114).** Mehitabel instantly saw that the answer was the word *INKSTAND. KST* appears in the middle. *In* begins the word (the question stated "*in* the beginning") and *and* ended the word (the question stated "*and* at the end"). The answer was really childishly simple.

**"Movie Star" Puzzle (page 115).** This is one hard puzzle! Ima is $27\frac{1}{2}$ years old, and Sucha is $16\frac{1}{2}$. To get the answer, you have to work backward. It also takes a lot of trial and error to arrive at the correct starting ages when working backward. When Sucha was $5\frac{1}{2}$ years old, Ima was $16\frac{1}{2}$. When Sucha is three times that age, she will be $49\frac{1}{2}$ years old. Half of this is $24\frac{3}{4}$, and when Ima was that age, Sucha was $13\frac{3}{4}$. Thus, Ima's age is twice this, or $27\frac{1}{2}$.

**"Statuette" Puzzle (page 116).** I'm afraid Calvin took a loss on the deal. His profit on the first statuette came to $18. (Dividing $198 by 11 will give you the 10 percent profit.) However, his 10 percent loss on the second statuette came to $22. (Dividing $198 by 9 will give you the 10 percent loss.) Thus, the $22 loss minus the $18 profit nets a $4 loss overall.

**"Travel" Puzzle (page 117).** The *hidden places* are:

1. He thinks I *am her st*upid sister. (Amherst)
2. Let no woma*n or man dy*e his or her hair. (Normandy)
3. His overwrough*t exas*peration filled the enemy with dismay. (Texas)
4. The wounded were brought in *nine veh*icles. (Nineveh)
5. The calmest man is sometimes *made ira*te. (Madeira)
6. The *sale m*ust commence at one o'clock. (Salem)
7. I should be proud to entertain suc*ha gue*st. (The Hague)
8. The escaping prisoners crossed the ri*ver on a* raft. (Verona)
9. He ha*s my R. N. a*s a monogram on all his notepaper. (Smyrna)
10. He must cross the Atlanti*c or k*eep quiet. (Cork)

**"Radio" Puzzle (page 118).** The word DOZENS. Take away one letter, the S, and you have DOZEN, which of course is twelve.

**"Checkbook" Puzzle (page 120).** There is no reason why the totals of the two sides of the ledger should ever be the same. The total of the balances on the ledger's right side have nothing to do with a total of the sums withdrawn from the account.

**"Checkerboard" Puzzle (page 121).** White to move and win: (26 to 22), (18 to 25), (21 to 17), (14 to 21), (19 to 16), (12 to 26), (27 to 31). Black is now completely blocked from moving and, consequently, loses the game.

**"Plywood" Puzzle (page 122).** Cut along the dotted lines and rearrange as shown.

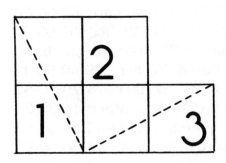 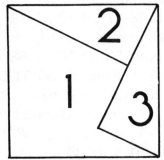

**"Line" Puzzle (page 123).**

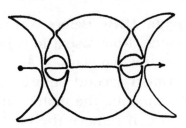

**"Flour" Puzzle (page 124).** On the first shelf exchange sacks (7) and (2). You now have a single sack (2) and a pair (78). Multiplied together we get 156. We then move single sack (5) and exchange it for sack (9) on the middle shelf. The total number on the middle shelf is now 156. Finally, we move sack (9) from the middle shelf down to shelf three, where it

takes the place of sack (4) in the pair. Sack (4) is moved to the right, where it becomes the single sack. Now on shelf three we have (39) times (4), which gives us a product of 156. We did this by moving only five sacks.

**"Animal" Puzzle (page 125).** Antelope: 22-33-24-25-16-15-14-4, ape: 22-14-6, bear: 55-46-38-47, beaver: 21-29-38-37-46-47, bison: 21-18-10-11-2, boar: 55-65-66-76, bull: 21-20-12-4, calf: 31-22-12-21, camel: 59-69-78-68-60, cat: 45-44-34, deer: 52-51-42-41, doe: 75-67-68, dog: 75-65-56, donkey: 52-43-53-61-71-72, elk: 68-60-61, elephant: 6-16-25-33-32-22-23-24, fox: 21-11-1, giraffe: 56-48-47-38-30-21-29, goat: 56-65-66-74, hare: 57-66-76-68, hen: 81-71-70, heron: 32-42-41-50-49, hog: 57-65-56, horse: 57-67-76-77-68, Hyena: 81-72-71-70-69, lamb: 16-7-8-9, leopard: 60-51-50-58-66-76-75, lion: 39-40-50-49, lynx: 12-3-2-1, mole: 78-79-80-71, monkey: 78-79-70-61-71-72, otter: 43-34-24-25-26, ox: 11-1, panther: 14-22-23-24-32-42-41, pig: 58-48-56, porcupine: 33-43-35-54-63-62-70, rat: 35-44-34, rhinoceros: 47-57-48-49-50-59-68-76-67-77, seal: 77-68-69-60, squirrel: 17-18-27-36-35-26-25-16, tiger: 74-64-56-46-47, toad: 74-65-66-75 or 34-43-44-52, weasel: 5-6-7-17-25-16, wolf: 5-13-12-21.

**"Glass" Puzzle (page 126).** Before you remove the glass, light the second match. Now, use it to light the head of the match being held by the two glasses. After the head of this match flares up, wait a second or two and blow out the flame. After a few moments, the match should be fused to the glass. Then you can remove the other glass, and the match will remain suspended in air. That's how J. Wellington took the guys down at Bits and Grits Coffee Shop.

**"Paper" Puzzle (page 127).** The length of the fold is 11.57 inches. The answer can be calculated from the measurements of two right triangles using the Pythagorean theorem (the square of the hypotenuse of a right triangle equals the sum of the squares of the other two sides).

Let's start with the small triangle at point $B$ on the paper (see figure 1). All calculations are rounded to two decimal places. Subtract 10.16 inches from 11 inches, which gives us .84 inches, the side of the small triangle. Now square .84, which gives us .71 square inches. Square the hypotenuse, 1.38, which gives us 1.90 square inches.

Subtract .71 from 1.90, which gives us 1.19 square inches. Taking the square root of this will give us 1.09 inches, the base of the triangle.

Now, look at figure 2. Add the 1.09 inches to the 3.82 inches on the right side of the paper, which gives us 4.91 inches. Subtract this 4.91 inches from the paper's width, 8.5 inches, witch equals 3.59 inches, the side of our second triangle. Square 3.59 inches, which gives us 12.89 square inches. Square the 11-inch base; that gives us 121 square inches. Add 12.89 and 121 square inches, which equals 133.89 square inches. Then, take the square root of this figure, and you will get the answer to our problem— 11.57 inches for the length of the line A–B.

Harriet should be running the company and not stuck in the secretarial pool, but will Herbert ever be able to swallow his pride?

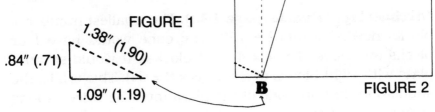

**FIGURE 1**

**FIGURE 2**

**"Division" Puzzle (page 128).**

```
         971
55 | 51463
     477
     376
     371
      53
      53
```

**"Hardware" Puzzle (page 129).** Nine washers are equal in weight to one bolt.

**"Age" Puzzle (page 130).** Madge is 30 years old; her sister Veronica is 10 years old.

**"Chess" Puzzle (page 131).**

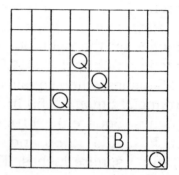

**"Antique" Puzzle (page 132).** There may be other solutions to this puzzle, but this is the only one the author knows.

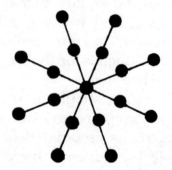

**"Archaeology" Puzzle (page 133).** The smallest number of blocks needed would be 128. The cube would have four blocks on a side (4 × 4 × 4 = 64 blocks). It would sit on a plaza with eight blocks to a side (8 × 8 = 64). This fulfills the stipulation that one side of the plaza must be twice as long as one side of the cube.

**"Number" Puzzle (page 134).**

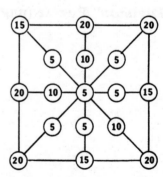

**"Dot" Puzzle (page 135).**

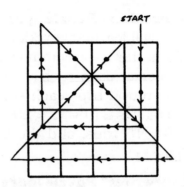

**"Rebus" Puzzle (page 136).** The answer is: To be always over "confident" in the midst of EXAMS diminishes ("dim" in "ISHES") one's chances for success in them (4 6 s in "THEM").

**"Floating Paper" Puzzle (page 137).** If you bet on this puzzle, you'd better make your first bet a large one, because this solution will only work once. Simply take sheet *a* and crumple it into a ball. When released, the crumpled sheet will drop straight down to the floor while sheet *b* will slowly float down.

**"Magic Square" Puzzle (page 138).**

| 16 | 3 | 2 | 13 |
|----|----|----|----|
| 5 | 10 | 11 | 8 |
| 9 | 6 | 7 | 12 |
| 4 | 15 | 14 | 1 |

**"Newspaper" Puzzle (page 139).** To solve this one, we've resorted to a mixture of English and Roman numerals. Devious, but it works.

$$
\begin{array}{r}
\text{SIX} \quad \text{IX} \quad \text{XL} \\
- \ \text{IX} \quad \text{X} \quad \underline{\text{L}} \\
\hline
\text{S} \quad\ \ \text{I} \quad\ \ \text{X}
\end{array}
$$

**"Steamship" Puzzle (page 140).** The next time all three ships will leave New York on the same day is 240 days later. This is the least common multiple of 12, 16, and 20, the number of days each completes a round trip. As for how many round trips each ship makes in this period, the first ship makes 240 ÷ 12 = 20 trips, the second ship makes 240 ÷ 16 = 15 trips, and the third ship makes 240 ÷ 20 = 12 trips.

**"Typewriter" Puzzle (page 141).** The answer to the doodle words are (1) hang-up, (2) dunderhead, (3) once upon a time, (4) head over heels in love, (5) day in, day out, (6) Sopwith Camel, (7) Unfinished Symphony, and (8) double bed.

**"Gold Bar" Puzzle (page 142).** The fewest number of pieces needed to cut the bar into are five. The pieces would measure one, two, four, eight, and sixteen inches in length. Using a combination of these five pieces, Patrick could always add an inch of gold to his daily bill at the Northern Lights Saloon. At the end of February and the months with just 30 days, Patrick used leftover gold to tip the waiters and show girls. What class!

**"Chicken" Puzzle (page 143).** On a regular day, Amy and Bessie brought in $15.00 and $10.00 for a total of $25.00. When Bessie brought the 60 chickens to market everything went fine until she ran out of Amy's chickens. Two of her chickens, together with three of Amy's were gone, she had to start selling the remaining ten chickens, which were hers. Since Bessie's chickens were worth $2.50 for five, she lost 50 cents for each of the last two transactions. I hope that she was able to convince Amy that she hadn't been cheated.

**"Progression" Puzzle (page 144).** The key to the progression is the number *3*. You must subtract 3, divide by 3, add 3, subtract 3, divide by 3, add 3, etc. Starting with hole 1, we subtract 3 from 12 and get 9, the score for hole 2. We then divide the 9 by 3 and get 3, the score for hole 3. We then add 3 to 3 to get 6, the score for hole 4. We then subtract 3 from 6 to get 3, the score for hole 5. We then divide 3 by 3 to get 1, the score for hole 6. Finally, for hole 7, we add 3 to 1 to get 4, the answer to the problem.

**"Coin" Puzzle (page 145).** The smallest number of coins needed to pay the exact cost of any item from one cent through one dollar is nine. The coins are: 4 pennies, 1 nickel, 2 dimes, 1 quarter, and 1 half dollar.

**"Logo" Puzzle (page 146).** First, fold a sheet of paper as shown in figure 1. Next, draw the three connecting lines. Now, without moving the pen, unfold the paper as shown in figure 2. You can now complete the logo without going over any line more than once and without lifting the pen from the paper.

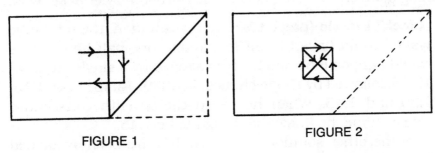

FIGURE 1     FIGURE 2

**"Rug" Puzzle (page 147).** He cut along the dotted lines shown in figure 1. Then he shifted the top half of the rug to the left and down, where it neatly fitted into the bottom half of the rug (figure 2). A few deft stitches with the old needle and thread and Abdul had sewn a perfect carpet before sundown.

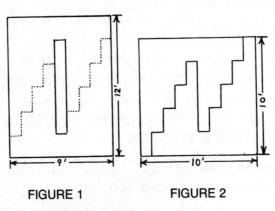

FIGURE 1     FIGURE 2

**"Gulliver" Puzzle (page 148).** The five "little airy creatures" hidden in the poem are the vowels *a, e, i, o,* and *u.* You'll find *a* in the word *glass, e* in the word *jet, i* in the work *tin, o* in the word *box,* and *u* in the word *you.* Swift called them airy because their sound is formed by air passing over the vocal cords when you say them.

**"Political" Puzzle (page 149).** Starting with the *T* on the left side, at the bottom of the frame, read around the frame clockwise. The campaign slogan comes from the 1840 presidential election when William Henry Harrison ran against Martin Van Buren. It was "Tippecanoe and Tyler, Too." *Tippecanoe* was a river in Indiana where Harrison fought some Native Americans, and *Tyler* was John Tyler, his running mate on the Whig ticket. The Harrison–Tyler ticket won.

**"Clock" Puzzle (page 150).** In one solution, the total time Waldo would have to wait is one and one-half hours. This would happen if he had been awakened by a single chime at 12:15, followed by single chimes at 12:30, 12:45, 1:00, 1:15, 1:30 and 1:45. When he heard the seventh consecutive single chime, he knew that it had to be 1:45.

In the other solution, Waldo could have been awakened by the last chime of 12:00. In this case, he would have to wait a full hour and three-quarters before he could be sure of the correct time.

**"Toy Box" Puzzle (page 151).** The length was 12 inches, the width, 10 inches, and the height, 8 inches.

**"Sports" Puzzle (page 152).** The outdoor sports are (1) CROQUET, (2) SOCCER, (3) BOCCIE, (4) FOOTBALL, (5) VOLLEYBALL, (6) TENNIS, (7) LACROSSE, (8) RACING, (9) STEEPLECHASE, (10) SHOOTING, (11) ARCHERY, (12) BOBSLEDDING (13) HOCKEY, (14) SAILING, (15) SKATING, (16) FISHING, (17) BIKING, (18) BALLOONING, (19) BASEBALL, (20) QUOITS, (21) HANDBALL, (22) RUGBY, (23) CRICKET, and (24) SWIMMING.

**"Word" Puzzle (page 153).** The word that Barlowe came up with is *attenuate* (at-ten-u-ate).

**"King" Puzzle (page 154).** The king was *David*. In Roman numerals *500* was "D." The first of all letters is *A*, and the first of all figures (Roman numerals, again) is *I*. Finally, five in the middle is *V*. Put them together and you have *DAVID*.

**"Racing" Puzzle (page 155).** The professor should bet as follows: $12 on Sway Belly, $15 on Aunt Sara, and $20 on Thunder Hooves, Of course, if any other horse comes in first, the professor is out of luck.

**"Nationality" Puzzle (page 156).** Myra was indicating that the lady was *Singhalese* (single *E*'s).

**"Route" Puzzle (page 157).** This solution is the one that this author knows. There may be others.

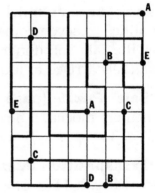

**"Inspirational" Puzzle (page 158).** And the message is: "To be overtenacious in the midst of trifles is the mark of a mean understanding."

**"Hopscotch" Puzzle (page 159).** What makes this puzzle so hard is that you must start at point *X* or at point *Y*. Did you chalk up a win here?

**"Wooden Match" Puzzle (page 160).** If we used the matches to form an equilateral triangle, the area within the triangle would be 8 inches times 6 inches divided by two, which is 24 inches (8" × 6" ÷ 2 = 24"). By stepping four of the matches in, as shown in the diagram, we drop 12

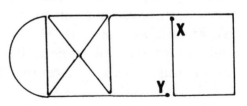

square inches of area, which leaves us with an enclosed area of 21 square inches, the solution required.

**"Circle" Puzzle (page 161).** Substitute the following numbers for letters: a = 2, b = 11, c = 8, d = 1, e = 14, f = 4, h = 13, i = 5, and j = 9.

**"Bread" Puzzle (page 162).** Since the bread was consumed equally by three men, then each one at $2^2/_3$ loaves. That means that the native with three loaves to start with only gave up $^1/_3$ of a loaf to Forsythe, while the native with five loaves gave up $2^1/_3$ loaves. This native then gave up seven times as much bread as the first native, so he was entitled to seven coins and the first native to one coin. This is the fair solution to the problem. Whether the natives actually arrived at it or not, we shall never know.

**"Safe" Puzzle (page 163).** Timothy must have had a bad memory indeed, if he couldn't remember 37—37—37. $37 \times 3 = 111.$    $37 \times 6 = 222.$    $37 \times 9 = 333.$

**"Transposition Puzzle (page 164).** The 22 moves are: 10 to 5, 1 to 8, 11 to 6, 2 to 9, 12 to 7, 3 to 4, 5 to 12, 8 to 3, 6 to 1, 9 to 10, 7 to 6, 4 to 9, 12 to 7, 3 to 4, 1 to 8, 10 to 5, 6 to 1, 9 to 10, 7 to 2, 4 to 11, 8 to 3, 5 to 12.

**"Poker Chip" Puzzle (page 165).** The most even rows that can be formed that we know about are 16. The drawing at right shows their placement. It's possible to arrange them differently, but the results will be the same.

**"Square" Puzzle (page 166).**

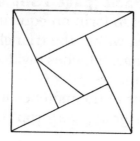

**"What?" Puzzle (page 167).** (1) the letter *n*, (2) a yardstick, (3) a police car, (4) a lawsuit, (5) music.

**"Moving" Puzzle (page 168).** First, light the fourth match, and then use it to light the heads of the three upright matches. Quickly extinguish the flames of all four matches. You will find that the heads of the pyramid matches have fused together, so that you can easily lift them from the table with the fourth match.

**"Cork Puzzle (page 169).** Fill the glass nearly to the top, and then place the cork in the water. Now, carefully pour more water into the glass until the water level is slightly above the glass's rim. If done with care, the surface tension of the liquid will allow the water to form a slightly convex shape. The cork will then "float" uphill to the center of the glass and stay there.

**"Rectangle" Puzzle (page 170).** You can draw 20 rectangles using the 12 black dots in the illustration. The two that everyone seems to miss are shown here. I hope that you didn't miss them.

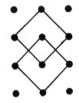

**"Ballooning" Puzzle (page 171).** The word hanging from the right balloon that should be moved over to the left balloon is . . . *DUNE*. All the words on the left can be preceded by *SAND*. Thus we have *SANDBAG*, *SANDBANK*, *SANDSTORM*, and *SANDBAR*. Add *DUNE* and we get *SAND-DUNE*.

**"Suitcase" Puzzle (page 172).** The Frontenacs placed two objects inside the suitcase. In the half that hung over the table edge, they placed a large piece of pig iron. At the other end of the case, they placed a large block of ice. The weight of the ice, plus the leverage gained by its being placed over the table, more than offset the pig iron's weight. However, as the ice melted,

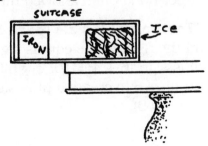

the water became evenly distributed throughout the suitcase, which caused the end with the pig iron to become heavy enough to tip the case off the table. This was certainly one of the most novel timing devices used in the entertainment world.

**"A to Z" Puzzle (page 173).**

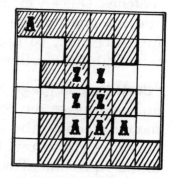

**"Submarine Net" Puzzle (page 174).** The fewest number of cuts needed to divide the net in two is eight. Starting at Section *A*, snip your way down to section *B*.

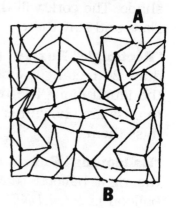

**"Will" Puzzle (page 175).** I'm afraid that the earl was more extravagant than anyone thought. It seems that he left his heirs . . . *nothing*.

**"Film" Puzzle (page 176).** That Christmas, Grandpa Townsend invited 16 relatives over, and one roll of the new super Kodak film allowed him to take 60 pictures.

**"Toothpick" Puzzle (page 177).** Shift the single toothpick on the right of the equals sign left to make the minus into a plus sign (6 + 4 = 10) *or* shift the single toothpick from the number *6* to create a plus sign from the original minus sign (5 + 4 = 9).

**"Billiard Ball" Puzzle (page 178).** The following four-move combination is a sure winner.

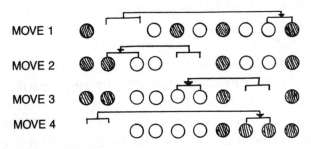

**"Keyboard" Puzzle (page 179).** The answer we were looking for is *TYPEWRITER*, but there are a few more ten-letter words that you can type from this single row of keys.

**"Doggie" Puzzle (page 180).** Fold the large link (b) in figure 1, and slip the small link over the end marked *d*. Now, hang the dog on the link as shown in figure 1, and slip the small link back over the end (d), then down onto the dog. Open up the large link and the puzzle is finished (figure 2). Hint: When you fold the large link just bend it; do not crease it. That way, when you open it out, there will be no indication that the large link was ever folded.

FIGURE 1

FIGURE 2

**"Astronomical" Puzzle (page 182).** I hope you didn't go ballistic trying to solve this one.

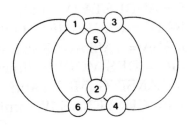

**"Abracadabra" Puzzle (page 183).** Starting at the top *A*, you have two ways to reach the row below. In turn, when going from either of the two *B*'s to the next row, you have four ways to reach the third row. Each succeeding row has twice as many ways of being reached. There are 10 steps below the top *A*. So, if you multiply 1 × 2, and then multiply the result by 2, and then multiply the new result again by 2—and if you do this 10 times altogether—you will get the number of possibilities, which is 1,024. This can be expressed mathematically as $2^{10}$, or $2 \times 2 \times 2 \times 2 \times 2 \times 2 \times 2 \times 2 \times 2 \times 2$.

**"Billiards" Puzzle (page 184).** During his five turns at the table he sank 8, 14, 20, 26, and 32 balls.

**"Egyptian" Puzzle (page 185).** Make the cuts where indicated in the figure on the left. The figure on the right shows how they are fitted back together into a square.

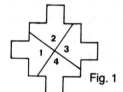
Fig. 1

Fig. 2

**"Age" Puzzle (page 186).** Ned was 60 when he graduated. It's rumored that he's active in Florida, in the Senior Citrus Sports League.

**"Rearranging Bee" Puzzle (page 187).** Six out of nine will get you an honorable mention:

1) OTKTLCIREL = LITTLE ROCK (Arkansas);
2) ARFRDHOT = HARTFORD (Connecticut);
3) PLGERSINFID = SPRINGFIELD (Illinois);
4) UAGATUS = AUGUSTA (Maine);
5) MSOCNARATE = SACRAMENTO (California);
6) HLEATESLASA = TALLAHASSEE (Florida);
7) ENSDSEMIO = DES MOINES (Iowa);
8) NILGANS = LANSING (Michigan);
9) YEECNEHN = CHEYENNE (Wyoming).

**"Gong" Puzzle (page 188).** Cross the cuts to divide the gong into five pieces.

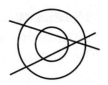

**"Substitution" Puzzle (page 189).** Pop got the following answer before they hit the first saltwater-taffy shop:

$$\begin{array}{r} 96{,}233 \\ +\ 62{,}513 \\ \hline 158{,}746 \end{array}$$

**"Math" Puzzle (page 190).** For the car polishers, and answer is:

$$\begin{array}{r} 173 \\ 4 \\ \hline 177 \end{array} \qquad \begin{array}{r} 85 \\ 92 \\ \hline 177 \end{array}$$

**"Coin Counter" Puzzle (page 191).** The fifty coins were: 40 pennies, eight nickels, and two dimes, for a total of $0.40 + $0.40 + $0.20 = $1.00.

**"Candy Store" Puzzle (page 192).** Hermione bought the following items:

| | | |
|---|---|---|
| 14 Jawbreakers | . . . . . . . . . . | $0.07 |
| 8 Stick candies | . . . . . . . . . | .08 |
| 2 Peerless butterscotch | . . . | .05 |
| 1 Cream chocolate drop | . . | .05 |
| 25 pieces of candy | . . . . . . | $0.25 |

**"Kite" Puzzle (page 193).** There are 17 squares in the kite. They are made up of four different-size squares. The number of each is:

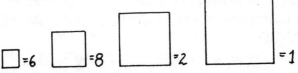

**"Soda Straw" Puzzle (page 194).**

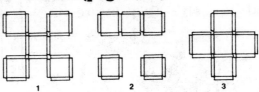

**"Hidden Word" Puzzles (page 195).** The first location is Bangor: "Rubens, just look at the super*b Angor*a cat!"
The second is Sing Sing: "Wonderful! He plays in A flat and she *sings in G* sharp!"

**"Bank Robber" Puzzle (page 196).** Starting with the *"B"* on the left side of the picture, read around the frame clockwise. Willie's famous quote says, "Because that's where the money is!"

**"Santa" Puzzle (page 197).** This is one of 14 possible solutions.

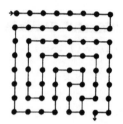

**"Packing Case" Puzzle (page 198).** For solids with plane surfaces and no holes in them, the sum of the faces and the corners is two more than the number of edges. Therefore, the packing case had nine faces.

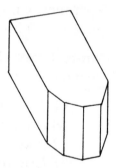

**"Puzzle Machine" Puzzle (page 199).** The word that doesn't fit is CHARCOAL. Remove this word from the column of words, and the first and last letters in each of the remaining words spell out the name GRETA GARBO.

**G**AN**G**
**R**EGATT**A**
**E**DUCATO**R**
**T**AXICA**B**
**A**KIMB**O**

**"Magic Square" Puzzle (page 200).** This is one of many ways that the numbers can be arranged to solve this interesting puzzle.

| 4 | 1 | 3 | 0 | 2 |
|---|---|---|---|---|
| 3 | 0 | 2 | 4 | 1 |
| 2 | 4 | 1 | 3 | 0 |
| 1 | 3 | 0 | 2 | 4 |
| 0 | 2 | 4 | 1 | 3 |

**"Knight's Tour" Puzzle (page 201).**

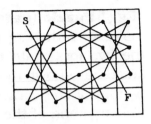

**"Line" Puzzle (page 202).**

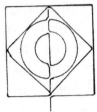

**"Cross" Puzzle (page 203).**

**"Racing" Puzzle (page 204).** Harry, Larry, Barry, and Bert could ride one mile in $1/6$, $1/9$, $1/12$, and $1/15$ of an hour, respectively. Therefore, they could ride around once in $1/18$, $1/27$, $1/36$, and $1/45$ of an hour, respectively. This would enable them to meet for the first time in $1/9$ of an hour ($6\frac{2}{3}$ minutes). Four times $6\frac{2}{3}$ minutes is $26\frac{2}{3}$ minutes, which is the amount of time that would elapse before they met for the fourth time.

**"Toy" Puzzle (page 205).**

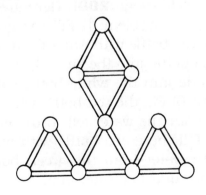

**"Egg" Puzzle (page 206).** To start with, make sure the egg is hard-boiled. Thrust the two forks into the cork at 60-degree angles, as shown in the picture. Hollow the bottom of the cork, so it fits snugly over the large end of the egg. Now pick up the egg, with the cork and forks on top of it, and place it on top of the end of the cane. With a little adjusting, you should be able to balance everything nicely, walk to the table, and scoop up your winnings.

**"Snake" Puzzle (page 207).**
This puzzle was invented by England's greatest puzzler, Henry Dudeney, back at the turn of the century. Unlike most line puzzles, this picture cannot be drawn using just one continuous line. It takes 12 lines to complete it. This puzzle asks for the longest of these lines. In the drawing at right, the line starting at *A*

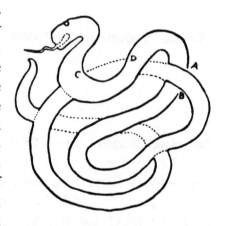

and ending at *B* is the answer. The other 11 lines are shown as dotted lines. Dotted line *C–D* is shorter than the solid line *C–D*, and was not used. This is an unusual puzzle. I've never seen another like it.

**"Measuring" Puzzle (page 208).** Here are the nine steps used in solving this problem: 1) Fill the green bottle with water. 2) Fill the red bottle with water from the green bottle. 3) Empty the red bottle into the sink. 4) Pour the water left in the green bottle into the white bottle. 5) Fill the green bottle with water. 6) Fill the red bottle with water from the green bottle. 7) Pour the water left in the green bottle into white bottle. 8) Fill the green bottle with water. 9) Fill the white bottle with water from the green bottle. The green bottle now has one quart of water in it.

**"Adam and Eve" Puzzle (page 209).** The answer is:

$$\frac{242}{303} = .798679867986798679867986\ldots$$

**"Taffy" Puzzle (page 210).** This is a tough one, so I guess Mrs. Murbles still has most of her taffy left. Here's how it's done: Divide up 21 candies so there are five on each of nine lines. Each appears in more than one line.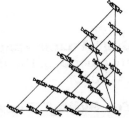

**"Transpositional" Puzzle (page 211).** Here's our answer to this puzzle: 1 to 4, 7 to 1, 6 to 7, 5 to 6, 3 to 5, 2 to 3, 1 to 2, 7 to 1, 6 to 7, 5 to 6, 3 to 5, 2 to 3, 1 to 2, 7 to 1, 4 to 7.

**"Domino" Puzzle (page 212).** The answer is a snap, indeed. Place domino *B* on its side in front of the tower. Position it so that, when made to stand upright, it will hit the edge of domino *A*. Reach your first finger in through the arch of the tower. Place your finger on the top edge of

domino *B*. Press down tightly on the domino, until it "snaps" up and smartly strikes domino *A*. Domino *A* will fly out of the tower. The pieces above it will drop down on the two upright ones, keeping the tower intact. This may take a little practice to master.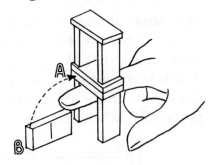

**"Executive" Puzzle (page 213).** The picture here tells all. You can make this puzzle by cutting eight cardboard squares all the same size. Next, cut four square in half, cutting on the diagonal, to make the triangles.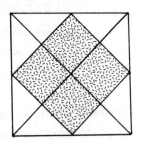

**"Rebus" Puzzle (page 214).**

First rebus: There's nothing like a good SQUARE MEAL!
Second rebus: You can't miss with AN INSIDE JOB!
Third rebus: A HOLE IN ONE!

**"Hero" Puzzle (page 215).** Here is the "hero's" answer:

$$\begin{array}{r} 98,765 \\ \underline{1,234} \\ 99,999 \end{array}$$

**"Bug" Puzzle (page 216).** There are 5,040 different arrangements of the letters LADYBUG. (7 × 6 × 5 × 4 × 3 × 2 × 1 = 5,040)

**"Toe Skiing" Puzzle (page 217).** A six-pointed star wins the day. Note the six small triangles and two large ones.

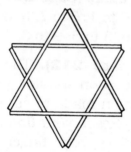

**"Fencing" Puzzle (page 218).** Looking at the whole fence from the road, every nine-foot section starts with a fence post on the left. All except the last section on the right, which starts with a fence post on the left and ends with a fence post on the right. Syms should have bought 34 fence posts, not 33. The rest of the order was correct.

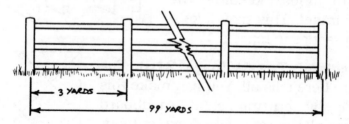

**"Party" Puzzle (page 219).** Here is one solution, starting at plate one, closest to the boy's hand: Move 1 to 4, 5 to 8, 9 to 12, 3 to 6, 7 to 10, and 11 to 2. Continue around the table to plate 1. You have now gone around the table three times. It's easy to solve this puzzle in four revolutions. Any solution using only three revolutions is considered a winner.

**"Battery" Puzzle (page 220).** Here is one way to solve this electrifying problem:

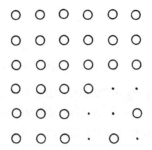

**"Teddy Bear" Puzzle (page 221).** They started by selling bears at three for $10. The first woman sold 30 bears for $100; the second sold 24 bears for $80; and the third sold 21 bears for $70. In the afternoon, they switched to one bear for $10. The first woman sold her last three bears for $30; the second sold her remaining five bears for $50; and the third sold her remaining six bears for $60. Thus, they each raised $130.

**"Medical" Puzzle (page 222).** The 10 most common body parts, which Doc Stall came up with, are: arm, ear, eye, gum, hip, jaw, leg, lip, rib, and toe.

**"Clock" Puzzle (page 223).** The answer is 11 times. Every hour, they meet about five minutes later than the previous hour. Starting at noon, the next times they'll meet are 1:05; 2:10; 3:16, 4:21; 5:27; 6:32; 7:38; 8:43; 9:49; 10:54; 12:00.

**"Robot" Puzzle (page 224).** The following is the solution that Robbie's internal computer came up with.

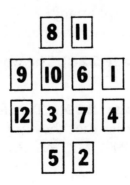

**"Stove" Puzzle (page 225).** The rebus goes like this:

(If) (the)   (B)   (empty) (put)   (:)
If   the  grate be  empty,   put  coal on.

(If) (the)   (B)   (full)  (.)  (putting)   (:)
If   the  grate be  full,  stop  putting  coal on.

**"Plywood" Puzzle (page 226).** Hiram will save the day if he makes the cuts indicated by the dotted lines in figure 1. He can then slide the top piece down, and to the right, thus forming the solid sheet pictured in figure 2.

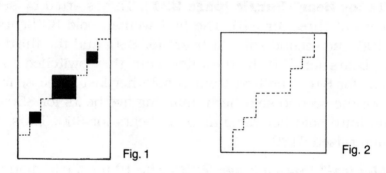

Fig. 1                    Fig. 2

**"Anagram" Puzzle (page 227).** The answers are:

1) Thelma = Hamlet
2) to love ruin = revolution
3) great help = telegraph
4) best in prayer = Presbyterian
5) a stew, sir? = waitress
6) Erin lad = Ireland
7) mad policy = diplomacy
8) moon-starers = astronomers

**"Spanish" Puzzle (page 228).** The word is *castanet* (cast a net).

**"Sailor" Puzzle (page 229).** The following words will explain it all. In the order that they appear we have: BIGHT, LIGHT, NIGHT, HEIGHT, MIGHT, RIGHT, SIGHT, TIGHT, FIGHT.

**"Dog Biscuit" Puzzle (page 230).** No growling if you missed this one.

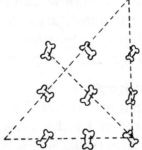

**"Carousel" Puzzle (page 231).** First, move in one direction only. Second, after you turn a coin over, skip the next coin before starting your next count.

**"Charade" Puzzle (page 232).** The first hint refers to a *mat*. The second to *rye*. The third, of course, was *money*. The whole then would be *mat-rye-money* (matrimony), which is certainly a *united state!*

**"Counting" Puzzle (page 233).** The three correct answers are: *thirty-one*, *thirty-three*, and *22*.

**"Scholar" Puzzle (page 234).** First scholar: The misspelled word is "*mispelled.*" Second scholar: The daughter's age today is 22.

**"Rumor" Puzzle (page 235).** Spoken like a real gentleman. The man's reply was, "Madam, I am above making mischief between man and wife."

**"Trolley" Puzzle (page 236).** It's possible to pare Barton's mileage down to 19 miles. He only needs to go over two lines twice. Our solution starts him off at station *E*. The journey goes as follows: *E, I, J, K, J, F, B, C, B, A, E, F, G, H, D, C, G, K, L, H.* The two lines that he goes over twice are *JK* and *BC*. You can change this route but never shorten it.

**"Cologne Bottle" Puzzle (page 237).** First, measure the height of the liquid in the bottle. Next, turn the bottle upside down and measure the height of the column of air in the bottle. Add these two heights together, and you get the height of an imaginary cylinder. Now, divide the height of the liquid by the height of the cylinder to get the percentage of volume of space inside the bottle that is filled with liquid. Let's say the height of the imaginary cylinder is five inches, and the height of the liquid is four inches. Four divided by five gives 80 percent, the volume of space filled by the liquid.

**"Progression" Puzzle (page 238).** The numbers are part of the series one through six. To get the value of a number, multiply the series number by the value of the preceding number. Thus, two is $2 \times 1$; six is $2 \times 3$; 24 is $6 \times 4$. The seventh series number is 5,040, or $720 \times 7$.

**"Contest" Puzzle (page 239).** The total number of coins in the jug is 2,521.

**"Robbery" Puzzle (page 240).** The travelling bag contained a half-dollar, 39 dimes, and 60 pennies.

**"Playing Card" Puzzle (page 241).** Professor Pepper's next slide revealed the following three cards: ace of diamonds, king of hearts, and two of spades.

**"Barber" Puzzle (page 242).** Henri would rather cut the hair of two Germans, because he makes twice as much money on two haircuts as on one! Since Henri was so well groomed and there is only one other barber in town, he must go to Pierre for haircuts. Pierre always needs a haircut because he's stuck with Henri, who's always too busy to cut his hair. So, if you visit that town, get your hair cut by Pierre.

**"Number" Puzzle (page 244).**

$$55^5/_5$$

**"Ornament" Puzzle (page 245).** Before cutting the string, take a loop of cord in the middle and knot it firmly together. Now take a pair of scissors and snip through the loop. As you promised, you have cut the string in two without causing any harm to the ornament. I'll take the red Mercedes, please!

**"Card" Puzzle (page 246).** The explanation is simplicity itself. Just be sure that the total of the first card plus the third card adds up to the value of the middle card. Simple . . . but very, very good!

**"Cross" Puzzle (page 247).** Here's the solution Sexton Winslow was looking for.

**"Business Survey" Puzzle (page 248).** Let's break down the results of Sylvester's mustard survey.

(1) Of the 234 people who use hot mustard, 90 of them only use hot mustard (234 – 144 = 90).
(2) Of the 213 people who use mild mustard, 69 of them only use mild mustard (213 – 144 = 69).

This means that we had 3 groups of people:

| | |
|---|---|
| (1) Those who used only hot mustard | = 90 |
| (2) Those who used only mild mustard | = 69 |
| (3) Those who used both hot and mild mustard | = 144 |
| | Total = 303 people |

Sylvester's figure indicate that 303 people had been surveyed, but their report stated that only 300 had been interviewed. Obviously, their report is flawed, something that the Volcano Mustard Company couldn't tolerate.

**"Water and Wine" Puzzle (page 249).** The answer is that there is as much water in the wine glass as there is wine in the water glass. The proof goes like this:

(1) Let's say that each glass contains 100 units of liquid and that the spoon holds 10 units of liquid.

(2) With the spoon Percy transfers 10 units of water from the water glass to the wine glass and stirs them both together.

(3) The wine glass now contains 110 units of liquid. When Percy now takes a spoonful of liquid from this glass he will be removing $1/11$ of each liquid. Thus he will have $9^1/11$ units of wine and $10/11$ units of water in his spoon. This he pours into the water glass.

(4) The water glass now contains $90^{10}/11$ units of water and $9^1/11$ units of wine which totals up to 100 units of liquid.

(5) The wine glass contains $90^{10}/11$ units of wine and $9^1/11$ units of water, also 100 units of liquid.

A fair exchange!

**"Planchette" Puzzle (page 250).**

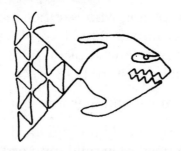

**"India Squares" Puzzle (page 251).** The puzzle measures 8 feet to a side. You'll find the following number of squares:

| | |
|---|---|
| 8 × 8 feet | 1 |
| 6 × 6 feet | 4 |
| 4 × 4 feet | 9 |
| 2 × 2 feet | 18 |
| 1 × 1 feet | 8 |
| Total | 40 squares |

**"Geography" Puzzle (page 252).** The letter in the question is the second *C* in the second line reading across. The four city names radiating from this letter are: Chattanooga, Chicago, Columbus, and Council Bluffs.

**"Cocoa Tin" Puzzle (page 253).** The secret to this problem is sweet indeed. Place the box on a square-topped table with one edge of the tin along one edge of the table. Position the tin one box width away from one corner of the table (the width *a* equals the width *b*). Now, take the ruler and place one end of it on the corner of the table and measure to the left top back corner of the box. This will be equal to the box's major diagonal line.

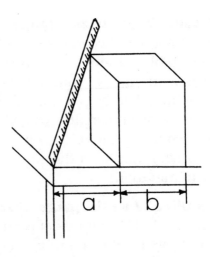

**"Counter" Puzzle (page 254).** The moves are: 2 to 6, 1 to 5, 8 to 2, 7 to 1, 4 to 8, 3 to 7, 10 to 4, 9 to 3, 6 to 10, 5 to 9.

**"Bathtub" Puzzle (page 255).** It will take exactly 5 minutes to fill Ma Bascomb's tub. To solve this problem we must first break down the times into seconds.

(1) The cold water tap takes 400 seconds to fill the tub, which comes to $1/400$ of the tub in 1 second.
(2) The hot water takes 480 seconds, which comes to $1/480$ of the tub in 1 second.
(3) The water drains out of the tub in 800 seconds, which comes to $1/800$ of the tub in 1 second.

If we use 4800 as the common denominator we come up with the equation:

$$\frac{12}{4800} + \frac{10}{4800} - \frac{6}{4800} = \frac{16}{4800} = \frac{1}{300}$$

This is equal to the net amount of water added to the tub every second. Thus, it will take 300 seconds, or 5 minutes, to fill the tub.

**"Touching" Puzzle (page 256).** First arrange two coins touching on the table. Then place two more coins on top so that all four are touching. Lastly, place the fifth coin upright as shown and you will have five coins all touching. All coins, of course, must be of the same size or denomination.

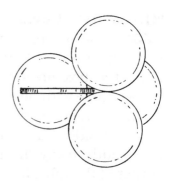

**"Milling" Puzzle (page 257).** Angus will have to bring exactly $111\frac{1}{9}$ pounds of corn to the mill if he wants to walk away with 100 pounds of cornmeal. (111.111 pounds minus 10% equals 100 pounds.)

**"Soda Straws" Puzzle (page 258).** Add the five straws to the ones on the table so that they spell out the number nine. How else?

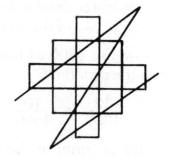

**"Math" Puzzle (page 259).**

$$123 - 45 - 67 + 89 = 100$$

**"Magic Square" Puzzle (page 260).** The answer to the Magic Square is 2, 3, 1 in the first row; 1, 2, 3 in the middle row; and 3, 1, 2 in the last row. Or, 3, 1, 2 in the first row; 1, 2, 3 in the middle row; and 2, 3, 1 in the last row.

**"Sculpture" Puzzle (page 261).**

**"Ports of Call" Puzzle (page 262).** (1) Los Angeles (2) London (3) Rio de Janeiro (4) Lisbon (5) Charleston (6) Marseilles (7) Montego Bay (8) Montevideo (9) Brest (10) Leningrad

**"Shooting" Puzzle (page 263).** The 3 birds are 25, 6, and 19.

**"Zoo" Puzzle (page 264).**

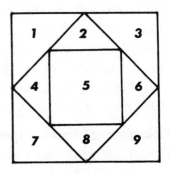

**"Clock" Puzzle (page 265).** Although several answers to this puzzle are possible, this one is usually considered the principal solution to this very old but good problem.

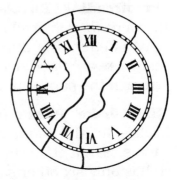

**"Poem" Puzzle (page 266).** Ms. Gotrock's ditty goes like this:

> Too wise you are;
>     too wise you be.
> I see you are
>     too wise for me.

**"Baseball" Puzzle (page 267).** Starting with the "I" on the bottom side of the frame, read around the frame clockwise. The quotation is Yogi Berra's famous observation, "It gets late out there early."

**"Big Fish" Puzzle (page 268).** We calculate that the head was 60 feet long, the tail 180 feet, and the body 240 feet, which gives an overall length of 480 feet. Now, that's some fish story!

**"State" Puzzle (page 269).** The great state of *ALABAMA*, of course!

**"Dice" Puzzle (page 270).** Before you pick up the dice, secretly moisten your right forefinger. Rub this finger across the face of one of the dice. Now place the second die against this moistened face, and press the two dice together with your thumb and forefinger. Still holding the two dice like that, place them across the die on the table and let go. The two dice will stick together and stay balanced on top of the third die. Once again, you've made your point!

**"Shopping" Puzzle (page 271).** She used a fifty, two twenties, a five and four twos.

**"Proofreading" Puzzle (page 272).** The first error is using the word *their* instead of *there*. The second error is spelling *error* as *errer*. The third error is saying, in the paragraph, that there are *three* errors, when in truth there are only *two* errors in the paragraph.

**"Handshake" Puzzle (page 273).** There will be 28 handshakes in all. Santa *A* shakes hands with seven other santas. Santa *B*, having already shaken hands with Santa *A*, has only six other santas to shake hands with. Santa *C* has only five to shake hands with, etc. The total number of shakes is:

$$7 + 6 + 5 + 4 + 3 + 2 + 1 = 28$$

**"Logic" Puzzle (page 274).** Every *INTERIOR* number in the triangle is found by multiplying together the two closest numbers to it in the line of numbers above it. Example: 8 is the product of $2 \times 4$, 32 is the product of $2 \times 16$, etc.

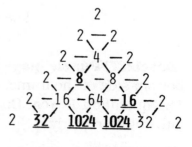

**"Crown" Puzzle (page 275).**

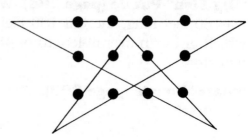

**"Waiter" Puzzle (page 276).** Put your face down close to the penny and blow on it. A good hefty gust of wind should get it off the plate. Choose a plate with a small sloping rim.

**"Mental" Puzzle (page 277).** The answer is simple. The first middle digit of any difference between two three-digit numbers (when the first three-digit number is reversed and the smaller is subtracted from the larger) will always be nine. Also, the first and third digits will always add up to nine. So, if the last digit is eight, the first digit must be one, and the second digit is, of course, nine. Works every time.

**"H$_2$O" Puzzle (page 278).** (a–bc) indicates $a$ moving from position $a$ to a position touching two other coins, $b$ and $c$. The moves are: (1–56), (3–14), (4–58), (5–23), (2–54).

**"Rearranging" Puzzle (page 279).**

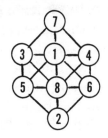

**"Real Estate" Puzzle (page 280).**

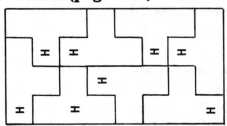

**"Weighing" Puzzle (page 281).** The weighings go as follows: (1) Put the 5-pound weight in one pan and the 9-pound weight in the other pan. Now, weigh out 4 pounds of tea in the 5-pound pan. (2) Remove the weights and place the 4 pounds of tea in one pan and weigh out another 4 pounds of tea. (3) Weigh another 4 pounds. (4) Weigh another 4 pounds. The remainder is also 4 pounds. For weighings (5), (6), (7), (8), and (9), divide each 4-pound portion into two 2-pound portions using the scales. Another mystery of the East solved!

**"Mystical Square" Puzzle (page 282).**

| 20 | 1 | 12 |
|----|----|----|
| 3 | 11 | 19 |
| 10 | 21 | 2 |

**"Substitution" Puzzle (page 283).**

$$\begin{array}{r} 850 \\ 850 \\ \underline{29786} \\ 31486 \end{array}$$

**"Progression" Puzzle (page 284).** The numbers are written in alphabetical order. *E*ight, *f*ive, *f*our, *n*ine, etc.

**"Train" Puzzle (page 285).** Engine *T* pushes car *B* up into *C. T* then goes around and pushes car *A* up and couples it onto *B, T* then goes around to the right side and pulls *B* and *A* down into the right siding. *T* then goes around and up the left siding into *C* and pushes *A* onto the main track. *T* leaves *B* on the right siding, goes to get *A*, and pushes *A* up into the left siding. *T* then returns to its starting position.

**"Stirring" Puzzle (page 286).**

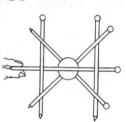

**"Time" Puzzle (page 287).** First off, the broken clock will show the correct time twice a day, for a total of fourteen times a week. On the other hand, the clock that loses an hour a day will be correct only once every twelve days. So, for accuracy, a stopped clock beats a slow one every time.

**"Pie" Puzzle (page 288).** The pie can be cut into eleven different-size pieces.

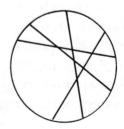

**"Domino" Puzzle (page 289).** The answer is that you cannot cover the checkerboard. Remember, one domino, while covering two squares, will always cover one red square and one black square. However, when we cut the two opposite end squares from the board, we removed two squares of the *same* color. In our example, the board was left with 32 black squares and 30 red squares. After you place 30 dominoes on the board, you will be left with two red squares that will *not* be touching, thus making it impossible to cover them with the last domino. On any checkerboard, no two squares of the same color will ever be side by side.

**"Chocolate Candy" Puzzle (page 290).** Let's work backwards from the eight pieces of candy. Since this was two-thirds of what the third traveller found when he woke up, he must have found twelve chocolates on the plate. In turn, twelve candies must have been two-thirds of what the second traveller found when he woke up. So, he saw eighteen candies on the plate. Finally, eighteen candies had to be two-thirds of what the first traveller found when he woke up. That means that the dish originally contained twenty-seven chocolates.

**"Tire" Puzzle (page 291).** She recommended that he take one lug nut off the other three tires and use them to mount the fourth tire. It worked, and we drove slowly into the next town. There we fixed our bad tire, and bought five new lug nuts.

**"Shape" Puzzle (page 292).** The object is a short wooden cylinder with a notch cut into it.

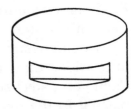

**"Family" Puzzle (page 293).** There are four daughters and three sons.

**"Unicycle" Puzzle (page 294).** The distance between Austin's home and that of his mother is 60 miles. Now, if he rode 15 miles an hour for four hours he would have arrived at 4 PM, an hour too early for dinner. On the other hand, if he rode 10 miles an hour for six hours, he would have arrived a full hour too late. So, Austin figured out that a steady 12 miles an hour for five hours would bring him to the table at exactly 5 PM, just as mom was putting the melon in front of his place at the table.

**"Groucho" Puzzle (page 295).** Well, the last number should be 18. Every number in the bottom row is the square of the number above it turned around. As an example, the first number in the top row is 4. The square of 4 is 16. Turn 16 around and you get 61, the first number in the bottom row. In the last row we have 9 squared, which gives us 81, when turned around we have 18, the answer.

**"Diet" Puzzle (page 296).** The number 102004180 translates: "I ought to owe nothing for I ate nothing."

**"Betting" Puzzle (page 297).** This answer only proves that it's how you look at a problem that counts. J. Wellington ignored the pencil and picked up the sheet of paper. He then proceeded to tear off the four corners of the paper. When he was done the sheet 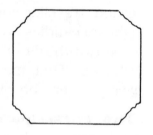 had eight corners, clearly proving that you can take away four corners from four corners and be left with eight.

**"Floating" Puzzle (page 298).** First, fill a wide-mouth glass to the top with water. Next, cut out a square of tissue paper that is a little wider than a sewing needle. Then get a steel sewing needle and place it in the middle of the paper. Gently place the tissue with the needle on it in the center of the glass of water. After a minute or two the paper will soak up enough  water to sink to the bottom of the glass, leaving the needle floating in the middle supported by the surface tension of the water. You'll then have a solid piece of steel floating in a glass of water.

**"Arrow" Puzzle (page 299).** All you need to perform this feat is a tall, straight-sided glass filled with water. Place the glass in front of the arrow on the card and see what happens. The water, acting like a lens, will cause the arrow to be optically reversed. When you look at the arrow through the glass, it will appear to be pointing left.

**"Monkey" Puzzle (page 300).** Jocko took the windows in the following order: 10, 11, 12, 8, 4, 3, 7, 6, 2, 1, 5, 9. This route travels the wide space between the bottom and middle rows of windows only twice. This puzzle is from Sam Loyd, America's greatest puzzle creator.

**"Dirt" Puzzle (page 301).** I'm afraid that President Roosevelt is having a little fun at Henderson's expense. There isn't any dirt in a ditch. It's empty.

**"Triangle" Puzzle (page 302).** There are four sizes of triangles in the drawing. The smallest size has 7 triangles. The next size has 3, the third largest has 3, and the largest has 1. This comes to a total of 14 triangles in all.

**"Entrance" Puzzle (page 303).** The sign says:

"TO OPEN GATE PUSH!"

**"Geometry" Puzzle (page 304).** Lines *BD*, *DG* and *GB* form an equilateral triangle. Therefore, the angle between lines *BD* and *DG* is 60°.

**"Tombstone" Puzzle (page 306).** According to the inscription Mrs. Sarah Fountain died before her husband. If this were so, how then could she have been his widow?

**"Magic Square" Puzzle (page 307).**

**"Tennis Ball" Puzzle (page 308).** Harriet gets the club grounds keeper, Thaddeus Rackencut, to fill the hole with

| 4 | 9 | 5 | |
|---|---|---|---|
| 1 | | | 8 |
| 7 | | | 3 |
| 6 | 10 | 2 | |

water from a nearby hose and the tennis ball promptly floats to the top. Game, set and match if you figured this one out.

**"Thimble" Puzzle (page 309).** The secret is quite simple. Always place the next thimble on a point that will allow you to slide it along to the point of the star your last thimble started from. For example: place the thimble on point *W* and slide it over to point *X*; then place the next thimble on point *Y* and slide it along to point *W*. Next, place a thimble on point *Z* and slide it over to point *Y*. Continue in this manner until all of the seven thimbles are in place.

**"Bakery" Puzzle (page 310).** The horizontal cut shown here will nicely divide the poppy seed loaf into ten pieces. The pieces are not all the same size or shape, but there is enough for everyone to have a taste.

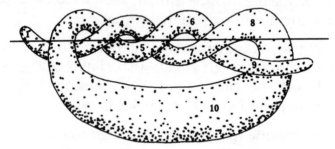

**"Bicycle" Puzzle (page 311).** Against the wind he could pedal 15 miles in an hour. With the wind he could pedal 20 miles in an hour. The difference is 5 miles an hour. Half of this is 2.5 miles. Therefore, the velocity of the wind was 2.5 miles per hour. So, on a calm day he could pedal 17.5 miles per hour, the difference between 15 miles and 20 miles.

$$\frac{60 \text{ minutes}}{17.5 \text{ miles}} = \frac{3{,}600 \text{ seconds}}{17.50 \text{ miles}} = 205.7 \text{ seconds per mile}$$

$$= 3 \text{ minutes } 26 \text{ seconds}$$
$$\text{per mile on a calm day.}$$

**"Coin" Puzzle (page 312).** Place the forefinger of your left hand firmly on the middle coin (the coin that can be touched but not moved). With your right hand move the quarter on the right a few inches away from the nickel (the coin that can be touched or moved). Now bring this quarter back smartly against the nickel. The nickel will not move, but the impact will cause the quarter on the left of the nickel to move away two or three inches from the nickel, thus creating an opening between them that you can now move the right-hand quarter into. Problem solved!

**"Magnet" Puzzle (page 313).** If you touch one end of one bar against the end of the other bar, there is an attraction, but you can't tell which bar is attracting the other. However, if you touch the end of one bar against the middle of the other bar the following happens: If the bar being touched against the middle of the other bar is the magnet, it attracts the other bar (Fig. 1). If, on the other hand, it is not the

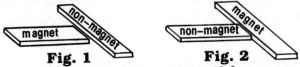

**Fig. 1**          **Fig. 2**

magnet, it doesn't attract the other bar because a bar magnet has almost no attracting power at its center (Fig. 2). Thus, if the touching bar is a magnet, it attracts, and if it is not a magnet, there is no visible attraction.

**"Card" Puzzle (page 314).** Place the four cards together as shown, with the upper right-hand corner of each card overlapped by the card above it.

**"Rope" Puzzle (page 315).**
The secret to this Eastern mystery is to cross your arms before bending down to pick up the ends of the rope. Once you have an end in each hand unfold your arms and the knot appears magically in the middle of the rope. And you never let go of the ends while doing it! Amazing!

**"Area" Puzzle (page 316).** The shaded area is one quarter of the area of the three-inch square. Since the area of the square is nine square inches, then the shaded area must be $2^1/_4$ square inches. You can rotate the four-inch square to any other position around the smaller square and the area covered will always remain the same, $2^1/_4$ square inches. If you rotate the larger square to bisect line *ac*, it will then cover an area on the smaller square measuring $1^1/_2$ inches by $1^1/_2$ inches, exactly $2^1/_4$ square inches.

**"Lunch" Puzzle (page 317).** He won by losing the bet! Treadmill picked up the basket and ate the boss's $6.00 triple-decker sandwich down to the last pickle. When he was finished, he gave the boss 50¢ and said, "I should have known better than to have wagered with you, Sir. You're a tough man to beat."

**"Rectangle" Puzzle (page 318).** Place the four rectangles together as shown. Note that the ends of the pieces make up the sides of an empty one-inch square formed in the middle (shaded area).

| | |
|---|---|
| 1 X 1 | |
| 1 X 3 | 1 X 4 |
| 1 X 2 | |

**"Cord" Puzzle (page 319).** Sir Goodwin retrieved all 160 feet of the Golden Cords and brought them safely back to England, where they provided for him in his old age. Here's how he did it. First, he took the two ends at the bottom and

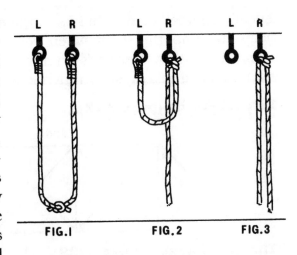

FIG.1            FIG.2            FIG.3

tied them tightly together (Fig. 1). Next, he climbed up the rope on the left until he reached the top. There he wrapped his legs around both pieces of rope and, while hanging on for dear life, he cut the right-hand rope free with his dagger. He then took the end of the right-hand rope and poked it back through the ring that had originally held it. He kept pulling the rope through until the knotted ends reached the ring (Fig. 2). Taking hold of the doubled rope that now hung from the right-hand ring, Sir Goodwin shifted around and cut the cord on the left side free from its supporting ring (Fig. 3). Sir Goodwin then carefully slid down the doubled cord to the floor. Once there, he pulled the cords free of the ring and hightailed it for home.

**"Number" Puzzle (page 320).** The selling of "products" was Distin's game and so is the solution to this puzzle. Each number is the product of the digits that make up the preceding number: 49 equals 7 times 7; 36 equals 4 times 9; and 18 equals 3 times 6. Therefore, the answer to our problem is 8 equals 1 times 8. A thumping good problem!

**"Salt and Pepper" Puzzle (page 321).** It helps to have a full head of hair for this puzzle. Take your comb and run it several times through your hair. Now lower it down so that the teeth are right above the specks of pepper. Miraculously, the pepper will leap from the salt and will cling to the magnetically charged comb, thanks to the charge of static electricity you imparted to it when you ran it through your locks. Judging by Herbert's thinning top, I'd say that he won't be doing this mystery much longer.

**"Pencil" Puzzle (page 322).**

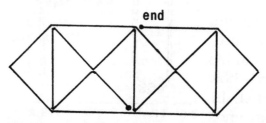

**"Theatre" Puzzle (page 323).** The breakdown of the admissions was: 11 men paid $55.00; 19 women paid $38.00; and 70 children paid $7.00—all told, a total of exactly $100.00 and 100 people.

**"Sting" Puzzle (page 324).** Okay, here's the sting. Turn over the quarter and place it on top of a "heads" nickel. Make sure that the quarter completely hides the nickel. Now, if you look at the table, you'll see that there is only 40¢ in heads showing. That's a honey of a puzzle.

**"Fish" Puzzle (page 325).**

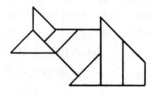

**"Buzz Saw" Puzzle (page 326).** The least number of pieces is two. Cut out the piece outlined by the dotted line, turn it end for end, and replace it in the board. The hole is now in the middle of the board.

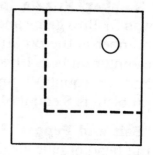

**"Word" Puzzle (page 327).** 1. Soap box  2. Circles under eyes  3. Backward glance  4. I understand  5. Zero degrees  6. Upper crust.

**"Perception" Puzzle (page 328).** The answer is that six F's are in the sentence. Why it's so difficult to count them the first time is hard to say. People seem to miss the F's in the "of's." Try this one on your friends and see how they do.

**"Spider" Puzzle (page 329).** To illustrate the solution imagine the cylinder opened out flat. The location of the fly is point *F* and the location of the spider is point *S*. Now extend the line of the left side upwards one inch to point *B*. Line *BS* cuts the top edge of the drawing at point *A*, the point where the spider goes over the edge of the cylinder. The spider's route is the hypotenuse of a right triangle with a base four inches long, and a high side three inches long. Thus, the hypotenuse has to be five inches long, the shortest route that the spider can take.

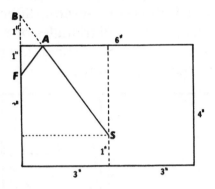

**"Earth" Puzzle (page 330).** In the following equations $C$ = circumference; $r$ = radius; and $\pi = 3.14$ ($r_1$ is the radius of the earth; $r_2$ is the radius of the steel band):

$$C = 2\pi r_1 \qquad C+10 = 2\pi r_2$$

$$r_1 = \frac{C}{2\pi} \qquad r_2 = .\frac{C+10}{2\pi}$$

$$r_1 = 4{,}000 \quad r_2 - r_1 = \frac{C+10}{2\pi} - \frac{C}{2\pi} = \frac{10}{2\pi} = \frac{5}{\pi}$$

$$r_2 - r_1 = 1.59 \text{ FEET}$$

**"Missing Letter" Puzzle (page 331).** Insert the letter *E* at the proper intervals, and it makes the inscription read as follows:

PERSEVERE YE PERFECT MEN
EVER KEEP THESE PRECEPTS TEN

**"Clown" Puzzle (page 332).** John is the golf player and the barber. Dick is the trumpeter and the writer. Roger is the computer technician and the truck driver.

**"Counting" Puzzle (page 333).** There are 34 squares and 104 triangles of several different sizes in the kite. Many of the squares and triangles overlap parts of other squares and triangles. Here are the different sizes of both figures as they appear in our drawing.

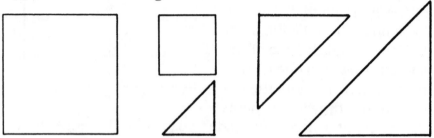

**"Mystery Word" Puzzle (page 334).** The word that Ms. Sunshine has in mind is *nowhere*. Put a space in its middle and you get *now here*.

**"Nuptial" Puzzle (page 335).** The day of the nuptials will be Sunday. You have to break the solution down into two parts.

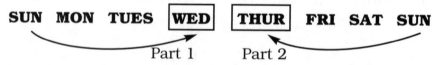

In Part 1 ("When the day after tomorrow is yesterday, then 'today' will be as far from Sunday . . ."), going from Sunday forward, we arrive at Wednesday, 3 days away. In Part 2 (". . . as that day was which was 'today' when the day before yesterday was tomorrow."), going from Sunday backwards, we arrive at Thursday, which is also 3 days away from Sunday. The answer, of course, has to be the day of the week given in the problem.

**"Golf" Puzzle (page 336).** Dashing Dan's two shots are a 150-yard drive and a 125-yard approach shot. The holes are made in the following manner: 150 yards: 1 drive. 300 yards: 2 drives. 250 yards: 2 approaches. 325 yards: 3

drives, 1 approach back. 275 yards: 1 drive, 1 approach. 350 yards: 4 approaches, 1 drive back. 225 yards: 3 approaches, 1 drive back. 400 yards: 1 drive, 2 approaches. 425 yards: 2 drives, 1 approach.

**"Pyramid" Puzzle (page 337).** First invert pyramids 2 and 3; then invert pyramids 3 and 4, and finally, invert pyramids 4 and 5.

**"College Boy" Puzzle (page 338).** Substituting the numbers for letters in our alphabetic equation, and adding a decimal point for the cents, we find that Junior needs exactly $106.52, the sum that his dad quickly dispatched to him.

$$
\begin{array}{rcr}
\text{SEND} & & 9567 \\
+\ \text{MORE} & = & +1085 \\
\hline
\text{MONEY} & & 10652 \\
\end{array}
$$

**"Punctuation" Puzzle (page 339).** The following punctuation brings order out of chaos: THAT THAT IS, IS. THAT THAT IS NOT, IS NOT. IS THAT IT? THAT IS IT.

**"Soup Tureen" Puzzle (page 340).** There were 400 of each type of coin.

$$
\begin{array}{r}
400 \text{ silver dollars} = \$400 \\
400 \text{ half-dollars} = \$200 \\
400 \text{ quarters} = \underline{\$100} \\
\$700 \\
\end{array}
$$

**"Bell" Puzzle (page 341).** When the Durango Kid started hauling on the rope, he found himself going up in the air the same distance as the bell. When the bell was four feet off the ground, so was Durango. No matter how fast or how slowly he hauled on the rope, he was the same distance above the ground as the bell. They both arrived at the tower together, which after all was what the Reverend wanted.

**"Castle" Puzzle (page 342).** The girl descended first, using the cannonball as a counterweight. The king and his son then took the cannonball out of the upper basket and the son descended, with the girl acting as counterweight. Then then sent the cannonball down alone and, when it reached the ground, the son got into the basket alone with the cannonball. Their joint weight allowed the king to descend. The prince got out and the cannonball went down alone. The girl then went down, the cannonball ascending. The son removed the cannonball and went down alone, his sister ascending. The girl then put the cannonball in the opposite basket, and lowered herself to the ground.

**"Square" Puzzle (page 343).**

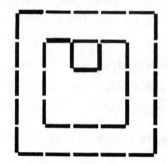

**"Web" Puzzle (page 344).** The following steps clearly describe the solution to the tangle:

Step 1: 20"× 4 = 80" circumference

Step 2: $\dfrac{80}{3.14}$ = 25.48 diameter

Step 3: 25.48 × 25.48 = 649.23 (area of square)

Step 4: $\dfrac{25.48}{3.14}$ = 12.74 (radius of circle)

Step 5: 12.74 × 12.74 × 3.14 = 509.65 (area of circle)

Step 6:  649.23
      − 509.65
      ‾‾‾‾‾‾‾
       139.58      = area of corners

Step 7: $\dfrac{139.58}{4}$ = 34.9 inches (area of spider's web)

**"Bridge" Puzzle (page 345).** All you have to do is to pleat the paper as shown and the puzzle is solved.

**"Bottle and Key" Puzzle (page 346).** This puzzle can only be solved on a sunny day, because the string must be in line with the sun. To remove the key from the string, just take a large magnifying glass and concentrate the sun's rays through the side of the bottle onto the knot. After a few moments the knot will burn through and the key will fall to the bottom of the bottle.

**"Horse" Puzzle (page 347).** Here's how Trevor Torts handled the case. He rode one of his own horses over to the Tralawny stable and added it to the seventeen horses of the inheritance, bringing the total to eighteen. He then gave John nine horses (half of eighteen), James six horses (one-third of eighteen), and William two horses (one-ninth of eighteen). This division disposed of the inheritance in the manner originally set forth by the Squire in his will. Having rendered a decision that satisfied all the parties involved, Trevor mounted his own horse and rode happily back home.

**"Counterfeit Coin" Puzzle (page 348).** The contestants took one coin from hat one, two from hat two, three from hat three, and so on. When they finished, they placed their pile of fifty coins on the scale for their one weighing. If the fifty coins were all genuine, their total weight would have been 500 grams, but since one or more of the coins was counterfeit, the total weight was less. When they subtracted the weight shown by the scale from 500, the difference was the number of the hat that contained the bogus coins. For example, if the counterfeit coins were in hat number six, the scale would have showed a total weight of 494 grams, since six coins in the pile came from this hat. 494 from 500 is six, the number of the hat with the counterfeit coins.

**"Scholar" Puzzle (page 349).** It's no word at all. The answer is *a postman.*

**"Shield" Puzzle (page 350).** Start at any dot, count six dots and place a coin on the sixth dot. Remember which dot you started counting from—that's where you want to place your second coin. Start counting from a dot that allows you to come to rest on the first dot. Start the third coin so that it comes to rest on the dot you started your second coin from. Continue like this for the rest of the coins.

**"Door" Puzzle (page 351).** Rearrange the letters to spell *one word.*

**"Eight Word" Puzzle (page 352).** The one thing that all eight words have in common is that each one contains three consecutive letters of the alphabet in a row.

**"Mental" Puzzle (page 353).** Pair the lowest and highest numbers (1 + 100 = 101; 2 + 99 = 101; 3 + 98 = 101; etc.), and you have fifty such pairs. Thus, 50 × 101 = 5050, the "mental" solution.

**"Hand" Puzzle (page 354).** Anyone not in on the secret usually tries to slowly draw away the card, inevitably failing. The proper method is to give the corner of the card a smart snap with the second finger of the left hand. If this is done exactly right, the card will shoot away with a sort of spinning motion, the coin remaining undisturbed on your right thumb. (Our thanks to Professor Hoffmann for this trick.)

**"Dress" Puzzle (page 356).** Since Mrs. Grey is the one who brought the subject up, she can't be wearing grey. She must have on either a white dress or a black dress. The woman who answered her observation was wearing a black dress so Mrs. Grey must then be wearing a white dress. The woman in the black dress can't be Mrs. Black since no one is wearing her own color, and she can't be Mrs. Grey since *she's* wearing white, so she must be Mrs. White. Finally, we come to Mrs. Black, who has to be wearing the grey dress.

**"Carpentry" Puzzle (page 357).** The drawing shows how the cuts are made and the pieces are reassembled:

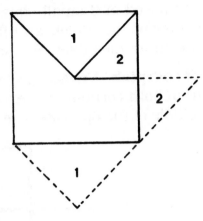

**"Real Estate" Puzzle (page 358).** Here's the solution Sydney came up with. Is it yours?

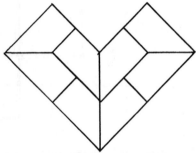

**"Match" Puzzle (page 359).** If you lay out the matches as a triangle, you will enclose an area of six square units. However, if you shift the three matches indicated by the broken lines, you will drop two square units and be left with a figure that encloses just four square units.

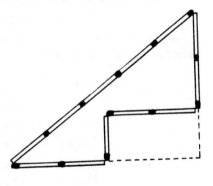

**"Find-the-Items" Puzzle (page 360).** The twenty we found are: BAT (BASEBALL), BED, BELL, CABLE (TV), CAT, CLOCK, CLOSET, COAT, COT, DESK, LOCK, SAFE, SOCK, SOFA, STOOL, STOVE, TABLE, TEA, TOOLS, VASE.

**"Archaeology" Puzzle (page 361).** The total number of squares is 31. There are 16 small squares; 9 squares composed of 4 smallish squares; 4 still larger squares composed of 9 small squares; 1 diamond square in the center of the tablet; and finally, 1 large square framing the entire tile tablet. You should now know perfection.

**"Toothpick" Puzzle (page 362).** Remove the toothpicks from both corners of one side and the toothpick from the middle of the opposite side.

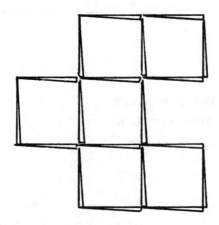

**"Treasure" Puzzle (page 363).** In this progression each bag contains fewer coins than the preceding bag. Each bag contains a specific fraction of the number of coins in the first bag, which contains 60 coins.

> Bag 1 = 60 coins
> Bag 2 = 30 coins ($^1/_2$)
> Bag 3 = 20 coins ($^1/_3$)
> Bag 4 = 15 coins ($^1/_4$)
> Bag 5 = 12 coins ($^1/_5$)
> Bag 6 = 10 coins ($^1/_6$)

**"Medieval" Puzzle (page 364).** The complete puzzle should read:

$$
\begin{array}{ccccc}
 & & 1 & 1 & 7 \\
 & & 3 & 1 & 9 \\
\hline
 & 1 & 0 & 5 & 3 \\
 & & 1 & 1 & 7 \\
 & 3 & 5 & 1 & \\
\hline
3 & 7 & 3 & 2 & 3 \\
\end{array}
$$

**"Butcher" Puzzle (page 365).** This is one of those "Gotcha" puzzles. Since a person's weight can't be calculated accurately just by knowing his waist size, the only correct answer to the question "What does a butcher weigh" would have to be "meat."

**"Easy 'Z'" Puzzle (page 366).** Figure 1 shows where the cuts are made and figure 2 shows how the pieces are reassembled to form a square.

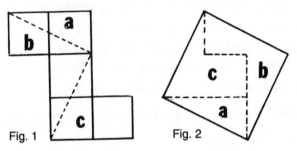

Fig. 1     Fig. 2

**"Toy" Puzzle (page 367).** Calvin paid $60.00 for each tractor, $15.00 for each shovel and $5.00 for each truck. The total for lot number three came to $950. The total for lot number four was $80.

**"Magic Coins" Puzzle (page 368).** Turn over coins 3 and 4, then coins 4 and 5, and finally coins 2 and 3.

**"Chicken" Puzzle (page 369).** The answer is 24 eggs. It works out that one chicken can lay $2/3$ of an egg in one day. Therefore, six chickens can lay four eggs in one day and 24 eggs in six days.

**"Weight" Puzzle (page 370).**

> Box 1 weighs $5^1/2$ pounds.
> Box 2 weighs $6^1/2$ pounds.
> Box 3 weighs 7 pounds.
> Box 4 weighs $4^1/2$ pounds.
> Box 5 weighs $3^1/2$ pounds.

**"Numero Uno" Puzzle (page 371).** The two numbers are 11 and 1.1. When added or multiplied together they give a result of 12.1.

**"Printing" Puzzle (page 372).** Philo will have to purchase twenty-seven pieces of type, for $135, in order to be able to print every month of the year. The letters needed are: AABCDEEEFGHIJLMNOOPRRSTUUVY

> January will need seven letters (JANUARY);
> February will need four letters (FEBR);
> March will need three letters (MCH);
> April will need three letters (PIL);
> August will need four letters (GUST);
> September will need two letters (EE);
> October will need two letters (OO);
> November will need one letter (V);
> December will need one letter (D).

**"Addition" Puzzle (page 373).** Charlie's answer is:

```
  1 X X          1 0 0
  3 3 X          3 3 0
  5 X 5          5 0 5
  X 7 7          0 7 7
  X 9 9          0 9 9
 ───────        ───────
  1, 1 1 1       1,11 1
```

**"Square" Puzzle (page 374).** The drawing contains exactly 100 squares and is drawn with only 15 straight lines. There are 40 with squares of one unit, 28 of four units, 18 of nine units; 10 of sixteen units; and four of twenty-five units.

**"Witch" Puzzle (page 375).** His statement was, "I will be fed to the bats!" If it is true, he will be boiled in oil. If it is false, he will be fed to the bats. There is no way to work out the correct punishment, so the witch was foiled until next Halloween.

**"Counterfeit Coin" Puzzle (page 376).** This is one of the most difficult of all counterfeit coin problems. The counterfeit coin could be either heavier or lighter than the other coins. You must find the answer in only 3 weighings. The schematic diagram presented here gives you the answer. The result of all comparisons (in boxes) is based on comparing the top figure(s) to the bottom figures(s). **L** stands for light. **H** stands for heavy.

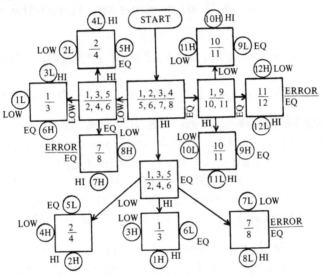

**"Abe Lincoln" Puzzle (page 377).** If you check a five-dollar bill you will find that Abe Lincoln is face up on both sides of the bill. On the back of the bill is a small statue of him looking out from the center of the columns on the Lincoln Memorial. Since he is looking out he is clearly face up on this side of the bill, too. As long as the bill keeps coming up heads when it is dropped, J. Wellington will win. When it comes up tails he will win again, but no one will bet with him again.

**"Scholar" Puzzle (page 378).** The word is *bookkeeper*, and the clue is *accountant.*

**"Route" Puzzle (page 379).** There are exactly 70 different routes Otto could take before he was forced to start over again.

**"Sears Hat" Puzzle (page 380).** If the hat cost $3.75 more than the fancy cord did, the cord must have cost 25 cents and the hat $4.00. Together, they cost $4.25.

**Bridge Puzzle (page 381).** Deirdre is married to Horace, Imogene is married to Charles, and Erika is married to Selwyn.

**"Superstition" Puzzle (page 382).** This is a tricky one, and it may have more than one answer. Here's the one we know:

$$(3)^3 + (3)^3 + (3)^3 + (3/3)^3 + (3 \times 3) + (3 \times 3) = 100$$

or

$$27 + 27 + 27 + 1 + 9 + 9 = 100$$

**"Birthday" Puzzle (page 383).** His birthday is on December 31st. In the puzzle picture on the train, Mr. Gotrocks is speaking to himself on January 1st. Two days previously, December 30th, he was 54. The next day, December 31st, he was 55. At the end of this new year he will become 56, and next year he will become 57.

**"Tree" Puzzle (page 384).** The trees are OAK, ELM, PINE, PEACH, PEAR, APPLE, MAPLE, PLUM, PALM, FIG, SUMAC (OR SUMACH), BEECH, WILLOW, SPRUCE, CEDAR, LARCH, and FIR.

**"Radio" Puzzle (page 385).** The answers are: 1. T (tea), 2. N-V (envy), 3. S-X (Essex), 4. X-S (excess), 5. S-A (essay), 6. T-P (teepee), 7. F-E-G (effigy), 8. C-D (seedy), 9. M-T (empty), 10. L (ell), 11. N-M-E (enemy), 12. L-E-G (elegy).

**"Mind Reading" Puzzle (page 386).** When the mists cleared, Madame Zorrina saw that the word that the gentleman was thinking about was . . . *forty.*

**"Indian" Puzzle (page 387).** Matches are, of course, made of *love.*

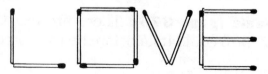

**"Prohibition" Puzzle (page 388).** Here's how Swifty's deliveries went: 1. Sal's received 8 cases—2 more than Hanratty's. 2. Hanratty's received 6 cases—2 more than the Dutchman's Cafe. 3. The Dutchman's Cafe received 4 cases—2 more than Edna's Hide-a-Way. 4. Edna's Hide-a-Way received 2 cases—6 fewer than Sal's Saloon.

**"Halloween" Puzzle (page 389).** The family consisted of two boys and two girls, their mother and father and both their mother's and father's parents (That is, their two grandfathers and two grandmothers.

**"Santa Claus" Puzzle (page 390).** The two solutions we know are:

$$
\begin{array}{r}
24,794 \\
-16,452 \\
\hline
8,342
\end{array}
\qquad
\begin{array}{r}
36,156 \\
-28,693 \\
\hline
7,463
\end{array}
$$

**"Subtraction" Puzzle (page 391).** Here is the good Professor's answer. "This is somewhat of a quibble. The number 45 is the sum of the digits 1, 2, 3, 4, 5, 6, 7, 8, 9. Solve the puzzle by arranging them in reverse order, and subtracting the original series. The remainder will to consist of the same digits in a different order, and therefore make the same total, *viz.*, 45."

$$
\begin{array}{r}
987654321 = 45 \\
123456789 = 45 \\
\hline
864197532 = 45
\end{array}
$$

**"Computer" Puzzle (page 392).** The answer is . . . 301. Do the divisions with pencil and paper to see the remainder.

**"Word" Puzzle (page 393).** The first word is *boldface*, a typesetting term. The second is *feedback*, the information you get in a survey, for example.

**"Beer" Puzzle (page 394).** In one day Brunhilda drinks:

$$
\frac{1}{14} - \frac{1}{20} = \frac{20}{280} - \frac{14}{280} = \frac{6}{280} = \frac{3}{140}
$$

Brunhilda drinks $3/140$ of a barrel of beer a day. Divide 140 by 3 and get $46^2/_3$ days, the length of time it used to take Brunhilda to knock off a barrel by herself.

**"Pyramid" Puzzle (page 395).** This design will keep him from being inventoried along with the canopic jars.

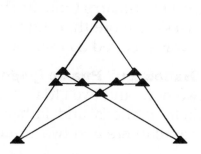

**"Geometry" Puzzle (page 396).** The following solution is the one that we know of:

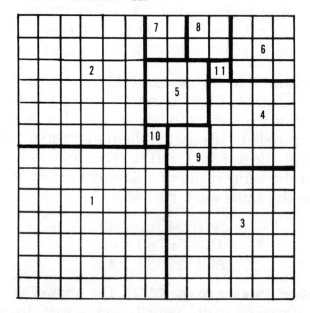

**"Poker Chip" Puzzle (page 397).** Move chips 2 and 3 to squares 9 and 10. Move 5 and 6 to squares 2 and 3. Move 8 and 9 to squares 5 and 6. Move 1 and 2 to squares 8 and 9.

**"Betting" Puzzle (page 398).** You will always win $26 with this bet. That's right, every pair will contain one red and one black card. Because the bottom card of each pile is a different color, when you riffle shuffle the deck together the cards will always fall in an alternating order. Try it and see for yourself. However, you are only allowed one riffle shuffle.

**"Shooting" Puzzle (page 399).** The words are *aspired*, *praised*, and *despair*.

**"Drink Stirrer" Puzzle (page 400).** One times one equals one.

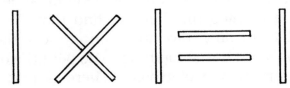

**"Golf" Puzzle (page 401).** At the end of 18 holes the young nobleman was left with 120 ducats. Here's how to solve it: First subtract the 80 ducats he lost on the back nine from the 500 he originally started with, leaving 420 ducats.

Next, let

$x$ = half what he had left at the end of the round;
$2x$ = what he had left at the end of the round;
$4x$ = twice what he had left.

Now, add them all together:

$x + 2x + 4x = 420$ ducats;
$7x = 420$ ducats;
$x = 60$ ducats;
$2x = 120$ ducats, the amount he was left with at the end of the round.

**"Vintage Car" Puzzle (page 402).** Harlow owns three cars.

**"Math Signs" Puzzle (page 404).** There is more than one answer to this problem. Here's one of them:

$123 - 45 - 67 + 89 = 100$

**"Bolt" Puzzle (page 405).** The heads of the bolts remain the same distance apart regardless of the direction you rotate them in.

**"Tin Man" Puzzle (page 406).** Starting with the "I" at the top right of the frame, read around the frame counterclockwise. The famous quote is, "It's better to wear out than to rust out!" The quote is by Richard Cumberland (from Boswell's *Tour of the Hebrides*).

**"Treasure" Puzzle (page 407).** What clues can we find in order to work this problem? First, there are no three-letter English words that do not contain at least one vowel. On examining the dials we find that "Y," on the middle dial, is the only vowel to be found. Next, the secret combination word has something to do with the owner of the chest, the bishop of Bristol. There is just such a three-letter word, "*PYX*." The dictionary defines pyx as "a box or vessel in which the reserved Eucharist or Host is kept."

**"Chocolate" Puzzle (page 408).** Piece *A* alone forms the first square. Then the two pieces marked *B* fit together to form the second. Next, the two pieces marked *C* make up the third square; and, finally, the four pieces marked *D* can be used to form the fourth square.

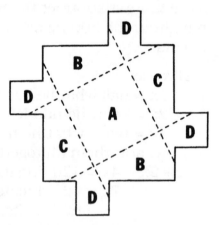

**"Animal" Puzzle (page 409).** The eight animal collective nouns are:

1) A doylt of swine.
2) A gaggle of geese.
3) A rout of wolves.
4) A troop of monkeys.
5) A leap of leopards.
6) A skulk of foxes.
7) A sloth of bears.
8) A muster of peacocks.

**"Match" Puzzle (page 410).** Remove two corner matches from the upper-right and bottom-left corners and the four matches from the inside of the figure. You now have one small square and two large squares, for a total of three squares.

**"Line" Puzzle (page 411).** To solve this problem you must start and stop the line at a junction where three parts of the line come together. In the drawing below, these parts are above the Bard's right eye and on his left shoulder next to his collar and hair.

**"Magic Square" Puzzle (page 412).** The following answer shows one way of distributing the numbers around the sides of the square.

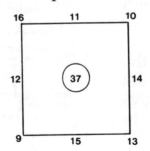

**"What, When, and Why?" Puzzles (page 413).** 1) It is matchless. 2) When it is scaled. 3) Because a good batter makes good dough. 4) One is hard to get up and the other is hard to get down. 5) When it is a skylight. 6) Because she has a head on one side and a tail on the other. 7) Ohio.

**...ks" Puzzle (page 414).** There were

Seven joke bottle corks @ \$0.01 = \$0.07
Seven Towers of Gold @ \$0.05 = \$0.35
Ten Laughing Uncles @ \$0.10 = \$1.00
Four Comical Nut Crackers @ \$0.25 = \$1.00

Total . . . \$2.42

**"Aces and Kings" Puzzle (page 415).** The setup of the eight cards, from the top down, in the deck is ace, king, king, ace, king, king, ace, ace. This is with the deck turned face-down.

**"Book" Puzzle (page 416).** The mystery was finally solved with the arrival of Algernon, the library's clerk. His explanation went something like this:

"Gee, what an easy puzzle that is, Pops. I learned it in sixth grade. Take a strong paper bag and lay it on the table with the open end hanging over the edge. Next, place the books on top of the other end of the bag. Now all you have to do is to blow into the open end of the bag while making sure that you keep the bag tight against your mouth so that none of the air escapes. A couple of good puffs and the books will tilt and fall over. Didn't you guys learn anything in school?"

**"Checker" Puzzle (page 417).** Black to move and win: 11–16, 19–15, 22–18, 14–23, 16–19, 23–16, 12–10, 3–8, 10–7. White is now trapped, making black the winnner.

**"Toothpick" Puzzle (page 418).** Move the three toothpicks on the extreme right of the original setup to the new positions indicated in the drawing. You now have 9 small squares, 4 medium-sized squares made up of 4 squares each, and 1 large square made up of the 9 small squares. It's reported that Roderick Sneakwell failed this test. Would you have won a Dusty Road cone?

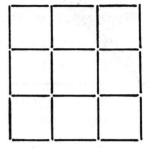

**"Sandwich" Puzzle (page 419).** The total number of watercress, asparagus, and cucumber sandwiches needed to satisfy the problem is 121.

**"Racing" Puzzle (page 420).** The following is only one of many solutions to this problem.

| 6 | 5 | 4 | 3 | 2 | 1 |
|---|---|---|---|---|---|
| 5 | 3 | 1 | 6 | 4 | 2 |
| 4 | 1 | 2 | 5 | 6 | 3 |
| 3 | 6 | 5 | 2 | 1 | 4 |
| 2 | 4 | 6 | 1 | 3 | 5 |
| 1 | 2 | 3 | 4 | 5 | 6 |

**"Synonym" Puzzle (page 421).** The winning synonyms were 1) quilt; 2) query; 3) quite; 4) quack; 5) quail; 6) queue; 7) quart; 8) queen; 9) quick; 10) quark; 11) quill; 12) qualm; 13) quest; 14) quiet; 15) quota; 16) quell; 17) quash; 18) quaff; 19) quake; 20) quirt.

**"Grand Prize" Puzzle (page 422).** Winthrop won the day by observing that each of the numbers above the line is spelled with three letters. Since the next number in the sequence, 10, is also spelled with three letters, Winthrop correctly ascertained that the number should go above the line. Another trophy for his collection.

**"Watch" Puzzle (page 423).** For all three watches again to register the correct time at noon it will be necessary for the watch that is losing one minute every 24 hours to lose 12 hours and for the other watch to gain 12 hours. At the rate of one minute a day, this will occur in exactly 720 days.

**"Rearranging" Puzzle (page 424).** The cities visited are:

TCLTUACA = CALCUTTA
RIZBRTIA = BIARRITZ
OULHNULO = HONOLULU
TENAWCOP = CAPE TOWN
YVRIKEKAJ = REYKJAVIK
GESPRIANO = SINGAPORE
TRHMUPTOOS = PORTSMOUTH
LENUMEOBR = MELBOURNE
BNACSAALAC = CASABLANCA
ORNONAG = RANGOON
SSRFACONCAIN = SAN FRANCISCO
NKGNGHOO = HONG KONG

**"Millennium" Puzzle (page 425).** For those of you who couldn't solve it and who don't remember the year 2000 we give the following solution. By the way, this square isn't limited to the ways of totaling 2000 that we mentioned earlier. The four center squares and the four corner squares also add up to 2000. Also, the four squares that make up the four quadrants of the square. There are also a couple of other ways for making 2000. See if you can find them.

| 499 | 502 | 507 | 492 |
|-----|-----|-----|-----|
| 506 | 493 | 498 | 503 |
| 494 | 509 | 500 | 497 |
| 501 | 496 | 495 | 508 |

**"Ancient" Puzzle (page 426).** When in Rome, do as the Romans do . . . and use the Roman numbering system. One-third of TWELVE (the word) would be the two letters LV, which equals 55. Also, one-fifth of SEVEN (the word) is the single letter V, which equals 5.

So, LV ÷ V = 55 ÷ 5 = 11.

**"Insect" Puzzle (page 427).** The eight insects we came up with are ANT, FLEA, FLY, GNAT, LICE, MITE, MOTH, WASP.

**"Triangle" Puzzle (page 428).** The dashes denote the three rods that must be removed from the figure. You are then left with three small triangles, three medium-sized triangles, and the seventh large triangle that contains the

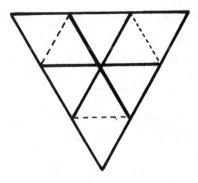

rest. After all, the young lady *didn't* specify that the seven remaining triangles would all be the same size.

**"Dog House" Puzzle (page 429).** The dotted lines indicate the matches moved.

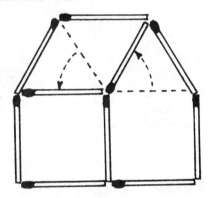

**"Chickenman" Puzzle (page 430).** The answer to the Chickenman's puzzle is the number 8.

**"Christmas" Puzzle (page 431).** Let's hope Santa was extra generous with these birthday kids. On Christmas morn Barton was 8, Wendel was 5, and Susan was 3.

**"Magic Kettle" Puzzle (page 432).** Since there are 35 heads, the minimum number of legs would be 70 (two for each bird). The farmer said the total number of legs was 94, which means that we have an extra 24 legs. Dividing the extra legs by 2 we get 12, the number of four-legged animals in the rabbit cage. Since we now know that 12 of the animals were rabbits, it follows that there were 23 pheasants in the other cage.

**"Santa" Puzzle (page 433).** Take a pencil and ruler and divide the square into 25 smaller squares, as shown in figure 1. Now, cut the square into four smaller pieces (cut along the heavy lines). We've numbered these four segments 1 through 4. If you now reassemble these four segments as indicated in figures 2 and 3, you will have two squares, each with a complete Santa.

Fig. 1

Fig. 2

**"Pentagram" Puzzle (page 434).** This is the one solution to this puzzle that we are aware of.

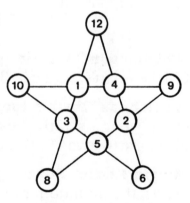

**"Solid Shape" Puzzle (page 435).** The six shapes called for by Merlin are 1) a ball; 2) a cone; 3) a cylinder; 4) a three-sided pyramid; 5) a four-sided pyramid; 6) a cube. Now let's get back and find out what in the world an infinite-sided solid is.

**"Musical" Puzzle (page 436).** Number the seven notes 1 through 7 as indicated in the drawing below. If you invert the following notes, in three moves, you will end up with all seven notes right side up. Turn notes 1, 2, and 3; then turn 3, 4, and 5; then turn 3, 6, and 7.

**"Color" Puzzle (page 437).** 1) On the ocean—*White*cap

2) A first starter—*Green*horn
3) Found in pies—*Black*bird
4) Some find it tasty—*Blue*grass
5) A type of building—*Brown*stone
6) Lacking in sense—*Dunce*
7) The ape man—*Grey*stoke
8) Best in the shade—*Lemon*ade
9) An unpleasant sight—*Pink*eye
10) A strong liquid—*Red*eye

**"Apple" Puzzle (page 438).** Sy gave each of his first five sons an apple from the basket. There was then one apple left in the basket. Sy then gave the basket with the apple in it to his sixth son. As the puzzle stated, Sy divided the six apples equally among his sons, and one apple was left in the basket.

**"Word Square" Puzzle (page 439).** The five words are: 1) *SATED*; 2) *ATONE*; 3) *TOAST*; 4) *ENSUE*; 5) *DETER*.

| S | A | T | E | D |
|---|---|---|---|---|
| A | T | O | N | E |
| T | O | A | S | T |
| E | N | S | U | E |
| D | E | T | E | R |

**"Sphinx" Puzzle (page 440).**
The drawing at right shows the arrangement of the four little "Sphinxlets" within the original Sphinx.

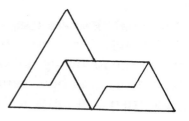

**"Radio" Puzzle (page 441).**

1) What's the difference between our king and a rejected lover? Our king kisses his missus, and the other misses his kisses.

2) What's the difference between our king and a flea? Our king can have fleas, but a flea can't have our king.

3) What's the difference between a hungry man and our king? A hungry man longs to eat while our king eats too long.

**"Detective" Puzzle (page 442).** The detectives are: 1) Charlie Chan; 2) Inspector Maigret; 3) The Saint; 4) Philip Marlowe; 5) Nero Wolfe; 6) Mr. and Mrs. North; 7) Ellery Queen; 8) Hercule Poirot; 9) Mike Hammer; 10) Miss Marple.

**"Anagrams" Puzzle (page 443).** 1) Revolution; 2) Telegraph; 3) Grover Cleveland; 4) Adolf Hitler; 5) Florence Nightingale; 6) Clint Eastwood; 7) HMS *Pinafore*.

**"Hopping" Puzzle (page 444).** The first to cross the finish line was the little frog. Although they stayed neck in neck down the course, when they reached the oak tree the frog's twenty-fourth hop landed him exactly on the twelve-foot line while the grasshopper's fifteenth hop sent him six inches beyond. At this point they both turned around and started hopping back to the starting line. Since the frog now had a six-inch lead over the grasshopper, he easily beat him when they came down to the finish.

**"Christmas Stocking" Puzzle (page 445).** There were 54 toys in the larger stocking and 45 toys in the smaller. The 54 is the reverse of 45. The sum of the toys in the two stockings is 99, and one-eleventh of that is 9, the difference between the number of toys in the two stockings.

## "Riddles" Puzzle (page 446).

1) P—because it is near O (Nero).
2) Neither, both burn shorter.
3) Job; he had the most patience.
4) Toast.
5) Wild oats.

## "Nails" Puzzle (page 447).

If you move the nails indicated by the dash lines to the positions shown, you will end up with five small squares and one large, for a total of six.

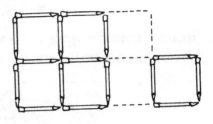

## "Echophone" Puzzle (page 448).

Pictured here is one possible solution to this puzzle.

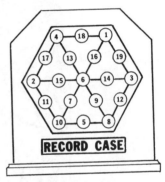

## "Picture" Puzzle (page 449).

The four words are:

1) GNAT—The bug buzzing around the minister's head.
2) NAME—The church's name on the tent.
3) AMEN—The missing word in the sermon.
4) TENT—The minister's tent church.

## "Addition" Puzzle (page 450).

In the solution, two odd digits are used to make an odd number: 13 + 3 + 3 + 1 = 20. (Note that 13 is composed of two digits.)

## "Diner" Puzzle (page 451).

"One on the city" is a glass of water. Here's one way to solve this problem:

$$759$$
$$75$$
$$629$$
$$\overline{1463}$$

**"Puzzle Poker" Puzzle (page 452).** Pictured below is one of several possible card arrangements that will solve this puzzle.

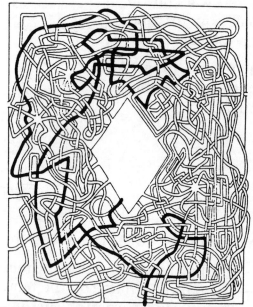

**"Maze" Puzzle (page 453).** Pictured below is the solution to Mr. Carroll's maze.

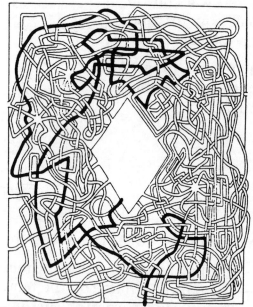

**"Sock Sale" Puzzle (page 454).** Here's how Aunt Hattie apportioned her purchases:

| | | | |
|---|---|---|---|
| Long winter socks | 3 pairs @ | $1.60 = | $4.80 |
| Calf-high socks | 15 pairs @ | .20 = | 3.00 |
| Short socks | 2 pairs @ | .10 = | .20 |
| | | Total | $8.00 |

**"Enigma" Puzzle (page 455).** The first two lines of the verse refer to the word "just" while the second two lines refer to the word "ice." Put them together and they refer to the commodity that the judge so liberally dispensed in his court, namely "justice."

**"Dictionary" Puzzle (page 456).** The answers are as follows: 1–G; 2–Q; 3–J; 4–B; 5–E; 6–O; 7–P; 8–K; 9–C; 10–H; 11–F; 12–M.

**"Lunch Tray" Puzzle (page 457).** "Muscles" carried 54 trays on the first trip and 45 trays on the second. Two-thirds of 54 equals 36, and 36 is four-fifths of 45. How did you stack up on this one?

**"Surveyor" Puzzle (page 458).** Draw a straight line from point **A** to point **D**. Point **D** is the midpoint of line **C-E**. This gives us the triangle **A-B-D**, which is half of the rectangle made up of side **AB** and side **BD**.

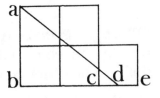

**"Poem" Puzzle (page 460).** Alas, the impossible is still impossible. In the confusion of the poem, at no time did it mention placing *the tenth man* in a room. Rather, it states that the landlord went back to the first room, where he had lodged man *one* and man *two*, and referred to one of them as *the tenth man*. I guess that the real tenth man ended up sleeping in the barn.

**"Coin" Puzzle (page 461).** Place a finger on the middle coin in the top row and slide the coin upwards and to the left. Keep sliding the coin around and down the left column of coins. Finally, slide it around the bottom and bring it into position beneath the middle coin in the bottom row. Now push the entire middle column of coins upward until you once again have four rows of 3 coins each. Each row will now have only all heads or all tails in it. During the entire operation you only touched one coin. Amazing!

**"Paper" Puzzle (page 462).** Take a stiff sheet of white paper and make three cuts in it as shown in the drawing. Each cut stops in the middle of the sheet. Now fold flap **A**, along the middle line, up to edge **BB**. Finally, take side **C** and rotate it 180°. Place the paper down onto the table and you will find that you have created the famous

"Paper Impossibility." It is most effective when glued down on top of a dark sheet of red or blue paper. The flap, of course, should be left unglued.

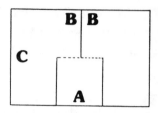 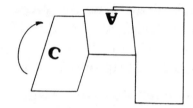

**"Change" Puzzle (page 463).** This is a "gotcha" type of puzzle. The coin that "is not a nickel" is, of course, a half-dollar. The other coin is a nickel. How else?

**"Archaeology" Puzzle (page 464).** The answer to this one is as old as puzzling itself . . . it's man. As a baby he crawls on all fours, in his prime he walks on two legs, and at twilight he walks with the aid of a cane.

**"Bell Ringer's" Puzzle (page 465).** It will take the brothers exactly $56\frac{1}{4}$ seconds to toll ten o'clock. Here's how it works: Between striking one and five there are four intervals. Therefore, dividing four into the total time of 25 seconds we get $6\frac{1}{4}$ seconds per interval. Now, between striking one and ten there are nine intervals. So, if we multiply nine times $6\frac{1}{4}$ seconds we get a total of $56\frac{1}{4}$ seconds, the time it takes to strike ten o'clock.

**"Talisman" Puzzle (page 466).**

**"Stocking" Puzzle (page 467).** The total number of stockings that Rodger had to take from the bottom drawer was three. If the first two stockings matched he had no problem. If not, the third stocking would match one of the first two stockings. Either way Rodger would be sure to arrive at his duel in sartorial splendor as usual.

**"Measuring" Puzzle (page 468).** Here's what Pew should have done;

1) Fill up the three-gallon jug; then pour the three gallons into the five-gallon cask.
2) Refill the three-gallon jug and again pour its contents into the five-gallon cask until the cask is full.
3) The three-gallon jug now contains one gallon. Empty the five-gallon cask back into the rum vat; then pour the one gallon from the three-gallon jug into it.
4) Finally, fill the three-gallon jug up again; then pour its contents into the five-gallon cask. The cask will now have the desired four gallons that Billy Bones came ashore to purchase.

**"Alice" Puzzle (page 469).** Alice asked, "If I had asked you yesterday, 'Which is the path that will lead me to the house of the Mad Hatter?' what would your answer have been?"

To such a question the truthful brother would again give the correct answer. The untruthful brother, however, would have to tell a lie as to what he would have answered the day before which, at that time, would also have been a lie. So his offsetting lie would also have been the correct path to take. Well done, Alice!

**"Sea Horse" Puzzle (page 470).** The winning moves go like this: Move 2 to 1; 5 to 2; 3 to 5; 6 to 3; 7 to 6; 4 to 7; 1 to 4; 3 to 1; 6 to 3; 7 to 6. The sea horses have now changed position and space 7 is empty.

**"Relation" Puzzle (page 471).** The person pictured in the portrait is the son of the gentleman who bought the painting.

**"Watch" Puzzle (page 472).**

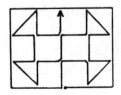

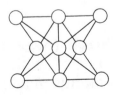

**"Contest" Puzzle (page 473).**

…**page 474).** Alexander and Sybilla
…two arrows in the 25 circle, two arrows
…and two arrows in the 3 circle.

**Puzzle (page 475).** Ned is out exactly …balls cost Ned $6 and he gave $8 in change …gentleman. Live and learn, Ned!

**"Orch… …" Puzzle (page 476).**

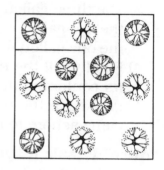

**"Button" Puzzle (page 477).** The drawing shows which two buttons to reposition.

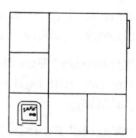

**"IQ" Puzzle (page 478).** Each pattern represents a number. In the first pattern there are three circles which gives us the number 3. The second pattern has one triangle, giving us the number 1. The rest of the patterns yield the numbers 4, 1, 5, 9 or, the value of Pi to five places. The next three patterns would therefore be two nested circles, six nested triangles and five nested squares. (The shapes of the patterns go in order: circle, triangle and square.)

**"Robbery Plans" Puzzle (page 479).**

**"Chess" Puzzle (page 480).** Here's how Bertram did it. Augustus opened with a white move on board one. Bertram promptly made the same opening move with white on board two. Augustus made his answering black move on board two. Bertram made this same answering move with black on board one. Back and forth they went with Bertram always using Augustus' moves on one board as his moves on the other board. Finally, Augustus realized that he was playing himself and that if he won one of the games he would also lose the other game, or, he could draw both games. In no case could he hope to win both of the games. In disgust he gave up and swore that he'd never play chess with his brother again.

**"Farmer" Puzzle (page 481).** The men built three enclosures and placed three heifers in each of them; then they built a fourth enclosure around the first three. In that way all of the enclosures came to hold an odd number of heifers.

**"Scholars" Puzzle (page 482).** The first scholar gives us a clue when he mentions that the answer is "devilishly" hard to solve. The word is "witchcraft." The second scholar also dropped a clue when he said that you will have to "line up" to get the answer. His word was "queueing."

**"Answerless" Puzzle (page 483).** Shame on Quimby, and shame on you if you missed this one. The letter "e," the most used of all the letters, is missing from the text of the puzzle that Quimby is editing.

**"River" Puzzle (page 484).** Any method of solution will show that the speed of the boat is irrelevant to the solution. The best solution is arrived at when one looks at the problem from Herbie's vantage point: To Herbie the hat is just sitting there in the water. First he sails away from it for five minutes, then he turns around and sails back for five minutes and picks it up. During that time the hat had traveled downstream one mile on the river current. It took the hat 10 minutes to travel that mile so we can calculate from that that the river was flowing at a rate of 6 miles per hour.

**"Hidden Sentence" Puzzle (page 485).** The coded sentence in the first puzzle is: "I understand you undertake to undermine my understanding."

The coded second sentence in the second puzzle is: "One ought to owe nothing, for one ate nothing."

**"Jumping" Puzzle (page 486).** The answer goes like this: For your first move jump 9 over 13, 14, 6, 4, 3, 1, 2, 7, 15, 17, 16, 11. Remove all pieces jumped. The next move is 12 over 8. The third play is 10 over 5 and 12. The final jump is 9 over 10 landing checker 9 back where it started.

**"Rearranging Bee" Puzzle (page 487).** Our global answers are as follow:

KLASAA = ALASKA
LHATDAIN = THAILAND
INDIRTDA = TRINIDAD
ACGIUNAAR = NICARAGUA
RUSLAITAA = AUSTRALIA
RISACFOAUHT = SOUTH AFRICA
ADEKMRN = DENMARK
GRBAAILU = BULGARIA
HPEITIAO = ETHIOPIA
DAUROHNS = HONDURAS
SHININECLTEET = LIECHTENSTEIN
HFNNAASTGAI = AFGHANISTAN

**"Circle" Puzzle (page 488).** The numbers in the inner circle are 5, 6, 7 and 8 which give us a total of 26. The numbers in the outer circle are 1, 2, 3, 4, 9, 10, 11 and 12 which give us a total of 52. This is exactly twice the total of the numbers in the inner circle. Puzzle solved!

**"Boarding House" Puzzle (page 489).** Since the taxi driver has never seen a ball game he must be Mr. Williams. Also, Mr. Edwards has never heard of approvals so he can't be a stamp collector. Therefore, the three occupations are: Mr. Williams is a taxi driver; Mr. Edwards is a fireman, and Mr. Barnet is a baker.

**"Utility" Puzzle (page 490).** To solve this one the builder was forced to run one of the lines, from the water works, underneath house number 1 to house number 3. After that, all the rest was easy.

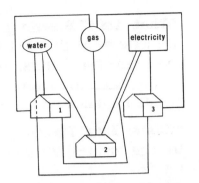

**"Speed" Puzzle (page 491).** The answer is arrived at by dividing the total distance Moriarty travelled by the total time of the journey. Let's say that the road on each side of Old Baldy Mountain was twenty miles long from base to top. It would take Moriarty two hours to reach the top and one hour to reach the bottom. Since the return trip would also take three hours, the total time for the trip is six hours. During that time he would have travelled a distance of eighty miles. The average speed then is 80 miles in 6 hours, which comes to $13^1/_3$ miles per hour.

**"Transpositional" Puzzle (page 492).** The winning moves are: 2 to 1, 6 to 2, 4 to 6, 7 to 4, 3 to 7, 5 to 3 and 1 to 5.

**"Brick Wall" Puzzle (page 493).** Wall **ab** is the same length as wall **bc**. If wall **bc** was sliced along the dotted line **1** and the upper section moved down to dotted line **2** we would have a brick wall of the same dimensions as wall **ab**. This clearly proves that both walls contain the same amount of material and thus should cost the same to build. Both Mr. Dumpty and the mason were wrong.

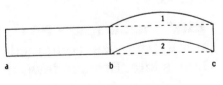

**"Trolley" Puzzle (page 494).** The amount of change that Amos was holding came to $1.19. This amount was made up of a half dollar, a quarter, four dimes, and four pennies.

**"What Am I" Puzzle (page 495).** The items in question are letters. In the first line twice ten is twenty, a word made up of six letters. In the word six there are three and in the word nine there are four, and so on with the remaining lines.

**"Easter Egg" Puzzle (page 496).** The toy costs 25¢ and the egg costs $4.25, which is $4 more than the cost of the toy.

**"Checkers" Puzzle (page 498).** Mr. Fogg's winning moves were: 7 to 10, 15 to 6, and 4 to 8. The white checkers were then locked in and couldn't make a move, thereby giving the game to the black side.

**"Dragon" Puzzle (page 499).** The answers to the dragon's puzzles are: 1) "Tarzan Strips Forever!" 2) You make a hippopotamus float with a large glass and a lot of root beer. 3) When spelling the numbers in the given series, each number is spelled with one more letter than the last: 1 = one; 4 = four; and 3 = three. Therefore, the next number in the series should be spelled with six letters. That number, in ascending numeric order, would be 11 (eleven).

**"Restaurant" Puzzle (page 500).** Ten people sat down to lunch. Each one's share of the $80.00 check was $8.00. After the Benson twins skipped out, leaving eight diners, those remaining had to add $2.00 each to their share to cover the balance. Thus, each of the eight paid $10.00.

**"Kite" Puzzle (page 501).** You'll find a total of 31 equilateral triangles contained in the construction of Mr. Okito's kite. Broken down they are:

1. 16 small triangles
2. 7 triangles made up of 4 smaller ones
3. 3 triangles made up of 9 smaller ones
4. 4 triangles made up of 16 smaller ones
5. 1 large outer triangle.

The hardest of the triangles to find is the seventh one, made up of four smaller triangles. You'll find it in the center of the kite with the three points of the triangle touching the centers of the lines that make up the inner triangle that is composed of 16 smaller triangles.

**"Sledding" Puzzle (page 502).** It took Harry and Harriet four minutes to finish the mile, while the Brodys covered the course in 10 minutes, a difference of six minutes. Thus, Harry's sled was two and a half times faster than the Brodys'.

**"Stick" Puzzle (page 503).** The drawing tells all. And remember, we didn't specify that the six squares all had to be the same size.

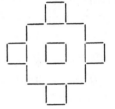

**"Riddle" Puzzle (page 504).** 1) Wheeling West Virginia; 2) the baby is a little bigger; 3) when it is adrift; 4) because it doesn't run long without winding.

**"Golf Tees" Puzzle (page 505).** The drawing shows how Nelda formed four perfect squares with 24 golf tees to win a new set of irons from MacDivot.

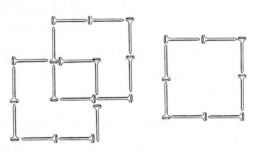

**"Word Square" Puzzle (page 506).**

| E | S | C | A | P | E |
|---|---|---|---|---|---|
| S | U | R | T | A | X |
| C | R | I | T | I | C |
| A | T | T | I | R | E |
| P | A | I | R | E | D |
| E | X | C | E | D | E |

**"Puzzle Spy" Puzzle (page 507).** The answer that came over the Snooper Phone was, <u>UNDERGROUND</u>. As for the hint, in London they call the subway the underground.

**"Cloth" Puzzle (page 508).** The solution to the draper's puzzle is to lay out the square of cloth and cut it twice along lines *A–A* and *B–B*. These lines are drawn from a point one-third up and one-third across on the sides of the square where they intersect. You are then left with squares *1* and *2*. The third square is created by taking pieces *3* and *4* and sewing them together along their long edges. This forms a square that is equal in size to square *2*.

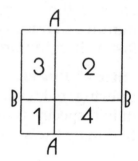

**"Betting" Puzzle (page 509).** Two-thirds of three-quarters is always equal to one half of any given amount.

$$(^2/_3 \times \,^3/_4) \times \$111.00 =$$
$$^6/_{12} \times \$111.00 =$$
$$^1/_2 \times \$111.00 = \$55.50$$

**"Bar Room" Puzzle (page 510).** The six coins that would get you one on the house are: one half dollar, one quarter and four dimes.

**"Rebus" Puzzle (page 511).** The first message, fully decoded, reads: "Captain Forbes arrived in the West Indies today with his forces."

The second message reads: "Captain Forbes mission a bust. He ran backward and forward across the island like a stranger in paradise, finding no one."

If you cracked those codes, you may be CIA material.

**"Weighing" Puzzle (page 512).** Here's how Linda and Mike solved Professor Kane's problem. First they divided the nine weights into three piles of three weights each. They then put two of these piles on the scale, one pile on each side. If either of the piles went up in the air, then that pile must contain the light weight. If they balanced evenly, then the third pile had to contain the light weight. Either way, after the first weighing, Mike and Linda knew which pile contained the light weight. For the second weighing they selected two of the coins from the light group and placed one on each side of the scales. If the scales balanced, then the third coin was the light one; otherwise the coin on the side of the scales that went up was the coin they were looking for. Either way, Mike and Linda solved the puzzle in two weighings.

**"Fishing" Puzzle (page 513).** Our fishing fools chalked up the following totals for the day: Emmet = 4 fish, Calvin = 3 fish, Quentin = 2 fish, and Wylie = 1 fish.

**"Poor Sport" Puzzle (page 514).** The first word is ANTIPERSPIRANT. The second is TORMENTOR.

**"What" Puzzles (page 515).** 1) A cat has claws at the tip of its paws; a comma had its pause at the end of a clause. 2) The letter "A," because it makes *her hear*. 3) DK (decay). 4) Bacon. 5) X-P-D-N-C (expediency).

**"Toy Train" Puzzle (page 516).** The sixteen individual moves are as follows: 1 to 5, 3 to 7, 7 to 1, 8 to 4, 4 to 3, 3 to 7, 6 to 2, 2 to 8, 8 to 4, 4 to 3, 5 to 6, 6 to 2, 2 to 8, 1 to 5, 5 to 6, and 7 to 1.

**"Quilting" Puzzle (page 517).** Sam Loyd listed 17 names in his original presentation of this puzzle. To date, we have been able to find 35 names. There may be, and probably are, more. However, readers able to come up with twenty or more names have solved this puzzle admirably. My listing is as follows, Ann, Anna, Annie, Cary Cindi, Diana, Diane, Dinah, Edna, Enid, Ina, Jane, Janel, Jean, Jenny, Judy, Jule, Lea, Lena, Mae, Maia, Mary, Maud, Minna, Minnie, Minny, Nan, Nana, Nancy, Nina, Rae, Raina, Rana, Rania, Rue.

**"Maze" Puzzle (page 518).** The following route will quickly take you to Rosamond's bower.

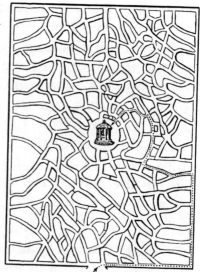

**"Candle" Puzzle (page 519).** As it turned out, the reverend made short work of the sexton's puzzle. The candles to be moved are indicated by the broken lines in the drawing.

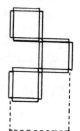

**"Square" Puzzle (page 520).** Consider that the smallest square is one unit wide by one unit high. There are 64 of these squares. Next, we have squares that are two units by two units. There are 49 of these squares. The breakdown is as follows:

$$
\begin{aligned}
1 \times 1 &= 64 \\
2 \times 2 &= 49 \\
3 \times 3 &= 36 \\
4 \times 4 &= 25 \\
5 \times 5 &= 16 \\
6 \times 6 &= 9 \\
7 \times 7 &= 4 \\
8 \times 8 &= \underline{1} \\
\text{Total} &= 204 \text{ squares}
\end{aligned}
$$

**"Vowel" Puzzle (page 521).** In the drawing, the heavy lines denote the edges of the five pieces. Each piece contains the letters "A," "E," "I," "O," and "U."

| E | U | O | A | U |
|---|---|---|---|---|
| O | A | I | O | E |
| A | I | E | A | I |
| O | U | I | U | A |
| E | U | I | O | E |

**"Motoring" Puzzle (page 522).** Aunt Hattie travelled 114 miles to reach Atlantic City. The following diagram tells all.

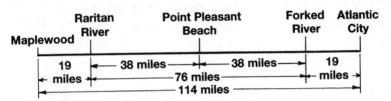

**"Archaeology" Puzzle (page 523).** The answer that Hawkings and Petrie came up with is pictured at right

| a | b | c | d | e | f | g |
|---|---|---|---|---|---|---|
| d | e | f | g | a | b | c |
| g | a | b | c | d | e | f |
| c | d | e | f | g | a | b |
| f | g | a | b | c | d | e |
| b | c | d | e | f | g | a |
| e | f | g | a | b | c | d |

**"Fencing" Puzzle (page 524).** The drawing shows Zebediah's solution to this grazing problem.

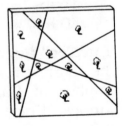

**"WWII" Puzzle (page 525).** This only appears to be a coincidence. The year in question is 1944. If we take the birthday of anyone born before 1944 and add the person's age in 1944 to the year of birth, the result will always be 1,944. So, if we take the year a political figure entered office and add the number of years the figure served to this number—once again, only up to 1944—the total will be 1,944. Adding these two totals together gives 3,888, the totals in the chart. Try making up your own "coincidence" charts using world leaders of today.

**"License" Puzzle (page 526).** The first "one" goes across the first two "ones" in the license plate to form the letter "H." The second "one" goes up against the "3," forming the letter "B." The plate now reads HOBO , a type of old-time tramp.

**"Mad Scientist" Puzzle (page 527).** He could have turned the tables on Smythe by . . . turning the chalkboard upside down. The numbers are now in a new arrangement giving us the expression 81 plus 19, which equals 100.

$$\begin{array}{r} 6L \\ 81 \\ 19 \\ \hline 100 \end{array}$$

**"Tea" Puzzle (page 528).** The four weights were 1 pound, 3 pounds, 9 pounds, and 27 pounds. Fu Ling Yu would sometimes have to put weights on both sides of the scale when weighing out certain amounts. Some examples are:

|          | Left side of scale | Right side of scale |
|----------|:----------:|:----------:|
| 7 lbs. =  | 1 + 9    | 3 + 7 lbs. of tea |
| 12 lbs. = | 3 + 9    | 12 lbs. of tea |
| 15 lbs. = | 27       | 9 + 3 + 15 lbs. of tea |
| 20 lbs. = | 27 + 3   | 1 + 9 + 20 lbs. of tea |

**"Hurdles" Puzzle (page 529).** The shortest route over an even number of hurdles is twelve hurdles. Since there is more than one route using twelve hurdles, we must find the one with the largest number total. That total is 36, and the route is indicated at right by following the dotted line.

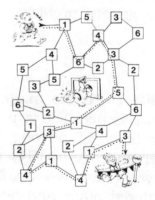

**"Gambling" Puzzle (page 530).** The player who goes second can be a sure winner if he, or she, knows the secret. Here it is: If the pigeon goes first and removes one card, the sharper removes two cards. If the pigeon removes two cards, the sharper removes one card. In either case, when the sharper removes his card(s), he makes sure the circle is divided into equal semi-circles each containing five cards. From that point on, the sharper removes from the opposite semi-circle the same number of cards the pigeon removes. This way, the sharper always takes up the last card and wins the bet.

When the sharper goes first, he removes just one card from the circle and waits for the opportunity to divide the cards in the circle into two contiguous sections, each section containing the same number of cards. With a little practice the sharper should be able to win 8, 9 or even 10 times out of 10 games. Unless, of course, he runs up against another player who is in the know. When this happens it's best to change trains and look for greener pastures.

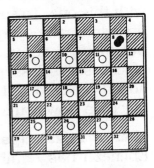

**"Checkerboard" Puzzle (page 531).** In the drawing at right we've rearranged and renumbered the squares in the solution to make it easier to give you the jumps in the winning move. Black jumps 8 to 15, 15 to 24, 24 to 31, 31 to 22, 22 to 15, 15 to 6, 6 to 13, 13 to 22, and 22 to 29.

**"Stone Carver" Puzzle (page 532).** The stone-carving team totalled three sculptors at full strength. If three can carve a calendar in three months, one can carve it in nine months, and nine can carve it in one month.

**"Egg" Puzzle (page 533).** When the water boiled, Albert dropped the egg in and turned both sand timers over. After the sand in the seven-minute timer ran out, he turned it over once again. At this point, four minutes of sand was left in the 11-minute timer. When the sand in the 11-minute timer ran out, four minutes of sand was in the *bottom* of the 7-minute timer. Albert turned this timer over and when the sand in it ran out, a full 15 minutes has passed and he removed the egg from the water.

**"Star" Puzzle (page 534).** The following nine moves will win the day. The first position is where the coin is originally placed. The second is where it ends up after hopping the intervening circle: 2 to 4; 8 to 2; 5 to 8; 3 to 5; 9 to 3; 7 to 9; 1 to 7; 6 to 1; and 10 to 6.

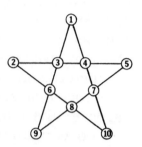

**"Underwater" Puzzle (page 535).** Mrs. Bellows is 30 years old and her daughter, Cecily, is 10. Today, Mrs. Bellows is three times as old as her daughter. Five years ago, when she was 25 and Cecily was 5, she was five times as old as her daughter.

**"Quibble" Puzzle (page 536).** A "quibble" puzzle is usually one that has a tricky solution. That's the case with this one. To solve it, when you add the 2 to 191, you first draw a line under the 1 on the right and then you put the 2 under it. The number now reads 19½, which, of course, is less than 20. In other words, when you added the 2 to 191 you just didn't sum the two figures together. Now you know what "quibbles" are all about!

**"Farm" Puzzle (page 537).** Zebediah has 11 animals, Ebenezer has 7 animals and Absalom has 21 animals.

**"Card" Puzzle (page 538).** The four face-down cards, left to right, are King of Hearts, Jack of Diamonds, Queen of Spades and Ace of Clubs.

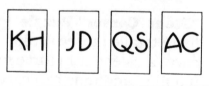

**"Anagram" Puzzle (page 539).** First off, let me say that this is not an Italian anagram club although Henri asked them if they were ready to order from *Today's Menu.* Fred's order should read *Salmon Steak* and *Carrot Raisin Cake.* Alice's should read *Waldorf Salad* and *Hamburger Patties.* .

**"Train" Puzzle (page 540).** At 75 miles per hour the passenger train can travel one-half mile in 24 seconds. (There are 3,600 seconds in an hour. Divided by 75 miles per hour, we get 48 seconds for the train to travel one mile. Thus, a half-mile can be travelled in 24 seconds.) This means that the engine will emerge from the tunnel three seconds before Fred reaches the exit, too late for him to catch the engineer's eye. However, since it took six seconds for the train to completely enter the tunnel, it will take six seconds before the last car, the caboose, will exit from it. This makes a total of 30 seconds from the time Fred started running towards the tunnel exit. Since Fred could reach the exit in 27 seconds, he had three seconds to spare, long enough to catch the brakeman's attention and save the train.

**"Word Pyramid" Puzzle (page 541).** In puzzles of this type there is usually more than one solution. We give the following solution, starting at the top word and working down: A, LA, ALE, GALE, ANGLE, DANGLE, and GLADDEN.

**"Q" Puzzles (page 542).**

| | | | |
|---|---|---|---|
| 1) Quell | 6) Quick | 11) Quaff | 16) Quiet |
| 2) Quill | 7) Quote | 12) Qualm | 17) Quake |
| 3) Quart | 8) Query | 13) Quasi | 18) Queen |
| 4) Quota | 9) Quail | 14) Quite | 19) Quirk |
| 5) Queue | 10) Queer | 15) Quest | 20) Quips |

**"Poem" Puzzle (page 543).** The poem is about the letter "E."

**"Fours" Puzzle (page 544).** Here's the solution Professor Flunkum finally came up with. Make-up class is Saturday, 7:00 A.M.

$$44 + \frac{44}{44} = 55$$

**"Store" Puzzle (page 545).** Bascomb filled Fleurette's order by giving her five two-cent blue spools, fifty one-cent red spools, and eight five-cent green spools. This neatly came to $1.00, which made an easy transaction for Neville, the cashier.

**"Subtraction" Puzzle (page 546).** Alice found the solution when she passed through the looking glass. Once inside she looked back and found that the subtraction problem when reversed now read, "Nine minus one equals eight," which, of course, is correct.

**"Contest" Puzzle (page 547).** 1) A sponge; 2) in the Arkhives (archives); 3) the Mississippi River; 4) when he is out of patients (patience).

**"Party" Puzzle (page 548).** There were seven party-goers in the group and each item purchased cost $2.90. Seven times $2.90 comes to $20.30, the total amount of the purchases as given in the problem.

**"Quotation" Puzzle (page 550).** To score a solid hit with this problem, start with the first "I" on the left side of the frame, just below the "K" in the corner, and proceed counterclockwise, reading every other letter around the frame. You will end up with the following famous quotation: "If you come to a fork in the road, take it."

**"Checkers" Puzzle (page 551).** To win, white moves as follows: 19 to 16, 11 to 27, 18 to 15, 10 to 26, and 32 to 5, a quintuple jump. What a player!

**"Concert" Puzzle (page 552).** When it comes to solving puzzles, Bertie plays second fiddle to no one. Here's the answer that he came up with. The original five-letter word had to be SMITE. The other four words that can be made from the letters in this word are: MITES, EMITS, ITEMS, and TIMES.

**"Liars" Puzzle (page 553).** Since Henry and Thelma can't both be liars, it follows then that Jeffrey must be lying. Therefore, since Henry called him a liar, Henry must be telling the truth. And since Henry is telling the truth, Thelma must also be lying. If you have any questions, direct them to Schnappsie. Dogs are always honest.

**"Fax" Puzzle (page 554).**

1) VEAGNE = GENEVA
2) LHTMOCOKS = STOCKHOLM
3) ARWCOC = CRACOW
4) NAOMRSINA = SAN MARINO
5) IOPVLELOR = LIVERPOOL
6) GRTSSORUAB = STRASBOURG
7) FSDRSODULE = DUSSELDORF
8) MKILECIR = LIMERICK

**"Money" Puzzle (page 555).** This is how Uncle Andrew divided the money up among the eight compartments.

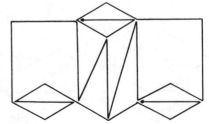

**"Watch" Puzzle (page 556).**

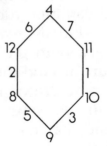

**"Line" Puzzle (page 557).** The drawing at right shows Biff's solution to his kite puzzle.

**"Counterfeit" Puzzle (page 558).** The breakdown of counterfeit bills liberated by Harry was as follows:

| Type | Number | Total |
|---|---|---|
| $1.00 × | 10 = | $ 10.00 |
| $5.00 × | 100 = | $ 500.00 |
| $10.00 × | 9 = | $ 90.00 |
| $50.00 × | 18 = | $ 900.00 |
| Totals | 137 | $1,500.00 |

**"Hidden Cities" Puzzle (page 559).** The city in the top picture is Alexandria. "Pa<u>lex and Ria</u>lto were the early trotting kings." The second city is Erie. "Like a weary trave<u>ler, I e</u>ntered the town."

**"Word Pyramid" Puzzle (page 560).** Puzzles of this type usually have more than one solution. Uncle Olaf gives the following one: R, RE, EAR, REAL, LATER, RETAIL, RELIANT, ENTRAILS.

**"Voting" Puzzle (page 561).** First, fold the top and bottom portions of a sheet of paper as shown in figure 1. Next, draw one side of the "X"; continue the line onto the top fold of paper (dotted line); then bring the line back down to the center of the paper and finish the other side of the "X" (figure 2). Next, fold the bottom part of the paper up and continue the line over to the side (dotted line figure 3). Finally, come off the folded part back onto the center and draw the square around the "X" (figure 4). You have now drawn the square, with the "X" in the center, using one continuous line that has not crossed itself at any point.

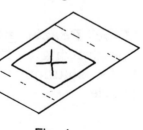

Fig. 1

Fig. 2          Fig. 3          Fig. 4

**"Blackboard" Puzzle (page 562).** The two positive numbers needed to solve this one are 1 and 2. These two numbers are combined and written as $^1/_2$. Added to 19 they give a total that is, of course, less than 20.

**"Hexagon" Puzzle (page 563).** The drawing shows where to place the nine lines.

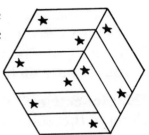

**"Miller's" Puzzle (page 564).** This is one solution to this crusty puzzle.

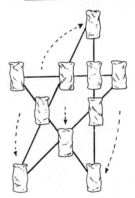

**"Butter Knife" Puzzle (page 565).** Actually, Valadon had two ways to win this bet, thus doubling his profits. In the first solution he moved the knife on the left to the left until it touched the outer edges of the two vertical knives. This formed a small square made up of the four blunt ends of the knives (figure 1).

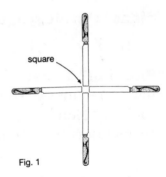

square

Fig. 1

In the second solution Valadon moved the rightmost knife over to the left, forming the number four (figure 2). In this case the number four is the "square" of two. After all, Valadon never did specify what kind of a square was to be formed.

Fig. 2

**"Platter" Puzzle (page 566).** The word that answers the question in our poem is . . . EMPTY. Regardless of which letter(s) is dropped, the remaining letters are pronounced the same; _MPTY, EMPT_, MPT_, _M_T_.

**"Cities" Puzzle (page 567).** 1) Erie (Pennsylvania); 2) Casper (Wyoming), the friendly ghost; 3) Billings (Montana); 4) Champaign (Illinois); 5) Phoenix (Arizona); 6) Ann Arbor (Michigan).

**"Magic Square" Puzzle (page 568).** Here is the solution to Mesmer's hypnotic problem. It should be noted that the four corner squares and the four center squares also add up to 79. There are also several other four-square combinations that add up to this same total. See how many you can find.

| 19 | 22 | 26 | 12 |
| 25 | 13 | 18 | 23 |
| 14 | 28 | 20 | 17 |
| 21 | 16 | 15 | 27 |

**"Billiard" Puzzle (page 569).** If you spell out the numbers of each ball, in English, you will see that Miss English pocketed the balls in alphabetical order: eleven, fifteen, nine, one, seven, and two.

**"Signs" Puzzle (page 570).**

$$9 + 8 + 7 - 6 - 5 - (4 \times 3) - 2 + 1 = 0$$

**"Banking" Puzzle (page 571).** There are many solutions to this problem. Here's the one that Mr. Spendenborrow submitted.

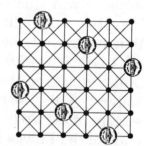

**"Card" Puzzle (page 572).** When the 12 cards have been set up in the correct order, and the deck has been turned face-down, the order of the cards, from the top card down, will be:

KH, KD, QH, KC, JH, QD, KS, JC, QS, JD, JS, and QC (KH = king of hearts; KD = king of diamonds, etc.)

**"Five Buck" Puzzle (page 573).** The hint in the picture is the fact that it's a five-dollar bill, which has a picture of Abraham Lincoln on one side. The answer to the puzzle is "Four score," the opening words of Lincoln's Gettysburg Address. Four score, or 4 × 20, when added together (as mentioned in the last line of the poem) make two dozen.

**"Contest" Puzzle (page 574).**

Mike's puzzle:
$$\frac{1}{3} \text{ of TW(EL)VE} = \text{EL}$$
$$\frac{4}{5} \text{ of S(EVEN)} = \text{EVEN}$$
$$\text{EL} + \text{EVEN} = \text{ELEVEN}$$

Linda's puzzle:

$$
\begin{array}{r}
A\ B\ C \\
\times\ \ \ \ D\ E \\
\hline
F\ G\ H\ I
\end{array}
\qquad
\begin{array}{r}
1\ 9\ 8 \\
\times\ \ \ \ 2\ 7 \\
\hline
5\ 3\ 4\ 6
\end{array}
$$

**"Limerick" Puzzle (page 575).** There may be more than one answer to this one, but here's the one the gentleman in the chair came up with:

$333,333 \times 3 + 1 = 1,000,000$

**"Roller Ship" Puzzle (page 576).** Port A is 300 miles from Port B.
Trip from A to B: 20mph × 15 hours = 300 miles
Trip from B to A: 15mph × (15 + 5) hours = 300 miles

**"Scholar" Puzzle (page 577).** Here are the 10 contractions our word scholars came up with. We're sure that there are several others.

1) I'll becomes ill.
2) He'll becomes hell.
3) She'll becomes shell.
4) We'd becomes wed.
5) She'd becomes shed.
6) Can't becomes cant.
7) Won't becomes wont.
8) We're becomes were.
9) I'd becomes id.
10) It's becomes its.

**"Penmanship" Puzzle (page 578).** The following drawing shows now Nellie performed this interesting exercise.

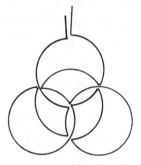

**"Alderman" Puzzle (page 579).**

Mr. Glandhander received    1,336 votes
Mr. Murphy received    1,314 votes — 22 less
Mr. Hoffmann received    1,306 votes — 30 less
Mr. Dangerfield received    1,263 votes — 73 less
Total   5,219 votes

**"Word Square" Puzzle (page 580).** The five words are: 1) niche; 2) idler; 3) Clara; 4) herds; 5) erase.

| N | I | C | H | E |
|---|---|---|---|---|
| I | D | L | E | R |
| C | L | A | R | A |
| H | E | R | D | S |
| E | R | A | S | E |

**"Acronym" Puzzle (page 581).** 1) Okcwamos = "Old King Cole was a merry old soul"; 2) Dddmsj = "Diddle diddle dumpling my son John"; 3) Twaowwlias = "There was an old woman who lived in a shoe"; 4) Pppapopp = "Peter Piper picked a peck of pickled peppers."

**"Automobile" Puzzle (page 582).** Back in 1948 the ages of the cars mentioned were:

1) The 1924 Essex Coach was 24 years old.
2) The 1928 Lincoln Victoria was 20 years old.
3) The 1932 Duesenberg Convertible was 16 years old.
4) The 1936 Cord 812 was 12 years old.

**"Row" Puzzle (page 583).** The following diagram shows how 12 checkers can be arranged into seven rows—three horizontal, three vertical, and one diagonal (beginning with the top left corner and going down to the lower right corner), each containing four checkers.

**"Auction" Puzzle (page 584).** Each phonograph was worth $600. Each gravy boat was worth $300. Each Toby mug was worth $100.

**"Garden" Puzzle (page 585).** The drawing shows how Colonel Pikestaff solved the puzzle.

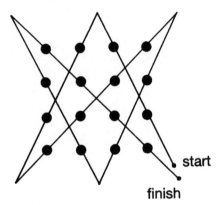

**"Breakfast" Puzzle (page 586).** The breakfast items on our menu board are:
1) French toast
2) granola
3) cheese omelet
4) tofu special
5) espresso
6) hotcakes
7) poached eggs
8) cinnamon roll

**"Gold Claim" Puzzle (page 587).** The boys went to see their lawyer, Trevor Torts. Here's how he helped them divide up their inheritance.

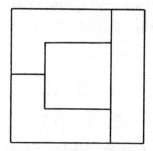

**"Puzzleman" Puzzle (page 588).** Here is one possible answer to this problem:

$$1 + 3 + 5 + 7 + \frac{75}{75} + \frac{33}{11} = 20$$